The Secret Treasury David Lipsey

VIKING

VIKING

Published by the Penguin Group
Penguin Books Ltd, 27 Wrights Lane, London w8 5tz, England
Penguin Putnam Inc., 375 Hudson Street, New York, New York 10014, USA
Penguin Books Australia Ltd, Ringwood, Victoria, Australia
Penguin Books Canada Ltd, 10 Alcorn Avenue, Toronto, Ontario, Canada m4v 3b2
Penguin Books (NZ) Ltd, Private Bag 102902, NSMC, Auckland, New Zealand

Penguin Books Ltd, Registered Offices: Harmondsworth, Middlesex, England

First published 2000
10 9 8 7 6 5 4 3 2 1

Set in 10.5/15pt Monotype Minion and Metaplus
Typeset by Rowland Phototypesetting Ltd,
Bury St Edmunds, Suffolk
Printed in England by Clays Ltd, St Ives plc

A CIP catalogue record for this book is available from the British Library

ISBN 0-670-88926-1

Contents

Preface

This book is not a history of the Treasury, though it contains some history. It is not a book about public administration, though it contains a lot about public administration. Nor is it about politics, though it is shot through with politics. Nor even is it about economic policy, though it contains some economics. It is, put simply, an attempt to paint in words a portrait of the Treasury as an institution as it stands today.

Other people have written good books from each of the other perspectives. Henry Rosebeare's history of the Treasury is comprehensive. Academic studies have largely covered the Treasury's role in the machinery of government: recent volumes include Colin Thain and Maurice Wright's monumental *The Treasury and Whitehall* (Clarendon, 1995) and Richard Chapman's useful, if patchy, text *The Treasury in Public Policy Making* (Routledge, 1997). Treasury politics and economics is also covered in the memoirs of several recent chancellors, all now lords: Roy Jenkins, James Callaghan, Geoffrey Howe, Nigel Lawson. In addition, Edmund Dell, who was never chancellor but was a Treasury minister, has written a wise if worldly history of occupants of the office since 1945 (*The Chancellors*, HarperCollins, 1996); and Lord Jenkins a delicious history of those before then, in *The Chancellors*. (The two overlap, both including Hugh Dalton.) The most recent serious history is covered by Philip Stephens's *Politics and the Pound* (Macmillan, 1996); and there is later material, both in

Paul Routledge's *Gordon Brown* and Hugh Pym and Nick Kochan's *Gordon Brown: the First Year in Power*. Simon Jenkins's splendid polemic *Accountable to None* is a sustained attack on Treasury centralism, which this book rebuts.

I have stolen shamelessly from these authors and many others. But I still hope to have added value. For none of these books alone can hope to capture what the Treasury is really like. It is a living, breathing institution, with its own strong values and its own foibles, its own way of looking at the world and its own way of relating to those who do not share it. Its essence is elusive, but fascinating – the more so since it affects every one of us, every single day of our life.

The one book that has ever got near to capturing that essence, *The Private Government of Public Money* by Hugh Heclo and the late Aaron Wildavsky, was first published in 1974 by Macmillan. (The authors updated it in 1981.) At that time I had just joined the Department of the Environment as political adviser to the late Anthony Crosland, MP, and was on a rapidly rising learning curve. Their book helped me to understand what would otherwise have been the puzzling relations between the department and the Treasury. Professor Wildavsky's next book was a biography of Moses – like the archetypal Treasury official, a man accustomed to handing down commandments on tablets of stone.

One occasionally meets young administrators in Whitehall who have never read Heclo and Wildavsky, which (to stick with Moses) is a bit like being a vicar who has never read the Old Testament. But their work still leaves room for the present volume.

First, Heclo and Wildavsky do not cover everything. Theirs is a volume about public spending, one of the most important activities of the Treasury but a long way from being the sole one. Secondly, it has aged. Even in its chosen field of public expenditure, the last seventeen years have seen, for example, the Financial Management Initiative, the Treasury's Fundamental Expenditure Review, the emergence of the Private Finance Initiative, privatization, resource cost accounting and the Comprehensive Spending Review. (If you do not know what some of these things are, by the end of this book you will.) Outside public finance there has been the death of Keynesianism, supply-side economics, globalization, EMU and the euro. The Treasury is (like most modern institutions) a rapidly changing place in a rapidly changing world. It seemed worth another look.

It has taken me some time. When I started in 1992, I had just left *The Times* for the civilized world of *The Economist*. Used to the frenetic pace of the former, I had spare capacity, which I wanted to fill. Then various things happened (including becoming 'Bagehot', the *nom de plume* of *The Economist*'s political editor in the run-up to the general election). Even after that, when Bill Emmott, the paper's editor, granted me a sabbatical to finish the book, I did not get uninterrupted time, serving (under Lord Jenkins) on Tony Blair's Independent Commission on the Voting System, on the Royal Commission on the Funding of the Long-term Care of the Elderly and on the Davies Commission on the funding of the BBC. So everyone, including Kate Jones, my saintly publisher at Hamish Hamilton, and Lisanne Radice, my no-less-saintly agent, has had to wait.

My own qualifications for writing the book include that spell at the Department of the Environment (and subsequently in Lord Callaghan's Policy Unit at Downing Street); four years as economics editor of the *Sunday Times* from 1982 to 1986; and an interest in public policy. (I have been a visiting professor in the subject at the University of Ulster.) But more important, Sir Terence (now Lord) Burns, the Treasury's permanent secretary, gave me permission to interview a large number of top Treasury officials, and his successor, Sir Andrew Turnbull, repeated that permission for a second round of interviews in 1999. They are quoted extensively unattributably through this book; hence the tedious references to 'one official said' or 'one senior official' (deputy director and above) said. But their insights have shaped much of what follows. I would like therefore to thank Owen Barder, John Beestock, David Bostock, Alan Budd, Terry Burns, Robert Culpin, Jon Cunliffe, Paula Diggle, Martin Donnelly, Huw Evans, Robin Fellgett, Darren Gibbs, John Gieve, Paul Gray, Joe Grice, Joe Halligan, Jeremy Heywood, Nick Ilett, Peter Kane, Chris Kelly, Sue Killen, Andrew Kilpatrick, Andrew Likierman, Paul McIntyre, Jamie Mortimer, Gill Noble, Gus O'Donnell, David Owen, Sue Owen, Mike Parsonage, John Pavel, David Peretz, Alice Perkins, Stephen Pickford, Steve Robson, Philip Rutnam, Adam Sharples, Judith Simpson, Caroline Slocock, Ruth Thompson, Andrew Turnbull, Simon Virley, Moira Wallace, Alan Whiting, Nigel Wicks, Mike Williams, Philip Wynn Owen and Edna Young among (then) serving Treasury officials for formal interviews. (No one should waste hours trying to guess who said what. I have ways of hiding sources. And in any case there were others, not enumerated here, in dark corners, at night.)

Outside the Treasury I would like to thank Howard Davies, Terry (now Lord) Higgins, Sarah (now Lady) Hogg, Tessa Keswick, Peter Mandelson, Sylvain de Forges and Giles Radice, MP, among many others for their time and insights. Giles Radice and Gavyn Davies among outsiders read the whole manuscript, as did Lord Burns, and I have benefited greatly from their comments.

Nearly everyone I spoke to outside the Treasury and many inside are more critical of the institution than I am myself. John Maynard Keynes, himself both an insider and an outsider, once compared Treasury control to conventional morality. 'There is a great deal of it rather tiresome and absurd once you . . . look into it . . . nevertheless it is an essential bulwark against overwhelming wickedness.' I am, on this point at least, a Keynesian.

The Treasury does lots of silly things for lots of silly reasons; and quite often ends up doing them badly. But most of what it has to do are things someone has to do: stopping us spending more than we earn; or inflating ourselves to bankruptcy; or wasting the taxpayers' money. Given the complexity of the world and the political pressures the miracle is, as with Johnson's woman preacher, not that it is done well but that it is done at all. In any case, much of it is done well, very well, by humane and intelligent people, working inhumane hours for unspectacular pay – most of them doing it, in part at least, not for their own sakes but for ours. We could do better. But we could easily do a good deal worse. If, after reading this book, you think the Treasury seems less like the enemy of the good, I shall have achieved my objective.

Introduction | 1

The ups and downs of recent Treasury history recorded; the views of its critics set out and assessed; and its fundamental character as a necessary evil described.

The Treasury has few friends. Inside government, it is loathed for its arrogance and its meanness. Outside government, it is reviled for its conservatism and its incompetence. Anthony Sampson, in his classic *The Anatomy of Britain*, described the Treasury as the 'central citadel' of British government. That citadel is constantly under siege.

The history of the Treasury suggests that it goes back nearly a millennium, before the Domesday Book; in the pages of that great reckoning of the country's wealth we glimpse the shadowy presence of a 'thesaurorius'. Two centuries earlier, Alfred the Great planned the budget of Wessex. The Exchequer itself refers to the chequered cloth used to count money by piling it up on squares. The Chancellor of the Exchequer was once the Lord Chancellor's Clerk. An apparatus of tally sticks – with notches as wide as a handspan for thousands of pounds and narrow as a hair for pence – was used to keep track. Henry Rosebeare, the historian of the Treasury, records that there was an element of ritual in all this, a symbol of the Treasury's pomp and power.

The themes that characterize the modern Treasury are apparent from earlier times. Here is King James I musing perceptively that 'All Treasurers, if they do good service to their masters, must be generally hated.' Here is Charles II's Treasury fretting as to whether it could meet the king's request for £300 to buy 'a little house near St James's

Park' for one of the king's mistresses. We see the beginnings of parliamentary accountability in 1340, though it was not completed in its modern form until two thirds of the way through the nineteenth century. 'As sure as the Exchequer' was an old English proverb.

Nor is there anything new about the ups and downs of Treasury fortunes which have characterized recent years, though the cycles seem to come and go rather quicker nowadays. One great accretion in Treasury power came between 1665 and 1714, but the eighteenth-century Treasury was often marred by corruption and sinecurism. Treasury hours at one point were from eleven in the morning until three in the afternoon.

Rosebeare records intense debates between the Treasury and its critics, reaching high points in the 1780s, the 1820s, the 1850s, 1900 and 1942, as its critics railed against the iniquities of 'Treasury control'. It has always had to fight for its place in the world. Behind every Treasury official today saying no to some plausible departmental spending bid stand the ghosts of his forefathers and their forefathers, fighting the unending battle for national fiscal continence.

The nineteenth century saw the Treasury's influence in that regard hugely on the up. This it owed as much to an improvement in its abilities as to any increase in its powers. The process in fact began with the reforms of 1782–3, when it was decided that promotion amongst the underclerks should go to those 'who have distinguished themselves most by their Diligence, Attention and Acquirement of the Knowledge of business without regard to seniority' – effectively the end of sinecurism. One clerk who had not attended for two years was actually dismissed. Reform then saw the abolition of the sinecures – public officials supplementing their salaries by charging fees – and the extension of audit.

This process was carried on in the wake of the Northcote–Trevelyan report of 1854, which modernized the public service. Sir Charles Trevelyan was a Treasury man, and wanted an efficient civil service. His report ushered in recruitment by open competition, promotion on merit and a division between the 'intellectual and mechanical work' of administration to free the top brains from drudgery. Thereafter, one member of a royal commission observed that the Treasury 'was not satisfied with an ordinary first-class man, but they want a double-first-class man of Balliol'.

The rise in Treasury power was reflected by a gradual rise in its manpower. In 1784, after the reforms, its core still consisted of four chief clerks, six senior clerks and six junior clerks, with administrative support. The numbers grew but not steadily: for example, in 1822, the number of junior clerks, sixteen, was reduced to eleven. But gradually it grew into its task. By 1904, its upper echelons numbered twenty-five.

Economy was still its principal objective. Over the twenty-five years of the Napoleonic Wars, the national debt rose from £240 million to £840 million, a frightening figure when annual taxation revenue amounted to only some £80 million a year. The Treasury's powers still had their limits. Though they could veto departmental expenditures, they could not actually control their inner workings. At one point, Trevelyan himself was to complain to the Select Committee on Miscellaneous Expenditure that, though it had managed to get the War Office and the Admiralty to use cheaper stationery, the Foreign Office and the Home Office continued to use a very expensive quality – *plus ça change*. Yet its veto power was still a powerful one.

It was further buttressed by the developments in political economy of the time, and in particular, the rise of liberalism. 'Economical reform' was the watchword of the age. Under Gladstone's seven great years as chancellor from 1859 to 1866, a purposeful Treasury made itself felt. Its instinctive austerity was reinforced by the doctrines of the economic liberals, who were the apostles of free markets, and low state spending. Their doctrines showed that the state could not combat recession either by spending more or by borrowing more: rather the reverse. Thus the Treasury buttressed its traditional belief in economy with a theoretical justification for it, based on the latest political economy.

It was able increasingly to use Parliament, an institution dominated by the taxpaying classes, as its ally in containing expenditure. The Public Accounts Committee, still Parliament's watchdog, dates from 1861. The Exchequer and Audit Departments Act of 1866 brought together estimates, appropriation, expenditure and audit into a more or less coherent system, which survived to an extraordinary extent into the last years of the twentieth century.

Lord Salisbury, the Tory prime minister, attacked the Treasury in 1900 for its power. 'It has,' he said perceptively, 'the power of the purse, and by exercising the power of the purse, it claims a voice in all decisions of administrative authority and policy. I think that much delay and many doubtful resolutions have been the result of the peculiar position which, through many generations, the Treasury has occupied.'

It should not be, though, that its power goes uncontested. 'You do not get any criticism at the Treasury – none whatsoever,' an assistant secretary at the Board of Trade told a royal commission. 'You get refusals, but you do not get any discussion. Treasury "reasons" are not worth considering at all . . . Reasons founded on entire ignorance . . . nothing can be more useless and absurd.'

The Times in 1980 attacked the Treasury's control of the civil service establishments. 'It is no ordinary storm which has burst upon the Treasury,' said a leading article of 20 January 1980. 'Sluices of bitterness long dammed up' poured out, sparking a bitter correspondence.

Nor was it successful in keeping spending down, as the rise of an industrial society led to new demands on the state. Indeed the rise of the working class, and its political representation in Parliament, led to the increase in public expenditure's share of the nation's wealth which seemed irreversible until the last quarter of the nineteenth century. Lloyd George's 'ninepence for fourpence', which launched the national insurance system before the First World War can hardly have been welcome to the official Treasury, whatever the political and social imperatives which underlay it.

War has often been the catalyst for increased Treasury power and influence, as the damages to the national finances are repaired. This was true for the Second World War, but less so for the First. However, the Treasury had a good record in that war, preventing a financial collapse in the City in 1914 by prompt action. It also raised government revenues considerably, with basic income tax raised from 1s 2d (6p) to 6s (30p) in the pound. The Haldane Committee of 1919 developed the Treasury's administrative machinery, and especially its expertise in establishment matters and its control of the civil service. At the end of the process its head was also the head of the civil service – a post which, however, remained controversial ever afterwards.

If the First World War represented a limited success for the Treasury, however, the twenties and thirties were disastrous. Britain's return to the Gold Standard in 1925 owed as much to the Bank of England as to the Treasury, but Winston Churchill, the chancellor, afterwards felt his officials had 'misled' him. The Treasury continued to apply its rules of balancing budgets and seeking economies even as slump and depression were rendering these policies counter-productive. In 1929, under Philip Snowden, Labour's chancellor, the Treasury insisted on cuts which destroyed the government and created a betrayal myth which haunted that party from then until the 1990s. The lack of economic expertise is obvious, at least in retrospect. Opponents of deflation, such as John Maynard Keynes (who had been a Treasury official from 1914 to 1918), argued against these policies in vain.

The experience of the 1930s conditioned the post-war Treasury. In the period after the Second World War, it was mostly criticized for being too deflationary, for 'stop–go' economic policies and for an excess of restraint. From today's perspective, however, it might at least as easily be regarded as excessively expansionist, over-optimistic about the capacity of the economy to expand and insufficiently sceptical of the influence of fiscal policy. Certainly, its emphasis on international credibility looks better with the benefit of hindsight, after the experience of the IMF crisis of 1975–6 had taught the nation a hard lesson in the realities of global economics.

For this was the period in which the cycle of Treasury ups and downs was at its most compressed, its reputation rising and falling almost as abruptly as that of the chancellor of the exchequer himself. At the time of writing, that is to say in mid-1999, it had emerged from a bad patch. Where, at the beginning of 1998, the talk was all of internal tensions and low morale, now it was of a new arrogance. But what goes up also comes down; and there is no guarantee that that will still be the case by the time this book is read.

For there is a cycle in the reputation of the Treasury almost as well established as the economic cycle itself. Consider the past decade. At the end of the 1980s, the Treasury went through a long down swing. Having ridden high, intellectually and politically, during the Lawson years, it was widely blamed for the bust that followed the irresponsible boom of those years. This culminated in recession for industry and repossession for home owners.

Worse was to come, though. In 1992, it copped the blame for Britain's unceremonial exit from the Exchange Rate Mechanism of the European Monetary System. Later this was to lead to the sacking of the chancellor, Norman Lamont. 'It is no small thing for the Treasury to lose a chancellor,' a senior Treasury mandarin observed later.

Under Mr Lamont's successor, Kenneth Clarke, the Treasury began to regain ground. Mr Clarke was at least a substantial political figure – albeit in an insubstantial government.

Nevertheless, the Treasury felt its creativity to be undermined by the government's weakness, and by the chancellor's conviction that he knew more about practically anything than they did. It was no affectation when, following Labour's victory in the 1997 general election, officials lined the staircase of the Treasury's monumental chambers in Whitehall to cheer Gordon Brown, the new chancellor, into office.

What followed was typical of the ups and downs of Treasury life. Over his first weekend in the Treasury, Mr Brown determined to put into effect a secret plan, drawn up in outline when Labour was in opposition, to give independence to the Bank of England. Senior officials such as Sir Terry Burns, then permanent secretary, and Sir Alan Budd, then chief economic adviser, worked round the clock on the details. The chancellor was, by all accounts, impressed.

The amity did not last. Little incidents combined to undermine Mr Brown's faith. There were budget leaks which he blamed (they think unfairly) on officials. The chancellor did not think highly of the official handling of his decision, only weeks after giving the Bank of England independence, to take away its job of supervising the financial system. He felt the Treasury had failed to warn the Bank of England that its supervisory powers would be reduced. They thought that he was not wise to embark on a second major reform affecting the bank so quickly and with such inadequate preparation.

For a while, many Treasury officials felt themselves to have been sidelined in favour of the chancellor's personal appointees – Ed Balls, his economic adviser in opposition, and his other personal adviser, Ed Miliband. Charlie Whelan, his personal press secretary, shouldered aside Jill Rutter, the official press spokesperson. Word began to get around that the chancellor did not think much of his senior officials. Sir Terry, in particular, was said to be out of the loop, and rumours that he would leave began to circulate.

Some senior Treasury officials thought from the first that this would prove a passing phase. This is what always happened, they comforted themselves, when a new chancellor comes to office in a new government, full of natural suspicion of those who served his predecessors. When, however, the chancellor settles in, he learns to distinguish the officials he trusts from the officials he does not trust.

The former become the Treasury's standard-bearers with him. The process is speeded up if a new chancellor gets into trouble. He will turn to them for the salvation that comes from their collective memory and experience.

By the end of 1998, Mr Brown had not yet got into serious trouble. Nevertheless, things had certainly changed. Sir Terry had left, for the House of Lords, the sadness of his passing eased when the chancellor found two World Cup final tickets for him as a parting present. Meanwhile some officials were impressing the chancellor.

It will always be Mr Brown's way to rely on a coterie of confidants of unimpeachable personal loyalty as well as great industry. Hence the 'hotel group' of his intimates – so called because of their supposed tendency to meet in the large suite at the Grosvenor House Hotel off Park Lane occupied by Geoffrey Robinson, until the end of 1998 himself a Treasury minister.

Equally, however, as the coterie ran through the ideas which it had worked up in opposition, it had increasingly to work with officials to force through the next wave of reform. Welfare-to-work, for example, a project close to the chancellor's heart, required detailed painstaking effort by Treasury officials. Officials also enjoyed the reflected power which came from the chancellor's dominance of large parts of the Blair government's domestic agenda.

But even aside from Mr Brown's personality, the future of the traditional mandarinate, swapping effortlessly from government to government, is in question at the Treasury, as it is throughout White-hall. Not everyone believes that the sceptical, non-partisan official, peddling his traditional remedies, can compete with the modern medicine of the political adviser and the spin doctor.

There is an analogy, not an exact one, to be sure, but one which perhaps illustrates the Treasury's difficulties. Britain's monarchy, too, is an institution with deep historical roots. The monarchy once had tremendous authority; it could ignore criticism. But then the criticism became too strong to ignore. Though the immediate crisis caused by the death of the Princess of Wales is over, the monarchy is struggling to reinvent itself for the future. So is the Treasury.

The Treasury is not likely to fall into the same moral traps as caught the monarchy. Treasury men and women – inclined still to regard a night playing chamber music as a pretty wild time – are not like that. But the proximate cause in both institutions were similar: the decline generally in inherited authority. In a rough democratic era, all institutions come under fire. Wherever you look – parliament, business, the professions – reputations have fallen, questions are asked and those in charge are held accountable. What before could be done by edict now has to be done by consent, and consent has to be earned. The Treasury is no exception.

The Treasury, like the monarchy, has been somewhat bewildered by the change. Of course, there were always those who criticized it, and a broad back was always a necessary attribute in its officials. And, like monarchs, Treasury people had always understood that there was a price to be paid for their position, which required discretion even when under fire.

However, at the Treasury's low point the level of criticism was deeply threatening. Since the monarchy does not have a real job to do, except in times of crisis, its troubles do not matter much. They involve, no doubt, angst in its members and entertainment for the populace, but public affairs would go on generally in much the same way if they went as they would if they stay.

The same cannot be said of the Treasury. If criticism goes too far, if it goes beyond differences on policy to questions of competence, if, worst of all, it suggests that the organization has lost its essential unity, then criticism can destroy its capacity to do its job. That undermines confidence in the financial markets and it reduces the Treasury's ability to influence the climate in which business operates.

It also makes it harder for its political leaders to deliver, in Cabinet, in Parliament and in public generally. Besides, no one likes to go from being the subject of awed reverence to being viewed with something approaching contempt. Even among men and women who rate intellectual toughness high amongst their virtues, the last few years of Treasury life have seen hard institutional pounding, from which they were relieved, at the time of writing, to be emerging.

Mr Brown may have disappointed some Treasury officials by his reluctance to let them come close to him. But that was outweighed for most, and certainly for most junior ones, by the immense boon he brought to them. A genuinely big figure, he dominated all save the prime minister in government. The Treasury's writ again ran where it had threatened not to run any more.

In the bad patches, the conversation of Treasury officials frequently mused on the chances of the Treasury recovering its position, and officials their position within it. No more. It was able under Mr Brown to return to its old attitudes: arrogant towards the views and capacities of others, and hungry for power. By 1999, the worry of some Treasury officials was that, under Mr Brown's leadership, they were again in danger of overplaying their hands.

The Treasury's critics

Still, better to be thought too strong than too weak. The Treasury did not enjoy its bad run. The unpopularity it suffers when it is doing well is more easily borne. For, as worldly wise Treasury officials are swift to tell you, criticism and unpopularity go with their territory.

Of course they will be unpopular with spending departments and their ministers. Treasury officials are daily made aware how each minister has a thousand plausible projects on which they would like public (i.e., taxpayers') money expended. Each spending department, moreover, is itself under siege: from pressure groups on behalf of clients from agriculture to zoological research, each with powerful claims as to the unsustainability of current funding and the great good to be derived from more spending. Departments, usually sym-

The Forward March of Expenditure Halted?

Year	Total managed expenditure as % of GDP	Financial year	Total managed expenditure as % of GDP
1948	36.1	1955/56	35.6
1949	36.6	1956/57	36.2
1950	36	1957/58	35.6
1951	38.3	1958/59	36.6
1952	39.4	1959/60	36.3
1953	39.4	1960/61	36.6
1954	37.7	1961/62	38.6
1955	35.7	1962/63	38.3
1956	36.1	1963/64	38.4
1957	35.7	1964/65	37.9
1958	36.4	1965/66	39.2
1959	36.7	1966/67	40.9
1960	36.4	1967/68	44.1
1961	37.8	1968/69	43
1962	38.5	1969/70	42
1963	38.1	1970/71	42.2
1964	38	1971/72	42.2
1965	38.9	1972/73	41.5
1966	39.9	1973/74	44.2
1967	43.4	1974/75	48.7
1968	43.6	1975/76	49.9
1969	42.1	1976/77	48.7
1970	42	1977/78	45.5
1971	41.9	1978/79	44.9
1972	41.9	1979/80	44.8
1973	42.3	1980/81	47.3
1974	48	1981/82	48.1
1975	49.8	1982/83	48.5
1976	49.5	1983/84	48.3
1977	45.8	1984/85	48
1978	45.1	1985/86	45.6
1979	44.4	1986/87	43.9
1980	46.8	1987/88	42.1
1981	48	1988/89	39.2
1982	48.3	1989/90	39.6
1983	48.3	1990/91	39.7
1984	48	1991/92	42.4
1985	46.3	1992/93	44.2
1986	44.5	1993/94	43.8
1987	42.4	1994/95	43.3
1988	39.8	1995/96	42.8
1989	39.4	1996/97	41.4
1990	39.7	1997/98	39.6
1991	41.5		
1992	43.9		
1993	44		
1994	43.5		
1995	43.1		
1996	41.6		
1997	39.9		

GDP starts in 1948 annually and in 1955 quarterly. Figures are consistent with data published on 21 December 1998.

pathetic to these causes, dislike saying no. When they do, they often find it politic to blame the Treasury, whose standing outside Whitehall is correspondingly undermined.

Yet Treasury men and women can fairly point out that these criticisms run in parallel with another criticism strongly made outside government: of the rise in public spending and the Treasury's failure to stop it. Over the past century, public expenditure has risen in fits and starts: starting at around 10 per cent of GDP in 1890; first approaching 50 per cent during the First World War before dropping back below 30 per cent in the 1930s; rising to 60 per cent during the Second World War before easing back to around a third in 1950; then steadily climbing above 40 per cent in the 1970s. It rose further to above 45 per cent in the early 1980s, thanks to the burden of welfare payments to the rising number of unemployed. It is at present declining somewhat, with a projection for the end of this parliament of around 40 per cent (see table). Compare this with other European nations, and it seems surprisingly low. Compare it with the United States, still more with the Far East, and it seems high.

So to one set of critics the Treasury is a supremely mean institution. To another set of critics it is a supremely weak one. Either may be right, but they cannot both be.

The same contradictions are apparent where the Treasury's wider management of the economy is concerned. Conveniently in this case, the same person was an eminent mouthpiece for both sets of criticisms. In 1964, Sam Brittan, a distinguished economic journalist, wrote his trenchant *The Treasury under the Tories*. It was a coruscating demolition of the stop–go policies of the time. As Brittan saw it, the Treasury slammed on the macroeconomic brakes whenever the British economy was picking up momentum. Then, when the economy juddered to a halt, the Treasury would press the accelerator too hard, too late. The result was deeply damaging to economic confidence and to the willingness of business to invest. Britain's growth rate was lower in consequence. As the title of his book suggested, he thought the Treasury was at least as much to blame as the Tories.

It was an influential critique. The Labour party took it up and ran with it. Harold Wilson became prime minister in 1964 with an inchoate determination to break the power of the Treasury. The Department of Economic Affairs, designed to plan the economy for a faster rate of growth, was the result. Wilson had not thought through precisely what planning in a mixed economy meant, and the DEA proved a failure. There was as much stopping and going in the first Wilson government as before.

But the 1960s gave way to the 1970s and the theory of stop–go gave way to another theory, later to be dubbed monetarism. The same distinguished economic journalist was converted to the new theory, and was joined by the other principal economic journalist of the day, Peter Jay.

Now inflation was the main peril threatening the economy. It could be countered only by tight monetary policy, which in turn required the government to borrow much less than it had habitually thought right.

In the 1980s, a Conservative government was elected which shared this analysis. So, though at first sceptical, did most Treasury officials. Mr Brittan became Sir Sam in 1993. Outside critics remained vocal, but the new philosophy won through. In the global economy of the 1980s and 1990s, it was no longer possible for one economy to inflate its way out of recession.

But within the new conventional wisdom new fractures swiftly appeared. There were fractures between devotees of pure monetarism, focusing on particular measures of the money supply to determine the stance of policy, and eclectic monetarism, which looked at a broader set of indicators. There was constant controversy about the role of the exchange rate in economic policy: the degree to which it should be left to market forces and the degree to which the authorities should influence it. From the mid-1980s on, this got tied up with another politically charged debate about Britain and the European Union. It so happened that Europhiles all thought that Britain's economy as well as its politics would be well served by linking its currency to those of the European Union, and that Europhobes all thought the reverse.

Here is not the place to go into the rights and wrongs of these controversies, which are now for historians. The Treasury itself ducked and weaved around them. What is clear is that the Treasury, whatever its policies, could never simultaneously have satisfied all its critics. It could not have satisfied the pressure groups for more spending on particular things while accommodating advocates of less spending overall. It could not sensibly tighten fiscal policy to please the inflation hawks and loosen fiscal policy to please the expansionists. It could not simultaneously peg the pound for price stability and lower it for competitiveness. Interest rates could be set to promote growth or to fight inflation, but not manipulated in the short term to achieve both.

The Treasury's actual stance has been pragmatic. Ministers have come and gone; parties have embraced their own pet theories; but the Treasury as an institution has rarely gone overboard for any particular economic and political fashion. As each has come into prominence, it has sought to absorb its more abiding elements, but without the zeal of the true convert. It has been ever sceptical, empirical, cautious, careful and where possible safe. Enthusiasts are not for the Treasury; nor the Treasury for enthusiasts.

What has been less often noticed, as the great theoretical economic arguments of the past die down, is that its policy, though inglorious, has also been reasonably successful. Take as a starting point 1991. Then, the critics of Treasury deflationism were again in the ascendancy. British membership of the Exchange Rate Mechanism of the European Monetary System was, they said, causing high interest rates in Britain, and therefore deep recession. Exit from the ERM was a precondition of recovery.

As we shall see, Britain did indeed leave the ERM. However, by then the British economy had already begun a slow recovery. It started in the autumn of 1991 and lasted for at least the following seven years. In that same period, despite Britain's proneness to bouts of inflation, the underlying rate of inflation had fallen to around 2.5 per cent. It was seven years before there was again any prospect of recession – a period of sustained growth without parallel in Britain's recent economic history and which, in 1999, showed no signs of ending.

It would be Panglossian to say that all problems had been solved. The danger of over-optimism was illustrated in the summer and autumn of 1998, when opinion swung from concern that the economy was overheating to concern that it might collapse in the wake of the Far East economic crisis and slumping stock markets. Swings from optimism to pessimism and back are as old as the economic cycle itself, and the Treasury tries not to get carried away by them. All that can be said with certainty of its middle-of-the-road caution is that no one has yet come up with a better way of managing the economy.

A necessary evil

If the Treasury did not exist, it would have to be invented. Two Treasury functions, at least, are essential to any system of government. One, which until recently most commentators would have identified as the most central, is that of running the economy. That does not of course mean, in a modern mixed economy, actually producing anything. It does not even mean planning, in any direct or even indicative way, for others to produce anything – though there have at odd moments popped up odd figures on the left who would have liked the Treasury to do a bit of each. It does, however, mean setting the parameters under which others produce, through, for example, the stance of fiscal policy and its related monetary policy.

In recent years, macroeconomic policy has declined in importance. Economists have become less confident of its power, at least to change things for the better; and politicians have found that they cannot even manipulate the economy to win elections. Whereas macroeconomic policy was in the post-war period regarded as a way of smoothing out economic fluctuations, its role is now seen as more modest. The aim, broadly, is to provide a stable framework for economic policy, no more, no less.

However, this does not mean that the Treasury has abandoned all its ambitions to improve the performance of the economy. As we shall see, its main tools, both under the Conservatives and under the New Labour administration, have been microeconomic: the promotion of competition, a preference for free trade, and measures, including welfare-to-work, designed to promote the better workings of the labour market. Cautious as ever, the Treasury does not yet claim that such measures have improved the growth of the productive capacity of the economy, which it puts at around 2.25 per cent per annum. But the coexistence of faster growth with low inflation plausibly owes much to this change.

The second function that has to be fulfilled is the control of the overall level of public spending. Perhaps when government was consuming only 10 or 15 per cent of national output, it was sufficient to leave individual departments to control their own spending, subject only to parliamentary oversight. But no one who has observed recent history can believe that that would be possible now. Ministers' bids for public spending always exceed the amount of money which could plausibly be made available to them. Moreover, they would exceed it by more were they not aware of the presence of the Treasury. Fear of too obvious a defeat over spending – not to mention of an intellectual savaging at the hands of the Treasury's brightest and best – is the only thing that keeps departments continent.

These two functions do not necessarily have to be combined in a single ministry; in Germany, for example, economic affairs is handled separately from expenditure control. The two functions do, however, both have to be fulfilled. The question to be asked about the Treasury is not: does the job need to be done? The question to be asked is: does the Treasury do it well? And the conclusion of this book is that it does it not at all badly.

2 | Dramatis Personae

The roles and characters of the chancellor, of Treasury ministers, of their special advisers and of senior officials, and the way in which they interrelate.

The chancellor of the exchequer

Punch's advice to those thinking of becoming chancellor: don't. Since 1945, Britain has had nineteen chancellors. Of these, only three – Harold Macmillan, James Callaghan and John Major – have gone on to become prime minister. Being chancellor cost Denis Healey certainly, and Roy Jenkins and Kenneth Clarke probably, the leadership of their party and perhaps of their country. It ruined Hugh Dalton and Norman Lamont and it killed Stafford Cripps. Lord Callaghan, who finally made it to the top job in 1976 after the Exchequer nearly destroyed him a decade earlier over the devaluation of the pound, once remarked, 'You either leave in time or in disgrace.'

The chancellor is not even titular king of his own department. The title 'First Lord of the Treasury' actually belongs to the prime minister, to Number 10 Downing Street, not Number 11. Lady Thatcher, to whom deference did not come naturally, would frequently remind her chancellors of the fact when they quarrelled with her.

Few would dispute that the chancellor is the second most important figure in the government after the prime minister. Foreign secretaries still keep up appearances, but their true power has diminished with Britain's position in the world. Home secretaries have awesome responsibilities, but in a relatively narrow field. But there is hardly anything governments do that does not affect either the economy of the country or the amount of its citizens' money that it spends. Chancellors of necessity roam wide.

They also roam alone. The most striking fact about any chancellor's position is its isolation. In general each of his colleagues has an interest in his success. After all, a successful economy with the right balance between public and private spending is the best ticket for re-election. In each particular case, however, each individual colleague may have an interest in his failure. The minister of agriculture of course accepts the general case for free markets, but he would just like something to be done for sheep farmers to get them off his back. The minister of social security of course accepts the case for public spending restraint, but surely no one would want it to affect the very poorest in our society. And besides, every other serious politician in the Cabinet bar the prime minister covets the chancellor's job.

What is the chancellor to do then? He is not without resource. He would not have the job unless he was a senior politician, with the support of the prime minister, but also, most likely, of a significant faction within his party. He also has considerable formal powers. Broadly speaking, no minister can spend money without his say-so. All major policy initiatives have to be cleared with the Treasury. Every department is marked by the Treasury. Nothing can be done (or not much) behind his back.

The chancellor, however, can still be overruled by the Cabinet. It follows that it must be his first duty to ensure that he is not.

His main strength here is his relationship with the prime minister. The prime minister has a power denied to the chancellor: namely the power to sack ministers. That means that a strong prime minister can usually deliver Cabinet support for the chancellor's policy if he wants to. The chancellor's aim must be to make sure that he does want to. He does this by ensuring both that he commands prime ministerial support for the basic thrust of his policy and that he is too strong himself to be sacrificed if his policy goes wrong. If the chancellor fails in that aim, he is doomed.

Tiffs between prime ministers and chancellors are endemic. Prime ministers always want, at the margins, to cut taxes a little more and to have interest rates a little lower, particularly in the run-ups to general elections. The good chancellor is more cautious.

However, if a tiff turns into a confrontation, the chancellor is dead, as the recent fatal rows between Nigel Lawson and Margaret Thatcher and eventually between Norman Lamont and John Major showed. This explains the extreme sensitivity in the early months of the New Labour government of Gordon Brown and Tony Blair over their relationship – a relationship complicated by the fact that the man who was initially the junior partner in it eventually got the top job.

But the chancellor cannot rely on his relationship with the prime minister alone. His ability to command his colleagues will depend on his wider political skills.

Different chancellors deploy different weapons. Sir Geoffrey Howe used sweet reason to bore his colleagues into submission; Nigel Lawson used the force of his logic; Mr Brown deploys the power of his personality.

Some chancellors rely on their party position to control their colleagues. Mr Callaghan, for example, could always draw on his strong trade-union support in the party. Others summon up outside powers. Denis Healey used first the power of the financial markets and then that of the International Monetary Fund to deal with the stabilization crisis of 1976–7. Others use their command of Parliament, and of the media. Kenneth Clarke, for example, was a fine parliamentary debater and a destructive broadcaster, which gave him the political clout to get his way.

Chancellors also differ greatly in their style. Sir Geoffrey Howe, who had the advantage of a barrister's training, was a man who required little sleep, devoured paper and loved meetings. Norman Lamont liked meetings too, though many thought that this was because they gave him new opportunities to defer decisions. Kenneth Clarke, by contrast, held few meetings and did not like lots of paper. Though it is untrue that he would not take advice, it is true that, after an unbroken run in government back to 1979, he thought he knew more than most officials; also that he was a man who found decision-taking easy. So much so that Mr Brown and his crew found that they had to do some re-education on taking office to re-accustom officials to the work demands of a different kind of chancellor.

Ministers

'We have at least one minister too many here,' says one Treasury official as the discussion turns to his titular masters. And then another says the same thing. And then another and then another, until you realize that this is not a considered verdict on ministerial workloads, but a piece of organizational theology. Since it is the Treasury's professional creed that everything can be cut, there seems no reason to make an exception for ministers. 'We have at least one minister too many here.'

There are many ministries in Whitehall which do indeed have at least one minister too many, but the Treasury is not one of them. When I met Helen Liddell, the tough and resilient economic secretary to the Treasury in the spring of 1998, she had that eye-tiredness which signals overwork, pressure and too little sleep.

This is not surprising. When Labour took office, Mrs Liddell took over responsibility for overseeing one of the great financial scandals of the century. Urged on by the Tories, private insurance companies had rushed into the market with personal pensions. Millions were sold in pursuit of commission with scant regard to their suitability. A review of every case was under way under the auspices of the Personal Investment Authority, the industry's regulator, but foot-dragging by the firms had slowed things down.

Allocation of Responsibilities of Treasury Ministers, Spring 1999

Chief secretary, Alan Milburn MP

- Public expenditure planning and control (including local authorities and nationalized industries finance)
- Value for money in the public services, including Public Service Agreements
- Departmental investment strategies including Capital Modernization Fund and Invest to Save budget
- Public/private partnerships including Private Finance Initiative
- Procurement policy
- Public sector pay, including parliamentary pay, allowances and superannuation
- Presentation of economic policy and economic briefing
- Welfare reform
- Devolution
- Strategic oversight of banking, financial services and insurance
- PSX (public services and expenditure), QFL (forward legislation), GL (local government), HS (home and social affairs) and EA (economic affairs) committees
- Resource accounting and budgeting

Paymaster-general, Dawn Primarolo MP

- Minister responsible for Inland Revenue, Customs and Excise and the Treasury and with overall responsibility for tax and the Finance Bill
- Personal taxation, NI contributions, tax credits
- Business taxation, including corporation tax
- Capital gains tax
- Inheritance tax
- VAT
- European and international tax issues

Financial secretary, Barbara Roche MP

- Growth, with responsibility for the growth unit and productivity agenda
- Small firms and venture capital
- Science, research and development
- Welfare-to-work issues
- Competition and deregulation policy
- Export Credit
- Customs and Excise taxes, except VAT and road fuel duties
- North Sea taxation
- Support to the Paymaster General on the Finance Bill
- Parliamentary financial business, PAC, NAO
- LEG Committee (current legislation)
- Support to the Chief Secretary on the Financial Services & Markets Bill

Economic secretary, Patricia Hewitt MP
- Banking, financial services and insurance and support to the Chief Secretary on the Financial Services & Markets Bill
- Foreign exchange reserves and debt management policy
- Support to the Chancellor on EU and international issues
- Responsibility for National Savings, the Debt Management Office, National Investment and Loans Office, Office of National Statistics, Royal Mint and the Government Actuary's Department
- Environmental issues, including 'green' taxes and other environmental economic instruments
- Taxation of company cars and road fuel: Vehicle Excise Duty
- Financial services tax issues (e.g. ISAs, stamp duty, pensions)
- Support to the paymaster-general on the Finance Bill
- ESOPs
- Treasury interest in general accountancy issues; support to the chief secretary on resource accounting and budgeting
- Charities and charity taxation
- Women's issues

Minister of state, Lord Simon
- EMU business preparations
- Economic reform in Europe
- Chairman of the inter-departmental taskforce on competitiveness in Europe
- Member of the (E)DOP Ministerial Sub Committee on European Issues

Mrs Liddell knew what it was to be diddled over a pension. Once an employee of the late Robert Maxwell, she had suffered from his robbery of his companies' pensions funds.

Mrs Liddell took a personal grip on the pensions scandal, summoning the industry's grandees before her and castigating their performance. All manner of retribution was threatened. It was not always clear that she had precisely the powers that she used to bludgeon them, but it worked anyway. Previous obstacles melted away; staff were hired and the compensation paid soon passed £1 billion. Mrs Liddell's stock rose. She was one of those chosen to accompany Tony Blair to America for an intellectual summit with Bill Clinton in 1998 and was later moved from the Treasury to spearhead Labour's campaign to defeat the Scottish Nationalists north of the border.

Her successor as economic secretary, Patricia Hewitt – who has since moved on – inherited her workload. She had responsibility for the new bill to reform regulation of the financial services industry – a bill which runs to 367 clauses. The job also involved a good deal of day-to-day work on, for example, answering questions on economic policy and covering for the chancellor in lesser media appearances, as well as the grinding round of Cabinet committees and the receiving of deputations which make up the life of a junior minister.

The economic secretary has plenty to do besides fixing financial services. He or she now bears the brunt of EU work and of preparations for EMU; does the detail on low pay and the minimum wages; looks after debt management and international economic matters; and is the Treasury minister for women.

That is just one Treasury ministerial job. If you consult the authoritative *Vacher's Parliamentary Companion*, you will find some twenty-three ministers listed for the Treasury, together with a clutch of parliamentary private secretaries (MPs who dogsbody for ministers in the Commons). This total is, however, misleading. It includes the prime minister. It includes the chief whip and his lesser whips. It includes Lord Simon, a trade minister who spent about half his time with the Treasury, dealing mostly with EU matters; and it includes Lord Haskell, who is a spokesman for the Treasury in the Lords.

There are five full-time Treasury ministers other than the chancellor. The chief secretary is the senior of them. It is a job that has been done in the recent past by some of the fastest rising men of government, such as Michael Portillo, as well as those riding for a fall, such as Jonathan Aitken. In the summer of 1998, the clever and sceptical Alastair Darling, a rising Scot, was replaced by Stephen Byers, an ultra-Blairite modernizer. He in turn was replaced by Alan Milburn, another rising modernizer, when he was moved to the Department of Trade and Industry following the resignation of Peter Mandelson in December 1998.

The chief secretary, who, like the chancellor, is a member of the cabinet, is responsible for public spending – the subject of Chapters 8 to 10 below. He also takes responsibility with the Treasury for public-sector pay, including parliamentary pay, allowances and superannuation. Devolution is his, as is export credit (see Chapter 14).

Next in the hierarchy is the paymaster-general. The names of most paymaster-generals are not much to conjure with, but the occupant in 1998 was an exception. Geoffrey Robinson is a rich and controversial figure with an eye for a deal. His closeness to Mr Blair and Mr Brown kept him in office despite controversy over his business interests and personal tax arrangements which ran on and on. The paymaster-general's job varies; in Mr Robinson's case it was tailored to his particular talents.

He was supposed to be responsible for growth. He looked after the government's welfare-to-work policy, as important as any to its strategy. Industry came his way as the sort of thing he, as a former chief executive of Rover, was supposed to know about; and he launched a one-man bid within government to increase its help to the coal-mining industry in 1997–8. Corporate taxation, small firms, public–private partnerships were his, as was the windfall levy on privatized utilities. At his peak, it was hard to think of a junior minister in Whitehall who had more power, but inevitably the continual sniping at his integrity undermined him. Long before he lost office – for lending Mr Mandelson the money for his house – his responsibilities had become exiguous.

It remains to be seen whether his successors, starting with Dawn Primarolo, previously financial secretary, can rebuild the job on a different basis. Ms Primarolo is a former left-winger who looks and sounds like a faintly flustered Sunday-school teacher but has become respected by her colleagues for her safe pair of hands. She became better known towards the end of 1998 when the work of the little-known Code of Conduct Group, a European Union committee on unfair tax aids, which she chaired, was used by Eurosceptics to raise the bogey of tax harmonization in the EU.

The two junior Treasury ministers are the economic secretary, whose job we have already discussed, and the financial secretary. Both have more power than most junior ministers in Whitehall. The financial secretary after Ms Primarolo was Barbara Roche, who came from the Department of Trade and Industry. The workload includes dealing with the Inland Revenue and with Customs and Excise. Tax is detailed and difficult work. The financial secretary is also responsible for parliamentary financial business, piloting through the Commons arcane legislation such as the Exchequer and Audit Acts.

Just as the chancellor is outnumbered by Cabinet colleagues, so this small band is outnumbered by the mass hordes of would-be spenders in other departments. Just as he and the prime minister must stick together, so must his team stick with him if it is to survive.

The men and the women come and go; indeed it would be surprising if, by the time this book is published, the names of the team were as they are now. Theoretically the job descriptions also change, since it is largely up to the chancellor to decide who does what. However, the junior ministerial responsibilities have tended to remain reasonably stable over the years.

Formal responsibilities, however, never tell you the whole story of what junior ministers do. It is perfectly possible, if they want to, for the chancellor and chief secretary to do all the exciting bits themselves, leaving their juniors only scraps. Indeed even the chief secretary may have difficulty asserting his autonomous zone over an industrious or greedy chancellor.

Some chancellor are natural consulters. Most have daily or weekly meetings with their juniors – usually without officials present – to coordinate their political thinking. Some, however, are more natural consulters than others. Sir Geoffrey (now Lord) Howe, a workaholic, would talk things over endlessly with his political colleagues. Nigel Lawson was more of an autocrat. Gordon Brown has succeeded in getting a team entirely of trusties.

Junior ministers have their own styles too. Jock Bruce-Gardyne, for example, a junior minister under Geoffrey Howe from 1991 to 1993, was something of a licensed court jester on economic policy, guarding the flame of the monetarism that he had embraced as an economic journalist. Stephen Dorrell, under Lamont and Clarke, set out to balance his reputation as a Tory 'wet' by becoming a passionate privatizer. He was rewarded with a place in Cabinet, and was briefly in vogue as a candidate to succeed John Major as Tory leader. But for every colourful character and every rising star, there are several Treasury junior ministers who disappeared, as they arrived, without trace.

Special advisers

Ed Balls, Gordon Brown's special adviser, is not a menacing man. Though intellectually formidable, he is charming and normally unaggressive, his voice softened by a near lisp. At least once in his lifetime he was betrayed by a lack of worldliness: when, as adviser to Gordon Brown as shadow chancellor, he inserted in one of his boss's less stirring orations a reference to 'neoclassical endogenous growth theory', he attracted a classic put-down from Michael Heseltine, then deputy prime minister. 'It's not Brown. It's Balls.'

Yet the power ascribed to Mr Balls during Mr Brown's first year as chancellor was huge. Mr Balls was said to control the gateway to the chancellor. Officials who wished to persuade the latter had first to carry the former. He was widely claimed not to get on with Sir Terry Burns, the permanent secretary, who announced his retirement, at the age of 55, on 1 June 1998. Was it right that a man who had never been elected to anything should enjoy such power?

This was not the first time the question had been asked in the Treasury. In the 1960s, its corridors were inhabited by 'B and K', Tommy Balogh and Nicky Kaldor, great economists who were also Labour supporters. Kaldor even invented a tax, the Selective

Employment Tax, which was levied on service industries but not on manufacturing. The idea was that productivity rose faster in manufacturing than in services, so that if workers were shifted from the latter to the former, the economy would grow faster. Weird though the concept seems in these free-market days, it was in its time an idea of breathtaking originality.

These were perhaps the grandest of the Treasury's special advisers, and the most distinguished amongst them as economists. But from 1974 on, special advisers have become a permanent feature of the departmental scene. Numbers have varied between one and four but with the exception of a brief hiatus between Adrian Ham and Derek Scott for Denis Healey in 1977 and between David Ruffley and Anthony Teasdale for Kenneth Clarke in 1996, the special adviser has always been there. Mr Brown did not enjoy the services of Mr Balls alone; Charlie Whelan, his press secretary until early 1999, was also a special adviser. As the rules limited each Cabinet minister to two special advisers, Ed Miliband, the delightful and cerebral brother of David Miliband, the head of the prime minister's Policy Unit, officially worked for the chief secretary. Andrew Maugham really did.

The title has covered a wide range of types from, at one end, real experts (like Kaldor) to, at the other, those whose skills were primarily political. The latter included Mr Ruffley, a cunning spin doctor who went on to become a Conservative MP, and Warwick Lightfoot – or 'running bear' as the Treasury dubbed him. Tessa Keswick, Kenneth Clarke's adviser, was much liked but would not claim any special knowledge of economics. 'I cannot see that they bring anything at all to the feast,' said one top official of the Tory team towards the end of their time in office.

There have been heavy hitters among Treasury political advisers, such as Sir Adam Ridley. Sir Adam had been an influential head of the Conservative Research Department. When his party won the 1979 general election, he moved into Downing Street to work for Lady Thatcher. A few days later, he moved out again, his urbanity and roundedness ill-suited to her pushy style. Sir Geoffrey Howe, more appreciative, benefited from the inheritance.

There have been true experts: Bill Robinson, for example, under Norman Lamont. A former head of the Institute for Fiscal Studies, Mr Robinson was able to take on officials on their own terms. His expertise gave a spurious authority to his costing of Labour's programme at the 1992 general election, which resulted in the Tories' 'tax bombshell' – that Labour would cost the average person an extra £1,250 in tax.

On the whole, the permanent civil service is disposed to welcome special advisers. This is because they can take on functions which regular civil servants, non-partisan as they are, find difficult.

The chancellor's speech to party conference is one of these. The convention of non-partisanship prevents the civil service from providing the required political knockabout, so it falls to special advisers. (Civil servants will, however, check it before delivery for fact and for potential embarrassment.) Putting the chancellor's side in some internal government row is another; again, this is best done by the political adviser, as officials serve not only him but the government as a whole. Keeping the party machine oiled and the activists happy is also a job for the special advisers.

There are a number of more contested functions. For example, the Treasury may provide one kind of brief for the chancellor, one that concentrates on pointing out the implications of his colleagues' costly proposals. The special adviser may provide another, for example concentrating on the implications for the government's chance of re-election. The two may conflict.

Then there is the area in which frictions between advisers and officials easily arise. The special adviser has an important job to do in explaining to officials where the chancellor is coming from. It is a waste of everybody's time, for example, if the Treasury is preparing papers arguing for (let us say) a clamping-down on tax loopholes if the chancellor and his political party are implacably opposed to it.

Equally, however, this is a function that falls to the chancellor's private office, the group of full-time officials who are responsible for the links between him and his department. Often, private offices and political advisers work well together. Sometimes they clash.

Most important, however, few advisers are content merely to parrot their minister's or their party's view. Most have their own views on policy, and will tend to fight for them. The Treasury is not unworldly; it understands this and is prepared to concede a measure of influence to special advisers in return for being spared the tasks that it does not want. However, a measure of influence can turn into real power, as it has with Mr Balls. Then what is at stake is much more than how different personalities get on. Even in the urbane world of Whitehall, power will always be contested.

Officials can get paranoid about the power of special advisers. It is indeed true that they are not elected; nor, unlike civil servants, do they owe their appointment to open competition. To that extent, they appear illegitimate. But they do have legitimacy: the legitimacy that comes from the legitimacy of their masters.

Every powerful figure in history has wanted his courtiers, who are beholden to him and who will do his will. Indeed, without such figures he could not be powerful. Treasury ministers are no different.

There is moreover a limit on the special advisers' power. Unlike the mandarins, the special adviser is the minister's creature. If the minister tires of them, they are out. If he is sacked, so are they.

It follows that their power is restricted, for if ever they seek to exercise it in ways of which their minister does not approve, they are finished. His patronage can be instantly withdrawn.

Like all the best of his breed, Mr Balls has flourished because he usually knows his master's mind. He has enjoyed his trust. He is able to make his will effective. The day, however, that he goes beyond that, is the day he goes. His power is both great and precarious.

The sensible mandarin does not fight the political adviser – at any rate, not directly. The sensible mandarin works with the political adviser. He can do so secure in the knowledge that any compromises that that may involve are not necessarily permanent. Political advisers come and go but mandarins go on for ever.

The mandarin class

One of the senior Treasury officials interviewed for this book lined the walls of his office with posters of Marilyn Monroe. Another, even more senior, wore a check suit which would enable him to pass without comment at a convention of Essex bookmakers. Another had the ruddy hue and rustic accent of a Somerset cider farmer. (Appropriately, he was responsible for EU spending on farming.) Some were members of the legendary Treasury madrigals choir; on the other hand there is at least one senior official who, advancing years notwithstanding, is reckoned fiercer than Vinnie Jones in the football tackle. One, sadly, has been convicted for the murder of his wife.

Treasury permanent officials have an image: intellectual, austere, even inhuman. You can therefore fall into the trap of thinking that they all fall into this category.

But one size does not fit all. The Treasury has an institutional persona, but it is superimposed on a range of individual personas. Treasury man does not constitute a homogenous type. Though (for example) it is still true that most officials go straight home after a long Treasury day, a hardy coterie was long found knocking back pints in the Red Lion in Whitehall.

Anyone who was not clever would not greatly enjoy working there; and the Treasury's idea of 'clever' is a good deal more elevated than that common in lesser circles. There are officials who did not get first-class degrees, but few of them choose to admit it.

Treasury man is highly intelligent. 'I can't imagine working anywhere else,' says one official. 'It is so full of bright, intelligent, interesting people. There is nobody who is slow on the uptake. It is what I expected university to be like.' But Treasury man is not on the whole intellectual. It does not encourage reflective types who doubt what they are doing.

'You get a draft speech for a minister from another department at five on a Friday evening,' one official says. 'You know they've been working on it for weeks, but you have to clear it in a couple of hours.' This way of life does not favour fundamental thinking.

Since Treasury officials work long hours in rotten conditions with inadequate support staff often using outdated technology for pay which is much lower than what they could expect elsewhere, why do they stay? 'Power,' one says. The work is interesting. The influence is huge. The sense of public service is real. A young man in his twenties can find himself the trusted aide to a senior member of the Cabinet. A woman in her thirties can control the budget of a major government department. More than anything else, Treasury officials know what is going on in government, with an intimacy denied to nearly anyone else outside the inner Cabinet.

There are all sorts in the Treasury – including a number of oddballs. 'The Treasury does have extremely good people. There are very few obvious duffers, though there are some pretty eccentric people who could scarcely be employed outside,' says one senior ex-Treasury man.

Though individuals differ, the existence of a type can hardly be denied. If three officials from the Foreign Office, the Home Office and the Treasury were to meet on their lunchtime stroll in St James's Park, it would not be hard to tell the three apart.

Suppose the subject turned to whether to legalize drugs. The Foreign Office mandarin would expound learnedly on the role of opium in the history of the Far East in the nineteenth century. The Home Office official would worry about the dangers to public morality and the difficulties of political management of liberalization. The Treasury official would ask: how much could we raise by taxing them? Would the savings on the police outweigh the extra cost to the health service? Would it make it harder or easier to move druggies from welfare to work?

The Treasury has its virtues. It is a relatively informal place. Christian names are universally used (disconcertingly for an outsider, who will be expected to know that 'Andrew' means Her Majesty's principal permanent under-secretary of state and 'Gus' her most senior economic adviser). It is also relatively democratic: junior officials are encouraged to cross intellectual swords with their seniors.

But a true male *esprit de corps* would imply much out-of-work bonding. The Red Lion types aside, Treasury man arrives at 9.30 and leaves at seven, not stopping to socialize. In few other institutions do so many people know so little about the private lives of their colleagues – nor, for that matter, do they seem to care. Nobody at the Treasury remembers your birthday. There is no corporate entertaining. No one asks you to dinner of a Saturday night. You never meet a fat Treasury official.

'I remember when I was away for a year,' says a former mandarin. 'I walked in the front door, passed three or four people with whom I'd worked reasonably closely. None of them said good morning.'

Economic man

Those outside the Treasury think of it as made up of economists. Until surprisingly recently, this was not true. Professional economists were a minority and the power remained with generalist administrators.

Often, economists were kept out of the front line at the Treasury – so much so that the organization became worried by it. Economists were undervalued in the Treasury; so when the City market for their skills boomed in the 1980s, there was a haemorrhaging of top economic talent. 'We recruit good economists,' says one senior official. 'The problem is keeping them. Wives started having children so they lost an income and they were attracted by the City.'

Treasury Senior Management Structure (November 1998)

Directorate management

Permanent Secretary Sir Andrew Turnbull (**) — PERM

Heads of directorate standing teams

Ministerial support	MIN	Tom Scholar
Communications and strategy	COM	John Kingman
Strategy (strategy, finance and purchasing)	SFP (1)	Rob Brightwell

Macroeconomic policy and prospects — MPP

Director: Gus O'Donnell
Deputy director: Joe Grice
Deputy director: Jonathan Taylor (**)

Economic assessment	EA	Chris Kelly
Fiscal and macroeconomic policy	FMP	Andrew Kilpatrick
Economic and Monetary Union	EMU	David Ramsden
European Preparation Unit	EPU	Sue Killen
Debt and reserves management	DRM	David Deaton
Economist group management unit	EGMU	Malcolm Bradbury

International finance — IFD

Director: Sir Nigel Wicks (**)
Deputy director: Paul McIntyre (**)
Deputy director: Jon Cunliffe

EU finances	EUF	Simon Brooks
EU coordination and strategy	EUCS	Ric Todd
Debt, development and export finance	DDX	Mike Richardson
Globalization, trade and institutions	GTI	Alex Gibbs
Country economic and policy	CEP	David Lawton

Budget and public finances — BPF

Director: Robert Culpin
Deputy director: Nicholas Macpherson
Deputy director: Colin Mowl (**)

Exchequer funds and accounts	EFA	Ian Taylor (2)
EU and international taxation	EUIT	Peter Curwen
Social security	SS	Mike Williams
Public sector finances	PSF	Ian Walker
Budget coordination	BUD	Phil Wynn Owen
Tax policy	TP	Michael Swan
Tax administration	TA	Melanie Dawes
Work incentive, poverty and distributional analysis	WIPA	Stephen Matthews
Public service pensions	PSP	

Public services — PS

Director: John Gieve (**)
Deputy director: Norman Glass (*)
Deputy director: Gill Noble
Deputy director: Peter Sedgwick
Deputy director: Adam Sharples (*)

General expenditure policy	GEP	Adam Sharples (4)
General expenditure statistics	GES	Allen Ritchie
Public-sector pay and efficiency	PSPE	Bernadette Kelly
Defence, diplomacy and intelligence	DDI	Tim Dowse
Agriculture	A	
Health	H	Alastair Bridges
Devolved countries and regions	DCR	Elwyn Evans
Culture and central departments	CCD	Mark Parkinson
Welfare to work	WW	Anita Charlesworth
Education and training	ET	Nicholas Holgate
Home and legal	HL	Helen Tuffs
Local government	LG	Peter Kane
Environment, transport and the regions	ETR	Jeremy Moore
Central operational research and economics	CORE (*)	Norman Glass (6)
Resources accounting and budgeting	RAB	Ros Dunn

Financial management reporting and audit — FMRA

Director: Andrew Likierman (**)
Deputy director: Jamie Mortimer (*)

Team	Code	Name
Treasury officer of accounts	TOA (*)	Jamie Mortimer (5)
Central accountancy	CA	David Loweth
Whole of government accounts	WGA	Ian Carruthers
Development of accountancy resources	DART	Kevin Ross
Audit policy and advice	APA	Chris Butler
Strategy finance and purchasing	SFP (1)	Rob Brightwell
Treasury internal audit	TIA	Anne Marie Jones

Finance regulation and industry — FRI

Director: Steve Robson
Deputy director: Brian Rigby
Deputy director: Robin Fellgett
Deputy director: Harry Bush (*)(3)

Team	Code	Name
European financial services	EFS	Colin Farthing
Home financial services	HFS	Paula Diggle
Financial stability and markets	FSM	Dilwyn Griffiths
International financial services	IFS	Joseph Halligan
Regulatory reform	RR	David Roe
Private finance policy	PFU	Tim Wilson
Procurement policy	PP	John Colling
Procurement practice and development	PPD	Mike Burt
Productivity	PROD	Sam Beckett
Banking review	BR	Sue Lewis
Public enterprise partnership	PEP	Peter Schofield
Enterprise issues	ENT	Philip Rutnam
Competition, regulation and energy markets	CRE	Chris Ford

Personnel, accommodation and information services — PAIS

Director: Margaret O'Mara

Team	Code	Name
Personnel management	PM	Jim Hibberd
Information systems	IS	John Dodds
Accommodation and security	AS	Ian Cooper

Standing cross-directorate team

Team	Code	Name
Treasury management board	TMB	Sir Andrew Turnbull
Deputy directors group	DDG	Gill Noble
EU budgetary issues	EUBI	Paul McIntyre
EU monetary developments	EUMD	Jon Cunliffe
Investment in People Project Team	IiP	Gus O'Donnell
Steering committee on resource accounts and budgeting	SCARAB	Andrew Likierman
Treasury economic forecast	TEF	Joe Grice
Tax issues	TI	Colin Mowl

(*) indicates combined deputy director and head of standing team

(**) indicates head of cross-directorate standing team

(1) reports to Sir Andrew Turnbull on strategy, and to Andrew Likierman on finance and purchasing

(2) Reports direct to Sir Andrew Turnbull on royal finance matters

(3) Heads Enterprise and Growth Unit, comprising PROD, PEP, ENT and CRE teams

(4) Supported by Caroline Siccock and Peter Brook

(5) Supported by Glenn Hull

(6) Supported by Donald Franklin

The Treasury responded by commissioning a report on the relationship between the Treasury's economists and the rest of the organization. It has led to changes.

'One of the decisions was that there should be a greater convergence between the economists and the generalists,' says one senior economist. 'Generalists should have more economics and economists should have a more diverse career. The economists shouldn't all end up as boffins.

'There was parallel posting: the idea was that the economist did the numbers and the administrator did the words. That has ceased to happen. There was a colonization of senior grades by economists five or ten years ago.'

For a generation, the Treasury supplemented its home-grown economists by importing on a grade scale. Sir Terence Burns, the permanent secretary, was the senior economist at the London Business School before being recruited as chief economic adviser by the Conservative government in 1980. (It does not follow from this that he is a Conservative.) Until recently, equal second to him in the rankings was Sir Alan Budd, his successor as chief economic adviser. Sir Alan was recruited from a dull job with Barclays, but previously did Sir Terry's job at the LBS. Another senior colleague is Andrew Likierman, in charge of the reform of government accounting and financial information. Mr Likierman too came from the London Business School.

Things are now changing rapidly. 'True, Nigel Wicks [the Treasury's senior official for international policy] is a historian. But Andrew Turnbull, I think, did study economics; he did one year of a postgraduate degree in it,' says an official who shares Whitehall's general obsession with educational background.

Under him, the coming men at the Treasury are proper economists. That is true of Steve Robson, the driving force behind microeconomic policy; and of Gus O'Donnell, who has become chief economic adviser. Mr O'Donnell has had a varied career, including a spell as John Major's press secretary at 10 Downing Street and as the British representative at the IMF and the World Bank in Washington. However, he was first a proper professional economist, who was briefly a junior economics don. Other prominent economists include Peter Sedgwick and Colin Mowl. In twenty years' time, it seems likely that the Treasury will be dominated by professional economists – and will probably be the better for it.

Treasury women

The Treasury is not good at keeping women. Some of the most senior of its female staff have left in recent years. For example, Rachel Lomax, a former private secretary to the chancellor and often tipped to be the Treasury's first female permanent secretary, left for a job with the World Bank. Her move was surrounded by hot talk, strenuously denied, of internal conflict. She later returned to Britain as permanent secretary of the Welsh Office.

Or take Alice Perkins, another senior woman, who joined from the Department of Health. Ms Perkins, the wife of Jack Straw, the home secretary, has now gone back to her old department, on promotion.

Of the twenty-three top Treasury officials at the end of 1998, only two were women: Gill Noble, a spending controller, and Margaret O'Mara, at personnel. It is true that there are many less senior women in the Treasury ranks: nearly one sixth of the next most senior band at the Treasury are female. And there are others waiting in the wings. It will be surprising in a few years' time if Moira Wallace, a feisty young Scot now seconded to run the government's Social Exclusion Unit in the Cabinet Office, doesn't reach the top if she ever returns.

Even so, she and the others will have to get through what seems to be a glass ceiling. Few Treasury women make it to the top. And this despite the fact that the skills that are supposed to be at a premium at director level, essentially personal management skills, are by common consent ones where women enjoy a comparative advantage.

The Treasury's inability to make and keep the best women is a disappointment. At one point, when men were leaving the Treasury in droves to make fortunes in the City of London, speculation was rife that the Treasury would become a female-dominated department. Now, Treasury women believe that they will never make it to the upper echelons.

It does not help that Treasury culture remains women-unfriendly. It is addicted to long hours; Ms Perkins had to apply her persistence to protect an agreement that she should only work a four-day week.

'My old department was very woman-friendly,' says one senior woman. 'We had lots of parties. We had lots of part-timers at senior levels. When I arrived at the Treasury, I was the only woman in the room. No one introduced me.'

'Talking to the other women,' says another, 'we find it less congenial than other departments. The atmosphere is less relaxed; it's harder; it's more competitive. The job requires you to be quite tough and all the women worry that it makes us slightly abrasive.'

'It's ten years behind the rest of Whitehall,' says another younger woman. 'It's male dominated; it's public school dominated, it's Oxbridge dominated. It's the last place in the world I'd choose to work.

'There is an *esprit de corps* here, but it is a male *esprit de corps*. There is a certain all-male boarding-school feeling – and if you are a woman you are excluded from that.'

Ministers and mandarins

Theory has it that the politicians in the Treasury are in charge. In the old phrase: 'Officials advise; ministers decide.' Moreover, mandarins are not supposed to have views different from those of ministers. Ministers, accountable to Parliament, are in charge. Mandarins are their humble servants.

The theory suits both sets of parties. Ministers are egoists;

otherwise they would not have entered the trade of politics. They have to maintain that they are the ones with the power. They want decisions to emanate from themselves.

Mandarins of course are interested in power, but are generally less egotistical. They are therefore happy to influence outcomes even if someone else claims the credit. Moreover, if ministers have the illusion of temporary omnipotence, mandarins have the reality of permanency. While chancellors and their colleagues are writing their memoirs, the mandarins rule on.

Current conventions have other advantages for mandarins too. Their advice is secret; otherwise ministers might be embarrassed by appearing to be in conflict with their advisers. That, however, incidentally means that they never need to be held to account for that advice. They avoid odium. They preserve the mystique of mandarinism. They are to some extent spared the attentions of the mass media and have only indirectly to worry about their accountability to the public that pays their salary. However, some of them are starting to worry. Lord Burns in retirement has been heard to muse that he would have preferred his advice to have been public rather than private – an idea that would have his less radical predecessors turning in their graves.

Mandarins are of course non-partisan. They will serve governments of any political complexion with equal dedication, though no doubt they serve some with more relish than others. That, however, is not to say that they are not political. For their job is not that of the academic giving Platonic advice as to the general good. It is that of the political administrator. The reality of the relationship is therefore both different from and much subtler than the theoretical constitutional model implies.

In his magnificent book *The Chancellors*, Edmund Dell, himself a former Cabinet minister, describes the Treasury's position on it (pp. 191–2):

High on the official Treasury's agenda is that it should stand well with the chancellor of the exchequer and that the chancellor of the exchequer should stand well with his Cabinet colleagues. Like all great institutions, the Treasury has its own agenda. Building its own reputation is high on that agenda. That is not an attitude to be despised. The Treasury's reputation will in the end depend on the success of the British economy. The nation has every reason for satisfaction if the Treasury's reputation is high.

The last thing the official Treasury wants is a chancellor who has lost his reputation. It knows that the chancellor cannot be expected always to win. But a chancellor must not be left helpless in the face of the arguments . . . The position of the chancellor must therefore be carefully preserved and protected.

In the interests of this, officials must of course allow the chancellor much latitude. If ever his colleagues think that a chancellor is proving a liability to his party and their chances of remaining in power, he is done for. 'The Treasury is politically sensitive and it understands the role of chancellors in winning elections,' says Dell.

Yet in reality the chancellor must not be allowed total latitude. Chancellors after all come and go, but the British economy goes on and on. It follows therefore that it is the duty of officials to advise from that wider perspective, and where necessary to fight the chancellor in its interests.

It is mostly politicians who write memoirs. Therefore it is on the whole politicians' views of the Treasury that we know about. And politicians generally find it too cautious, too restrictive, too *Yes, Minister* for their taste. Stafford Cripps complained to Hugh Gaitskell in the post-war Labour government that his difficulty was that 'my official advisers are all "liberals" and I cannot rely on them to carry through a "socialist" policy'. Gaitskell when chancellor, though a different kind of socialist from Cripps, criticized 'reactionary' officials. Equally, the incoming Tory government of 1979 was soon at loggerheads with permanent officials whom ministers thought too Keynesian, too expansionist and too cautious. Sir Douglas Wass, a humane and urbane civil servant, was excoriated more severely than Sir Terence Burns nearly two decades later.

There is, however, room for a different view. It is again summed up by Dell in a telling, dangerous sentence, where he accuses the Treasury of demonstrating its 'typical professional deformation, its tendency to treat ministers too seriously'.

Governments intermittently, for good or bad reasons, do their best to ruin the British economy. Labour did it in 1974–5, by unleashing a public expenditure explosion under the plausible but misguided hope of avoiding the world deflation caused by the oil price hike. It took the Treasury three years to extinguish. The Tories did it in the late 1980s when Nigel Lawson persuaded his awed officials that he had made inflation a thing of the past, and again in 1991–2 when they failed to resist the temptation to spend their way to election victory.

Politicians have a legitimacy through election and an account-ability through Parliament that must always be respected. But officials have legitimacy too, based on permanence, collective memory and experience. They offer a disinterested devotion to the long-term national weal as they see it. When things are working, ministers and mandarins respect each other's contribution. When one or the other dominates, things go wrong.

There is a further complication in the relationship. Officials do not merely serve one minister, the chancellor. They are supposed to serve other ministers, his juniors, too.

This relationship between junior ministers and officials is not entirely straightforward. In theory junior ministers are elected. Appointed officials exist to serve them. Many a junior minister has sought to prove the point by summoning the permanent secretary and the department's highest officials to his presence.

The permanent secretary will do his best to respond. Where a junior minister has a difficulty of an organizational or procedural kind, he will be eager to sort it out. There are, all the same, two difficulties. Firstly, there is only one permanent secretary to five junior ministers, and if the permanent secretary and his senior colleagues sought to satisfy the potential demands of every junior, they would not be doing the rest of the job.

Secondly, the permanent secretary owes his whole loyalty to his department, and to the chancellor as its head. Junior ministers occupy a more ambiguous position. They have their own legitimacy as Members of Parliament and as prime ministerial appointees. They certainly have their own career agendas. They exist for their own sakes as well as for the chancellor's. They dare not go far out on a limb against him; at times (the present is one), they will mostly be his allies. But the potential for conflict exists; and the permanent officials must seek to stay above it.

Real relationships therefore cannot follow the master–servant model. In practice, they are governed by subtle understandings based on an appreciation of the strengths and weaknesses of the differing sinews of power. The civil service has its ways of dealing with uppity junior ministers. And it is ruthless with incompetent junior ministers. Bureaucratic assassination, as many failed politicians can attest, leaves corpses without marks.

Inside Relations | 3

The relationship between the Treasury and Number 10, between the chancellor and the Treasury and the Cabinet Office; between the Treasury and the Bank of England; and the complex considerations which determine the balance of power.

The Treasury and Number 10

The chancellor and the prime minister are next-door neighbours. All they have to do when they want to talk about something is drop by. They can be in daily touch; if they fall out it will be for reasons of personality and power, not mechanics.

So you might think; and so, under Tony Blair and Gordon Brown, it has mostly been. But it has to be said that their highly personal way of managing things is exceptional.

Generally, policy has not been run as if between neighbours. Instead, it has been quite highly formalized. By tradition, the prime minister's private office has included a private secretary with responsibility for economic matters. Day-to-day liaison with the Treasury has been conducted between him and a member of the chancellor's office, the chancellor's principal private secretary. In addition, the permanent secretary of the Treasury has generally kept his own relationship with the Treasury private secretary at Number 10. The private secretary concerned has every incentive to play ball. The prime minister may be his current employer but the Treasury permanent secretary will decide his next job. It would be a brave man who put all his trust in his current prince.

Obviously, the degree to which relations are conducted through these formal channels has varied. Sir Geoffrey Howe, for example, could rarely be allowed to seek to circumvent them by talking personally to Lady Thatcher since his pedantic stubbornness drove her up the wall. Between Kenneth Clarke and John Major, however, informal chatter was more common, as each sought to probe the other's bottom line.

Mr Blair and Mr Brown started off entirely informally. The habits of working together in opposition survived into government. The chancellor would drop by at Number 10 (or vice versa) once, twice, three times a day. Often no official was present to record what they talked about, or even what they decided.

But this turned out to be too informal. The official Treasury felt increasingly that they did not know what was going on. Senior officials were desperate, not just out of natural human curiosity but because they felt that, out of the loop, they could not do their jobs. When reports started to circulate that the chancellor and the prime minister did not see eye to eye about Britain's entry into the European Single Currency, this began to look serious. If you did not know what happened when they talked, you could not know where truth lay. And so efforts were made to make matters less informal. Jeremy Heywood, who had been Norman Lamont's private secretary, came into Mr Blair's office with a remit which included improving communications. By all accounts, he has succeeded; he became the prime minister's principal private secretary.

That is common enough. The prime minister's principal private secretary, a more senior official than the prime minister's private secretary responsible for economic matters, has often been a Treasury man. Andrew Turnbull, now the permanent secretary at the Treasury, was private secretary to Mrs Thatcher between 1983 and 1985. Even if he was not a Treasury man, the top private secretary in Number 10 inevitably got involved in the big stuff, and sometimes took over. 'Demarcations in the prime minister's office break down when the temperature rises. On Black Wednesday, it was Alex Allen, the principal private secretary, who was involved on a day-to-day basis, not Mary Francis, the Treasury private secretary,' says one Number 10 observer.

Whatever the structures may be, what in the end matters is the relationship between the two most powerful men in the kingdom. It is this to which we now turn.

The prime minister and the chancellor

The prime minister is also the first lord of the exchequer. At moments of high tension, few prime ministers resist reminding their chancellor of this fact, though the wise ones do it with a twinkle in their eye. For in this, the central and most complex relationship in government, formal titles do not matter. What matters is the relative power of the two, lubricated or made stickier by their personal relationship. Tensions are built in, and all too often the relationship ends in tears.

Why so? Surely the two individuals have an entirely common interest? Both the prime minister and the chancellor have overriding responsibilities for the success of the government as a whole. As splits between them all but ensure that it will not succeed, you might expect them always to pull together.

The prime minister relies on his chancellor. No modern prime minister could seriously contemplate taking on the dual burden of the exchequer and Downing Street (though it has been done in the past, most notably by William Gladstone). The prime minister's other essential commitments, notably in foreign affairs and in party management, mean that he must perforce leave much central control of the government's domestic policy to the occupant of Number 11.

Nor, in truth, is he well equipped to argue with his chancellor over the details of economic policy. Typically, the prime minister's Policy Unit will include a serious economist. Gavyn Davies, who served Jim Callaghan from 1974 to 1979 in his twenties, went on to become Britain's leading private-sector economist. John Major's Policy Unit was headed by Sarah Hogg, whose economic qualifications included a spell as economics editor of *The Times*. Tony Blair has Derek Scott, a former adviser to Denis Healey as chancellor; he has also been a city economist. Lady Thatcher relied on Alan Walters, a forthright monetarist, though that ended in disaster when Nigel Lawson resigned in 1989 over his influence.

But one individual alone, however great their capacity, cannot take on the Treasury. The wisest do not try. 'Everyone told me that playing games behind the Treasury's back was disastrous,' says one recent occupant. 'When I took over I had a sweet letter from Alan Walters saying "I hope you cause less trouble than I did."'

The involvement of the Number 10 Policy Unit also varies over time. If the head of the unit is economically minded, he will tend to talk to the Treasury off his own bat. If not, he may prefer to proffer his political judgements and leave the economics to the Treasury.

Personal contacts count. Mr Blair's Policy Unit consisted at first entirely of political appointees, though some had great expertise in their particular field. When, however, it was decided that it could also do with a civil service input – albeit only a token one – Sharon White, a talented young Treasury official, was the first recruit.

The Policy Unit may also have contacts with the political advisers in the Treasury, a powerful gang. David Miliband, head of the Number 10 Policy Unit, is the older brother of Ed Miliband, who works for Mr Brown.

Mr Brown has not apparently been allowed to set up a policy unit of his own, though one group around him seems to act very much as if observing the letter of the interdiction was more important than following its spirit. He has set up an embryo council of economic advisers in the Treasury, with Paul Gregg, a specialist in labour markets, and Chris Wales, a tax specialist, as members. But they function more as extra outside advisers to the chancellor on particular subjects than as a high-powered advisory committee, and they do not complicate relations between the chancellor and the prime minister.

Any prime minister knows how great is his chancellor's capacity to damage him. The resignation of a chancellor can prove calamitous. It will unsettle the prime minister's party in Parliament. Typically, it will worry financial markets, as signalling that policy will let up. In the end, it can even destroy the prime minister. If Nigel Lawson had not gone in 1989, it is unlikely that Lady Thatcher would have been defeated in 1990.

Obviously, the potency of a threat of a chancellor's resignation will vary. Thus Norman Lamont after Black Wednesday posed very little threat, since the prime minister was generally reckoned wrong not to have sacked him anyway. When he did quit, however, he caused greater damage than expected, thanks to an effective resignation speech.

A prime minister does not only need a chancellor to do the job. He must worry also about the consequences for his own position if the chancellor decides not to do it any more. It is a strong weapon in most chancellor's hands.

Equally, the chancellor relies on his prime minister. This is not merely a matter of the obvious constitutional point that it is the prime minister who gives him the job and the prime minister who can at any moment take it away. Without the prime minister, as we have seen, the chancellor would frequently be in a minority of one in Cabinet. He could not resist the combined weight of would-be spenders. The prime minister brings not only his vote but the vote of his claque – those ministers who are in the Cabinet not because of their individual weight or ability but because of his patronage. He brings his ability, as the chair of Cabinet, to manipulate its proceedings or keep matters away from it. He also brings the power of dismissal. He can in the last resort sack any minister who is too obstreperous about spending. His chancellor cannot.

The prime minister is also essential to the chancellor on really big international economic issues which are resolved at heads-of-government level. The chancellor of the exchequer cannot place a call to the German chancellor knowing it will be returned. The prime minister can.

You might expect therefore that chancellor and prime minister would have every reason to work together. Harmony between Number 10 and Number 11 might be expected to be the norm. Yet a glance at the record shows that it is not so.

There have been some notable breakdowns. Mrs Thatcher fell out with Nigel Lawson over the style and content of relations with Europe and Britain's membership of the Exchange Rate Mechanism of the European Monetary Union. John Major fell out with Norman Lamont over Europe and personally.

Under less stressful conditions and with more emollient personalities, things rarely get to that pass. But recent years have seen a number of devices used by prime ministers in an attempt to increase their powers vis-à-vis their chancellors. Harold Wilson in 1964 experimented with the Department of Economic Affairs as an alternative economic centre in Whitehall. Jim Callaghan invented the Number 10 seminar. This was an irregular meeting at Downing Street, including the chancellor but also including the Bank of England. Its apparently innocuous title suggested a talking shop, but its purpose was more serious: to get the prime minister's hands on levers of economic power hitherto monopolized by the Treasury and the Old Lady of Threadneedle Street.

Lady Thatcher had Professor Walters. She also set up the Efficiency Unit, based in the Cabinet Office and designed to carry out studies to get maximum value for public spending. Some would deny it, but the message conveyed to many in Whitehall was that she had doubts about the Treasury's ability to do its job of cutting spending and improving value-for-money.

Tony Blair has sought to upgrade the Cabinet Office as a more proactive arm of policy. Exactly how this will work is not yet clear;

but one interpretation is that this represents a threat to the Treasury's hegemony over much domestic policy.

What motivates these repeated prime-ministerial efforts? What is the in-built tension in the relationship between prime ministers and chancellors which makes conflict endemic to their dealings?

Both the prime minister and the chancellor have responsibilities for the success of the government as a whole. But they are not quite the same responsibilities. The chancellor has pretty well a single job: to deliver, in so far as it is within his gift, a strongly performing economy, with the right level of public spending and the right taxes to pay for it. At the margin, he is politically influenced. It is obviously better that the economy should be doing well at election time than in between elections. But even this no longer has the influence it once did. The chancellor's ability to control the economy in the short term is now widely questioned. After 1992, when the Tories won a difficult election in a recession, and 1997, where they were humiliated despite a stable recovery, the conventional wisdom about the relationship between economic and political success is in doubt. Chancellors may still think they are acting politically: Gordon Brown's initial two-year freeze on spending plans was designed to make a later relaxation in the run-up to an election easier. But in practice, Kenneth Clarke may have been right in declaring during his chancellorship: 'Good economics is good politics.'

The prime minister will be more strongly influenced by the immediate politics of economic policy, however. For one thing, he has the task of political management of his own party. When the economy is weak, his MPs get jumpy. The governing party performs worse in by-elections held in hard times, even if the same cannot be said with certainty about general elections. Moreover, a poorly performing economy will agitate his party in the country and particularly its activists. They will seek more radical measures of left or right which prime ministers (most of whom understand that elections are won in the middle ground) have to resist. All these factors mean that a prime minister is likely to be more reluctant to back economic restraint than a chancellor. There are many occasions in recent history where chancellors have wanted higher interest rates and prime ministers have not. There is no instance of the opposite case.

An element of rivalry between the prime minister and the chancellor is inevitable. Yes, they are members of the same party. Yes, they must cooperate in the same government. But most chancellors are at one time or another touted to take over the prime minister's job. Excepting the moot case of Norman Lamont, you have to look back to Anthony Barber, Edward Heath's chancellor in 1970–74, to find a chancellor who could not be prime minister and knew it. Nigel Lawson could, but claimed not to want it; Jim Callaghan and John Major actually got the top job; Denis Healey and Geoffrey Howe were serious contenders for it as, of course, is Gordon Brown.

Sometimes the political tensions are overt. Hugh Dalton as chancellor from 1945 to 1948 was constantly involved in plots against Clement Attlee, the prime minister (see Roy Jenkins's *The Chancellors*) though not on his own behalf. Roy Jenkins too was promoted by his friends to take over from Harold Wilson in the late 1960s, though he himself was probably less thickly involved in the plotting than the prime minister thought.

More usually, the rivalry is suppressed. If it gets out of hand, the chancellor may simply be sacked. Even if he is not, too overt a conflict will weaken the government; as John Major found out, there is little point in gaining the throne if the process that led up to its being vacant has rendered it irredeemably precarious. If a chancellor seeks to destroy a prime minister, he may succeed, but only at the cost of destroying himself too.

Moreover, a calculating chancellor will in most circumstances conclude that his chances are the stronger the less he plots. John Major succeeded Lady Thatcher because his fingerprints were not on the knife. Wilson saw off Jim Callaghan in the 1960s when the latter made a play for it, but then made sure Mr Callaghan got it in 1976 when he didn't. Any sensible adviser to Gordon Brown now would recommend him to be loyal to Mr Blair so that, when the time for the top man to quit comes, he will be the chosen successor.

Politicians, however, are not calculating machines. High office is addictive, but also stressful. It seems likely that Nigel Lawson could have gone on through his brush with Lady Thatcher had he really wanted to: she claims in her memoirs to be sorry that their 'long and generally fruitful' relationship ended as it did. Roy Jenkins's chums probably lost their perspective because they developed an exaggerated contempt for Harold Wilson. Similarly, Mr Lamont was frustrated by his old ally John Major. In other words, rivalry does lie at the core of many of the conflicts between prime ministers and chancellors, but if the rivals calculated correctly, the conflicts would be resolved. Where big egos clash good sense is frequently a victim.

Power realities

Who holds the cards? The prime minister or the chancellor? This is not a question to which there is any straightforward answer.

First, the balance of power depends on their political standing. If, for example, a chancellor has the backing of a large proportion of his party's MPs, he will obviously have allies denied to a less well-supported chancellor in fending off a prime minister. Roy Jenkins's unsackability between 1967 and 1970 owed something to this. The chancellor will also be better placed if he has his own supporting claque of ministers in the government, preferably ministers whom the prime minister fears he might lose if he loses the chancellor.

Hence the preoccupation in the summer of 1998 with whether Gordon Brown's supposed supporters or Mr Blair's did best in the Cabinet reshuffle. The sacking of Harriet Harman was widely portrayed as a decision by the prime minister to keep his chancellor in check by punishing one of his allies. Whether this is true or not is a moot point: Ms Harman after all was a friend of Mr Blair's long before she was a friend of Mr Brown's. In any case, her imperfect grasp of her portfolio would adequately explain her demotion. But the point is not whether it was a prime ministerial move against Mr Brown; the point is that it was *perceived* as a move against Mr Brown – which he was also perceived as being unable to prevent.

The balance of power may also depend on the mechanics of policy. For example, public expenditure used to be decided essentially bilaterally, in negotiations between individual departments and the Treasury. The prime minister found it hard to stick his oar in. Once negotiations were under way, the prime minister only got involved if there were difficulties. Individual ministers might appeal to him to intervene against the Treasury. Alternatively, they might appeal to Cabinet collectively. In either case, the prime minister was powerfully placed to decide the outcome. Very often, however, this amounted to no more than a power to split the difference, in the interests of a quiet life. In any event, such cases were the exception rather than the rule, as ministers who appealed soon found that their colleagues' patience with them was limited.

The new system involved the creation of a Cabinet committee, the EDX committee, which altered all that. The prime minister did not chair EDX, reserving his overt power as before for the resolution of serious disputes. But he appointed the chancellor to head the EDX committee; and he appointed its members. Having benefited from his patronage they could hardly deny him an influence. The process was also more open and long-drawn-out than in the past. The prime minister's chances to intervene were multiplied. 'Not only is the prime minister able to say, "The ones I want protected are the health service and law and order", he can say, "When it comes to education, why don't you do A rather than B?",' says one observer.

EDX now plays a somewhat reduced role. Gordon Brown has abolished annual public spending rounds, and so the annual session before the committee no longer exists. The prime minister and his Policy Unit were deeply involved in the fundamental review of spending which preceded abolition. But in future spending decisions may again be settled bilaterally with the spending departments, and the prime minister's position will be weaker relative to the chancellor's.

Another change has certainly weakened the prime minister's ability to meddle in economic policy. It concerns the emerging independence of the Bank of England in the determination of interest rates.

The first step, under the Tories, came with the publication of the minutes of the meetings between the chancellor and the Bank of England in which interest rates were decided; because the minutes became public, the government found it harder to twist arms.

Then, following the Brown reforms, interest rates became a matter for the bank alone to decide. The chancellor was responsible only for setting the targets which they were to seek to deliver.

At first sight, under these arrangements, it is the chancellor who has lost power. Before, he set interest rates; now the bank does. In fact, however, the prime minister loses much more heavily. Before, he could – and frequently did – lean on the chancellor to keep interest rates down. The chancellor might resist, but he did not always win. Now a prime minister who seeks to push his chancellor would be told: 'Sorry, prime minister; not my responsibility.'

Nor can the prime minister easily push the Bank of England. A monetary committee of nine decides policy, not just the governor. They hold longish appointments and cannot readily be sacked. They are not likely to be inflationists, otherwise the government would not have dared to appoint them for fear of market reaction.

The Treasury attends meetings of the monetary policy committee of the bank. Its representative can speak, but not vote – though he has to be careful not to intervene too overtly. The prime minister's powers over the monetary committee, compared with what they used to be vis-à-vis a recalcitrant chancellor, are nugatory vis-à-vis the monetary committee.

The Treasury and the Cabinet Office

Britain takes its civil service for granted. Smugly assured of its excellence, and discouraged from taking a closer interest by the plethora of acronyms and the proliferation of management jargon, the civil service is allowed to go its sweet way with the minimum of outside debate.

Thanks to this indifference, one of the most dramatic changes in the machinery of government in recent years has gone almost unnoticed. The Treasury has given up – and given up voluntarily – its responsibility for civil service management, on to which it has hung for years.

Its responsibilities for senior civil service pay, civil service recruitment, retirement and redundancy and the management of civil service pensions have been handed lock, stock and barrel to the Office of Public Service and Science (OPSS) within the Cabinet Office. The Treasury retains an interest in civil service pay, but only through its job of containing expenditure rather than as employer. It is a tenuous fingerhold.

Bureaucracies rarely give up anything without a fight. In this case, it was a fight that had gone on for more than thirty years. In 1968, Harold Wilson's government had set up the Civil Service Department (CSD). There was a widespread perception that Whitehall had become old-fashioned and fuddy-duddy, entirely unsuited to the white heat of the technological revolution which Wilson's government was unleashing. Nowhere was seen as more fuddy-duddy than the Treasury, whose dead hand inhibited civil service reform. Following the report of the Fulton Committee, the new CSD was created to change all that. But it was created only over ferocious Treasury opposition.

This is not a history of the Treasury. We shall not dwell on the gory thirty years' war that followed the change: the heads on Treasury pikestaffs attest to it. The late Lord Bancroft, the head of the civil service, was sacked for resisting Treasury ambitions. The Efficiency

Unit within the Cabinet Office, set up by Lady Thatcher under Derek Rayner in 1979, was a setback for the Treasury, since it advertised ministers' lack of confidence in the Treasury's ability to ensure value for public money. So the battle went on. It was a struggle that absorbed disproportionate amounts of Treasury energy.

The Treasury did not base its claim to remain involved in these issues on its special skill in the field or its special knowledge of management. Few Treasury hands would count those amongst its chief strengths. The Treasury's case for keeping its hands on management was based on its needs in an area where it did have a special locus: public-spending control.

For example, suppose the Department of Transport decided to pay a bit extra to recruit an outside expert. To the department, the cost might seem exiguous. But if Transport paid extra today, then tomorrow Housing would want to do it, and then Education. Before you knew where you were the floodgates of extravagance would be thrown open and the exchequer bankrupted. So the Treasury sought at all times to keep its hands on pay and rations.

The new division of responsibilities stressed the ongoing nature of the Treasury's interest in expenditure implications, but the reality was that the change represented a surrender for the Treasury. This was entirely right. For the Treasury's traditional Stalinist control had in fact already been undermined by civil service developments during the 1980s.

The most significant of these was 'Next Steps'. The Conservative government had to admit that there were some functions of central government that simply could not be privatized. But they also perceived that many of these functions were basically executive functions: paying out social security benefits, running the civil service college, buying computers. The traditional Whitehall model whereby these were theoretically run by ministers responsible to Parliament was a recipe for inefficiency. What they required was an appropriate measure of managerial autonomy. Functions of this kind were to be devolved to Next Steps agencies, the prime minister announced in 1988. These were to be quasi-autonomous bodies which would deliver the services to departments according to a broad contractual agreement between the two.

Next Steps both attracted and repelled the Treasury. It was attracted because it was itself moving ideologically away from centralization towards the virtues of markets, incentives and devolution. It was repelled because of the old peril: loss of control. In particular it was terrified that the creation of Next Steps would lead to a loss of its control over public spending. As Sir Robin Butler, the emollient ex-Treasury mandarin who headed the civil service told MPs, '. . . the Treasury was very anxious – and in my view rightly so – that this approach should not weaken the overall control of public expenditure which is necessary for macroeconomic purposes and for control over the pay bill.'

The Treasury did not win its battle. Next Steps happened. From an initial twelve candidates, the number of agencies has grown to more than 135 and 77 per cent of civil servants now work in them.

The Treasury negotiated some pretty powerful controls to compensate for its losses. Agencies were subject to annually revised framework documents setting out their objectives and methods. Departments had to discuss and agree these with the Treasury too.

The Treasury retained an important role in determining how much money they could spend and on what. For those agencies which are money-making trading bodies, it laid down strict rules for trading accounts. Unlike private firms, they would still be limited as to the amount of external finance they could seek. The relevant act of Parliament, the 1990 Government Trading Act, includes some thirty-six significant references to the Treasury. And the Treasury has devoted a good deal of effort to telling departments how to monitor the agencies.

Whether because of, or despite, Treasury efforts, the agencies have been a success. Obviously, a certain flexibility over pay is part of the reason for that success, and the agencies could argue powerfully that they should not be over-subject to central control in that area. As for the floodgates, Gordon Brown has managed to run a policy of the utmost restraint over public-sector pay without the powers that old-style Treasury officials would have regarded as vital to making it work.

Pay and rations are not now the main battleground between the two arms of central control in government, the Cabinet Office and the Treasury. However, it is possible to discern already what is likely to prove the next battleground. It emerges from Tony Blair's ambitions to beef up the Cabinet Office, and the potential conflict with Gordon Brown's ambitions to govern Britain on the home front.

In theory, the line between the Cabinet Office's role and that of the Treasury has been reasonably clear. The Treasury has been concerned with the content of policy. The Cabinet Office has been concerned with its coordination and delivery. So the Cabinet Office has made sure that departments submit their proposals to ministers collectively on time; that everyone with an interest is properly consulted; that one bit of policy does not conflict with another bit of policy; and that ministers in general (and the prime minister in particular) are properly briefed. Sir Robin Butler, a hands-off cabinet secretary, ran the Cabinet Office strictly along these lines, content to keep the show on the road and not much interested, apparently, in where that road was running. Under John Major, the prime minister who was seeking to keep a show on the road when many of his party passengers were determined to run off it, that was arguably what his role required.

Mr Blair has much wider ambitions. He is concerned to drive through his party's programme from the centre. There has been much chatter amongst his personal advisers about the need to beef up the Cabinet Office. Peter Mandelson co-authored in 1996 a manifesto which included the creation of a stronger 'Department of the Prime Minister and Cabinet'.

Mr Blair has been particularly concerned with the many issues which fall between the responsibilities of individual departments. One highly visible sign of this was his creation, within the Cabinet Office, of the Social Exclusion Unit under Moira Wallace, formerly one of his private secretaries.

By chance, Mr Blair's coming to power as the nation's highest elected officer was followed, soon after, by a change in the nation's highest civil servant. Having managed the change of government with silky skill, Sir Robin Butler retired as Cabinet secretary and head of the civil service. He was replaced by Sir Richard Wilson, who, though he had immediately before been permanent secretary at the Home Office, was originally a Treasury man. A man of compelling charm and drive, Sir Richard's first task was to report to the prime minister on the effectiveness of the centre of government in general and the role of the Cabinet Office in particular.

Mr Blair announced the results of that review to Parliament on 28 July 1998. Sir Richard, he said, had 'concluded that the linkage between policy formulation and implementation needed further improvement. He found that cross-departmental issues of policy and service delivery are often not handled well . . . He diagnosed a weakness in looking ahead to future opportunities and threats, and in reviewing the outcome of government policies and the achievement of government objectives.'

Several new initiatives emerged. The Office of Public Service was fully merged into the Cabinet Office, the aim being to bring the design and implementation of policy more closely together. A new Performance and Innovation Unit was set up in the Cabinet Office, under a high-flying Treasury official, to 'complement the Treasury's role in monitoring departments, both by looking at cross-departmental issues and by selecting aspects of policy that needed review'. Despite the conciliatory reference to 'complementing the Treasury', the message would escape few in Whitehall that the Treasury was failing in these regards. There was to be a new stronger Centre for Management and Policy Studies in the Cabinet Office, incorporating the civil service college, and a management board for the civil service.

Yet the prime minister's announcement was perhaps as significant for what it did not say as for what it did. It did not explain why, when Sir Richard had been asked to report within weeks, the report was delayed for more than six months. It did not say why the report, which was to have been published, remained private. It must be speculation, but there seems every reason to suppose that the Treasury would have resisted the emergence of a body potentially able to compete with it as the centre of power in government. And the chancellor can hardly have been chuffed either.

In principle, it ought to be possible to find a better *modus vivendi* between Number 10, the Cabinet Office and the Treasury than has existed up to now. A stronger Number 10, based on a strong Policy Unit, should remain responsible for ensuring that the government's political programme is driven through. A stronger Treasury ought to ensure that the economic strategy responds to the year-to-year vicissitudes of economic life, and that sound economics underlies both the government's spending decisions and their implementation. A stronger Cabinet Office ought to do more than coordinate policy formulation, important though that is: it needs to coordinate policy delivery across departments. It should be responsible for long-term thinking in a way that a department burdened with day-to-day work finds difficult. It should be looking at constitutional, legal and international dimensions of policy in a wider way than an economically focused Treasury can. And it should be making sure that the civil service of tomorrow is up to the job that ministers want done. Those are the principles. The practice remains to be seen.

The Treasury and the bank

After his first frenetic weekend in office, Gordon Brown announced that the Bank of England was to be independent. No longer would it be subject to directives on interest rates from the chancellor. Rather, he would give it a target for inflation and the bank would then decide the level of interest rates which would deliver that target.

Independence of the bank had been the remedy for Britain's macroeconomic ills preferred by most serious economists for years. Successive Tory chancellors had flirted with it, drawing back, however, for fear of the opposition of their neighbours in Downing Street. Now, in a *coup de théâtre*, Mr Brown had cut short the debate.

As Bank of England men went, Eddie George, the governor, had been less gung-ho for independence than most. Mr George had always had a reservation about independence. If the economy went wrong and unemployment rose, the mob might not be at the door of Parliament, where it belonged; it might be his parlour they invaded. But most people in the bank were delighted. Central bank independence is the fashionable economic nostrum of the 1990s. They were thrilled that a government was at last putting it into effect.

The euphoria was not to last. A few weeks later, the chancellor announced a change scarcely less revolutionary than independence for the bank. He decided to set up a new super-regulator, later christened the Financial Services Authority (FSA). And the FSA would take over all the bank's work of supervising the City of London. This would leave the bank with only residual prudential responsibilities for the financial system. Howard Davies, a Treasury man who had become deputy governor of the Bank of England, was to head the FSA. The Treasury was also to take away the bank's responsibility for managing public debt. There followed an unseemly row between the Treasury and the bank. Mr George felt he had been misled by Mr Brown's first announcement, which made no mention of the second revolutionary change. The Treasury retorts that he had been given a letter by Mr Brown telling him.

The relationship between the bank and the Treasury is traditionally fraught, as we shall see. It would therefore be tempting to characterize what happened as tit for tat. You take away our monetary policy, we take away your City responsibilities.

Tempting, but wrong. Most heavyweight opinion in the Treasury was delighted with bank independence on monetary policy, which in principle removed for ever the politicians' temptation to short-termism. And most heavyweight opinion in the Treasury was sceptical about the super-regulator. 'The immense costs of change in this area outweigh the predictable gains over the long term on any discounted present analysis,' one official said privately before the Brown move on regulation. 'The frictional costs are huge.'

Still, it was not the frictional costs which made the governor so furious that he is reported briefly to have contemplated resignation. Not only did Mr George feel he had been misled in his early discussions with Mr Brown, he had gone away convinced that regulatory reform was on the back burner. Instead, the policy was publicly launched before Mr George (or the Treasury, come to that) had had time to do any serious policy work on it at all.

'Steady Eddie', Mr George's sobriquet, is not well earned. Though good in a crisis, he also has a notoriously short fuse. On this occasion, it comprehensively blew. And his staff egged him on.

It was by no means the first occasion on which Threadneedle Street and Great George Street came to blows (see Stephen Fay, *Portrait of an Old Lady*, Viking, 1987). They have genuinely different perspectives. For the Bank of England, monetary issues – inflation, the strength of sterling – are always pre-eminent. For the Treasury, they have to contend with other economic desiderata, such as economic growth. The bank feels that it alone understands financial markets. The Treasury suspects that the bank is subservient to financial markets. The bank shamelessly acts as industrial lobbyist for one particular British industry, that based in the City of London. The Treasury does not like industrial lobbyists. 'If I'd been reviewing the Bank of England,' said one Treasury official, 'I'd have been seriously questioning whether it was worth putting top management time and resources into City sponsorship.'

There is also a question of lifestyles. Despite Mr Davies's best efforts when he was deputy governor of the bank, it still employs footmen in pink livery to guide you around. The Treasury privatized its down-at-heel but wonderfully helpful front-desk staff after the Fundamental Spending Review of 1994. When the deep carpet around the bank's inner sanctum wore out, the bank employed a specialist carpet firm to customize a new one at a cost of £40,000. The chancellor's corridors are clad in a shabby grey carpet. The rest of the Treasury does not even have that. The bank has several private dining rooms, and the butler still serves a fine luncheon claret. The Treasury makes do with the canteen, or sandwiches.

The Bank of England does less than the Treasury but manning levels are opulent. The Treasury is sparely staffed. The bank traditionally pays well. The governor received £232,675 in 1998–9. Treasury pay is modest. Only five officials were paid more than £100,000 in 1998–9, most of them only a slither more. The bank's employees get the money, but ultimately, the Treasury, with more access to ministers and from them to Parliament, has the power. So both have plenty to be jealous of in the other.

Of course, professionalism keeps such emotions in check. Rather sensibly, when Sir Alan Budd stepped down as the government's chief economic adviser, Mr Brown put him on the key monetary policy committee of the bank, which respects him highly. There are also areas in which the two institutions work closely alongside each other. For example, though the British director at the IMF has traditionally been a Treasury man, he has generally had a Bank of England man as his alternate.

The rivalries between the two may yet come to be overshadowed by a much wider reality. If (when?) Britain joins the European Monetary Union, the bank will lose its power over interest rates to the European central bank. The governor will be a mere member of its board. The Treasury will then lose its ultimate sanction against a bank-driven policy it does not like. It can legislate against a British central bank but not easily against a European one. It can sack a British governor but not a European governor. One of the great institutional conflicts of history will have ended, and not before time.

4 | Changing the Organization

The building remains the same, but inside, the Treasury has undergone a revolutionary period of change.

From the outside, the Treasury's building looks impressive. Now known as GOGGS (Government Offices, Great George Street), it was described until the 1960s as the New Public Offices (the Old Public Offices being the Foreign Office next door). But it is not that new: it was actually built in 1907, to a design by John Brydon. This in turn was based on a design which Inigo Jones prepared for Charles II to replace a building on the site which burned down.

The style is English Renaissance. An important feature is the circular court, 160 ft in diameter, approached through archways from Charles Street. Allegorical sculptures depicting dutiful government abound.

The outside of the inside is also impressive, with that huge sweeping staircase on which Gordon Brown was applauded. He has a decent office too, once the board room of the Board of Education. In 1998, during an open buildings day in London, he opened it to the public – a gesture that would have shocked the instinctively secretive chancellors of earlier times.

For lesser mortals, however, the building is not much of a place to work. The inside features large rooms with high ceilings, wide corridors and much monumental marble. It could be made into stunning offices. But that would need imposing desks, smart sofas, posh drapings: in other words, it would cost. The Treasury never likes to do things that cost. Austerity, for officials, begins at home.

So in reality most Treasury offices are furnished in standard-issue government tat, the odd picture breaking up the grey and often peeling paintwork. The result is a poor working environment. Senior figures sit behind their desks, which may be a route march from the entrance. 'My door is always open' is not convincing in such circumstances. The furniture is minimal and uncomfortable. The corridors are massive and not discriminated. It is easy to get lost. Though some attempt has been made to bring groups that work together closer together, teams are still often separated by corridors and thick walls. The corridors themselves are as clattery as those in hospitals. Chat is easily overheard. Informality is discouraged. Nor do the exiguous catering facilities help.

Before the election, the Tories planned to do something about this. The Treasury would move temporarily to new premises in Vauxhall while the old building was refurbished under a joint public/private partnership scheme. Then a minister went over to the proposed new building to test if he could get from his office to Westminster in the eight minutes allowed for him to vote once a division had been called in the House of Commons. Accounts differ as to whether he just made it or just didn't; in any event, it was a tight call. The move was off.

All hope of better accommodation has not been lost. At the time of writing, another attempt is being made to resuscitate the project to improve the Treasury but without mass decanting and the bureaucratic infighting that would accompany it.

Recently, a section of the Treasury had to be moved out to Victoria to accommodate changes. Senior officials vied with each other in arguing that they could not possibly move.

'No one wanted to go there,' the man in charge remembers. 'There was a tremendous fight. It was seen as a black spot. If you were sent to Allington Towers you were not very important, you had been sent away from ministers and all the rest of it. There was meeting after meeting of the management board, mandarin pitted against mandarin. In the end, the permanent secretary decreed who should go.'

The answer was that 'support services' went. Personnel always was at the bottom of the Whitehall pecking order.

But there was a sequel. Visitors to the new office in Victoria could not help but remark on its virtues: an open-plan office, warmth in winter, air-conditioned comfort in summer. When next the prospect of a partial move was mooted, the same officials who had fought to stay where they were before argued with equal passion that they should be selected for relocation.

Reconstructing the unreconstructed

If one of the great post-war Treasury mandarins returned to the Treasury from the grave, he would instantly find much, besides the building itself, which he recognized. There are still permanent secretaries, private secretaries and personal private secretaries, spanning between them everything from the highest of the high to the lowest of the low. There are still minutes, memos and meetings; still double envelopes for confidential documents and old-fashioned security cupboards and safes; and still the comforting secret language which can call the end of the day 'close of play' and 'I am copying this to –' rather than 'I am sending a copy of this to –.' The computer screens on people's desks notwithstanding, the first impression might be of a place where time has stood still.

Yet, if he was permitted longer leave from Hades, the returnee would find more and more that was foreign to his experience. He would particularly find this following the Treasury quiet revolution, now universally known by its initials 'FER' (which stands for Fundamental Expenditure Review), which has led to revolutionary changes in the way the Treasury is staffed and organized.

As with many revolutions, the cause of this one is much debated. Some put it down to the debacle of Britain's 1992 exit from the

European Exchange Rate Mechanism. 'ERM exit was one of the most extraordinary events in the history of the Treasury,' says one senior official. 'It would have been extraordinary if afterwards we didn't think why it had happened, what it might be about the organization of the Treasury which allowed it.'

There is something in this – but not much. For one thing, ERM exit was a failure of policy (for which the Treasury may be more or less severely blamed). It was not obviously, however, a failure caused by poor management. Indeed, if there were management failures, they were in its overseas side, which was a part of the Treasury least affected by the post-ERM FER changes.

In any case, the timetable does not fit. The FER started before ERM exit.

Early in 1992, Brian Fox, a senior official, came back from a course on the government's elite senior management programme. A mix of people attend these courses, including senior staff from government agencies and from outside. Fox came back convinced that the Treasury was a very old-fashioned organization. He told Sir Terence Burns that he should get his senior people together and think about the direction in which the Treasury should be going. And Sir Terry responded. Though the Treasury, like other departments, was enjoined to look at its senior management structure, the FER went much wider. 'The remarkable thing about the FER,' says another top Treasury official looking back on Sir Terry's retirement, 'is that it was an unforced change. There was no need to do it.'

At the time, Burns had been permanent secretary for only a few months. He had three thousand people under his command, including the Chessington computer centre, the civil service catering organization and HMSO. He had had little contact with most of these organizations in his previous job as the government's chief economic adviser. Nor had a keen interest in management characterized previous occupants of his new job. Sir Douglas Wass, the permanent secretary in the late 1970s and early 1980s, was too busy fighting against the new monetarism. His successor, Sir Peter Middleton, was a great crisis manager. 'He was brilliant at bringing people together to sort out a mess and good at saying after the event "Of course, that was the right thing to do,"' one official recalls. Neither came from a management culture; and neither took much interest in managing.

Sir Terry was interested in management. He was (as we have seen) from the London Business School, which taught the subject. Moreover, he had friends in the business. Perhaps the most influential was John (now Sir John) Birt, the director-general of the BBC, who had a cottage close to Sir Terry's near Brecon in Wales. Sir John had had to force through management change in the BBC if only because it did not have the cash to continue as it was. But he had become a management guru, and Sir Terry picked up his enthusiasm. 'It initially stimulated his intellectual curiosity but then it became a bit deeper,' says a colleague.

'This is very much a Cleopatra's Nose theory of the review but I genuinely believe that a lot of this comes down to Terry's personality. When he came to the permanent secretary's job, he came to see how remote a lot of people were from what was going on,' says a member of the review team.

Early in 1992, Sir Terry recruited Howard Davies, then running the Audit Commission, to the task. Mr Davies, who has a top-drawer practical mind, had worked both as a Treasury official and for McKinsey's, a firm of management consultants. He spoke to lots of people referred to in modern management jargon as 'customers and clients' of the Treasury: the Bank of England, a dozen industrialists, some permanent secretaries in other departments, the top fifteen Treasury officials. His findings, presented to a day think-in of officials at Chevening in March 1992, were not favourable.

'The Treasury was rude, abrupt and lacking in corporate memory. It makes decisions for the day, not for the long term. It mixed up control and influence. People had no clear view as to their relations with those who work for them or their superiors. There is at least one bureaucratic layer too many. It had no real top management group; the policy coordinating committee which talked about policy spent its time on "travellers' tales" gossip. There was no systematic process of deciding what the Treasury should be doing,' is how officials recall Mr Davies's presentation.

The findings were buttressed by a damning survey of opinion among the Treasury staff. People felt neglected. They were not respected or valued, especially those not in the golden stream of power and influence. People were moved on whim and managed by rumour.

The case for change was thus apparent. However, it was far from assured. Most organizations change fundamentally only when they are confronted with crisis: imminent bankruptcy, takeover or public humiliation. The Treasury faced none of these. Having bumbled on for centuries, it could have bumbled on some more.

In getting change going, therefore, Sir Terry faced a problem. But this time, luck was on his side. The government had just decided (as governments from time to time do) that all government spending should be looked at, from the bottom up. Each department would conduct a fundamental expenditure review. There would be no sacred cows.

Such reviews always raise a difficulty for the Treasury. Spending by the chancellor's departments is very small. In 1992, it amounted to about £3 billion, around 1 per cent of government spending. The great bulk of this is spent by the Inland Revenue and Customs collecting taxes. Central Treasury spending amounts to just £164 million, down from £198 million in 1992–3. However, though it is small, the Treasury feels that it cannot be laxly managed. For it is an article of Treasury faith that it has to be able to take its own medicine if it is to dispense it to others.

'We were required to do an FER as part of the process. We had to do it well. It became the agent for having to carry through quite quickly a number of ideas that had been crystallizing. We would have got there anyway but it might have taken a bit longer,' say Sir Terry's friends.

There was a minus to tying the management changes to the FER. It brought with it an understandable connotation that it was all about money and sacking people rather than improving the way the place ran. But there was a plus too. 'The thing the FER achieved was to give the whole thing a kick, the drive, the emotion,' says a senior FER official. At Chevening, the initial commitment to change was made.

Mr Davies was sounded out to take it on, but he was too busy. (Over the next six years he was to become successively director-general of the Confederation of British Industry; deputy governor of the Bank of England; and chairman of the Financial Services Authority.) The Treasury eventually turned to Sir Colin Southgate, chairman of EMI, as the senior outside person on the review. Wendy Pritchard, a management consultant, was also involved from the start. Ms Pritchard was an occupational psychologist by training, who had nearly become a doctor in her youth – a background that probably helped in dealing with the bruised psyches thrown up by the review. She had spent five years with Rank Xerox, and fifteen with Shell managing change. But she had also done odd jobs involving change management in the public service.

Meanwhile, Jeremy Heywood, the youngest and highest-flying of Treasury officials, got the job of running the review. Mr Heywood had been Norman Lamont's principal private secretary, and was to go on to be Tony Blair's. Mr Heywood is brilliant and, even by the standards of his profession, hard-working. In an institution where in any case hierarchy is rarely accompanied by deference, he was also outspoken, and ready to fight his corner. His appointment signalled that change was for real.

By May 1994, when Mr Heywood got back from a sabbatical at Harvard preparing for the review, not much had been achieved. The aftermath of ERM exit had put the process on hold for at least six months. 'There was a heightened sense of dissatisfaction with senior management. There was a reaction against the long-hours culture, the secrecy; and there was a feeling that the Treasury was not the same institution that we thought it was. But there was no particular consensus as to what had to be done,' says one of the review team.

Among some senior officials, initial enthusiasm had been blunted as the implications for Treasury jobs became clear. 'There were few constituencies for change,' recalls one official.

The only strong supporters of change were the Treasury's young thrusters. They knew that in the private sector people had lots and lots of responsibility in their late twenties and early thirties. But the Young Turks were not a defined group.

And there was a further problem. The ERM affair had not only distracted attention from the review. It had shattered morale. The rule of fundamental organizational change is that morale goes down before (if you are lucky) it goes up. You can generally reckon on three years of things getting worse before they get better. There was genuine reason for doubt, at this stage, as to whether the Treasury was in a position to cope with three more years of declining morale.

Change therefore was risky. Yet the risk was run. The return of Mr Heywood meant that things got going in earnest. The final report, disguised under the modest title of *The Fundamental Review of HM Treasury's Running Costs*, came out in October 1994.

The FER and its findings

The FER report is not a prepossessing document. Its red covers are of flimsy cardboard, distinguished only by the royal crest on the front. It is bound by a staple. Its authors are listed as 'Sir Colin Southgate, Jeremy Heywood, Richard Thomas and Suzanne Cook, assisted by Anna Molloy, Jessie Finbow' without any indication of who these people actually are. Most of its 218 pages are, to an outsider, clear but turgid. Paragraph 4A.3 of Annex 4.A begins 'In part II we set out three key ideas for the future organizational structure.'

The hard bits were lubricated with soft soap. 'The Treasury is an extremely effective and impressive department full of dedicated, professional and public-spirited staff. But in any organization, there is room for improvement.'

The prose suffered severely from the jargon of management consultants. The Treasury's 'focus' should be on 'core' activities. 'Delayering' will go with 'a more strategic approach'. 'The Grade 7 cadre' will sometimes provide 'team leaders' thanks to the findings of the 'Management Levels Project Team' – that is, when they are not 'bedded out' in other organizations.

Yet, cutting the crap, the FER report has much of the tough clarity which is the hallmark of successful Treasury officials. It starts from objectives: what the Treasury's objectives are. It tries to tie structure to those objectives. It says what the Treasury should not do and what should be done outside; what it might do better and how, crucially, to establish 'a management structure which pushes more responsibility down the line, while leaving room for creative and strategic thinking throughout the department'.

Sir Colin Southgate's introductory chapter was particularly forthright. 'I am amazed,' he said, 'by the number of "grades" of staff the Treasury has and how central these still are to the department's thinking and vocabulary. The sooner we can get away from that, the better the Treasury will work.' 'If there is any message I would want to leave with you . . . it is that you must put your people first.' And again, 'Personnel has sometimes been regarded almost as a "no-go" area for the Treasury's brightest stars, training has been neglected, and career planning and development for most staff seems to have lost their way.' ('Doesn't Sir Colin know that Robin Butler [later the Cabinet secretary] was once head of personnel here?', Treasury critics chortled. But in essence Sir Colin is right: not all the occupants of the post have shared Sir Robin's distinction.)

The Treasury was to be reorganized under seven directorates. They covered: macroeconomic policy and prospects; public finance; expenditure and policy analysis; financial reporting and audit; finance regulation and industry; international finance; and human resources and support.

The most controversial aspect of this bit of the reorganization concerned public spending. Here responsibility was divided. 'Macro' public spending – the setting of its overall level to meet the Treasury's economic responsibilities – was given to the public finance and expenditure director. But 'micro' public spending – governing which departments got what – was given to the expenditure and policy analysis director.

Under the review, the Treasury would go on having standing teams, responsible for specific subjects. But it would also have floating teams, or 'project teams'. These were to deal with new issues as they arose, and in particular to deal with subjects which fell across the responsibilities of different standing teams.

The directors would generally have the support of assistant directors. They would sometimes act as substitutes, sometimes as team leaders, and would sometimes contribute to particular bits of work. But in the process, a scythe was taken to a whole layer of management, the medium-grand Grade 3s (or under-secretaries in old Whitehall-speak). The top people would manage. The people at team level, Grade 5s or lower, would do the work. 'I know I'm not supposed to correct their English any more,' said one faintly bemused director after the review. 'But does this mean that I am not supposed to correct their economics either?'

One whole chunk of Treasury work was let go. The Treasury has always insisted that it is its job to monitor what other departments do on pay and rations. The rationale was that if department A paid (say) more to its cleaners, the wielders of the mop in department B would want it too. Given the relatively high level of unionization in the public sector, contagion was likely, and could damage spending control. It was therefore no mean thing for the Treasury to divest itself of this work as the review recommended. Such of it as was still to be done was to be handed – along with 125 staff – to the Office of Public Service and Science (OPSS) in the Cabinet Office – traditionally the Treasury's rival for central power.

The report's implications for the Treasury's work on overseas finance, on accountancy and on financial service industry monitoring are dealt with in the bits on these subjects that follow (see respectively chapters, 14, 11 and 12). However, one final set of review recommendations should be dealt with here simply because they were ones to which Sir Colin in particular attached the highest importance. They are those concerning personnel matters: career development, training, support systems, even the building.

Treasury officials, the FER said, were to take much more responsibility for designing their own careers. Jobs would not become known of through the grapevine and handed out by fiat; they would be advertised and people could apply.

Then there was the Treasury's IT. The Treasury had stumbled into IT quite early. But its system was clumsy, and not that much used. Until quite recently, you could find senior officials drafting in longhand and/or dictating into machines. Their labours were then sent to typing pools for transcription.

That was to change. The review here recommended substantial outsourcing. A separate project, the Efficient Office Project, looked at ways of making the Treasury more efficient.

Finally, the review recommended that officials should be given more time between jobs to be trained up for their new responsibilities. No longer would they be plunged into the middle of things to learn from the files on the job. And when they got jobs they would have them for longer. Typically, officials would have 'career anchors' in particular areas of work on which they would concentrate and to which, after a move, they would expect to return.

Life after FER

'It's like we have swum across a river and made the other bank,' said one official a while after the report was complete. 'Most people are lying in the sunshine saying "phew, we've made it". No one has quite noticed that right next door to the bank is a mountain range that we now have to get over.'

The first flush of organizational change is hard to manage. 'It's one thing to say: "There is no proper role for Grade 3 civil servants in the Treasury." It's another to stand up in front of fifty of them and tell them "You're hopeless," ' says an adviser to the review.

Around a quarter of the top jobs had to go. The Treasury was able to achieve this by voluntary redundancies. Though there are no private-sector-style pay-offs in the public service, there is the early pension, and it is by any standards generous. Besides, most of the discarded officials expected to do quite well as consultants after they left, and many have.

The Treasury had to go through the standard set of responses to such changes, which bear an uncanny resemblance to mourning. 'You get denial. You get anger.' And they were made worse by the fact that the Treasury is generally a collegial sort of a place, where people speak highly of their colleagues. Whereas in many organizations the departure of top people would be seen as an opportunity, in the Treasury it saddened many officials.

The mandarins had to change too. Sir Terry was at least interested in managing. But this was something new for many. They had after all gone into government to run the economy and it was a bit disappointing to have to run people instead. 'You not only have to remember that x wants job y,' says one. 'You have to know that he's going skiing next week, or it's the nanny's holiday.'

It is now reckoned that a senior director will spend perhaps half his time on management.

The reconstructed Treasury

Management is an activity which our reincarnated mandarin hardly knew existed. But as he wandered around the New Treasury, the returned mandarin would find many other things that were outside his experience.

Dictation and the typing pool have gone. Practically everyone now works direct into a terminal on their desks. Memos are circulated electronically, though this is not altogether a boon. It is harder to flick through a document on screen than on paper.

E-mail is growing exponentially. And personal secretaries, who used to sit there transcribing tapes, are developing new roles. Budget liaison officer is one of the more common – though it has to be said that developing roles and careers for support staff is still not one of the Treasury's strengths.

Nor would the returning mandarin find people gossiping about what jobs might be opening up in the organization. Jobs are all publicly advertised. People have to apply for them. Indeed there is now a procedure, so fair as to be bordering on the absurd, where everyone who does not get shortlisted for a job is sent a written note explaining why, and everyone who is shortlisted but doesn't get the job gets an even longer written note.

The returner would find fewer people. Before the FER, the Treasury employed some 1,300 staff. In early 1999 that was down to 1,055 staff on the Treasury books, and just 904 actually in post. The senior staff, now described as Range F and above (Grade 5 and above in oldspeak and assistant secretary and above in very oldspeak), numbers just seventy-three.

Perhaps the greatest change of all is in the level at which decisions are taken. The retired mandarin would expect to see submissions to ministers which had been drafted by juniors, but then commented on by their seniors and their seniors' seniors up a long hierarchy. Today, most submissions will go forward from quite junior officials in their thirties and forties direct to ministers, without prior vetting. If the minister wants a meeting, it will be with the officials responsible rather than a cast list of senior figures with a less detailed knowledge.

This is not cost-free. For one thing, there has been a certain loss of quality control: senior officials admit that some submissions are substandard. For another, though officials at the more junior level may be expert in the subject at hand, they may not have the same broad knowledge as others who are more senior, nor be able to spot all the ways in which policy in one area relates to policy in another.

Nevertheless, it is intrinsic to the new shape of the Treasury. One top official compares it with a Mateus Rosé bottle. Most staff will be concentrated in the wide bit of the bottle a bit above the bottom. The base is narrow and few will ever get promoted into the neck.

Denied the opportunities for top jobs, then, ambitious officials will have to satisfy themselves with making more out of more junior jobs. And the way to do that is to let them make the policy themselves, without interference from their superiors, and present it to ministers off their own bats. This is what the Treasury calls the 'New Settlement' between it and its staff; and it claims that it will work.

The other great change following the FER is a greater organizational flexibility. Before the FER, the structure was fixed, with clear lines of responsibility and reporting. Now it is much more fluid.

There is a greater use of cross-cutting teams, combining people from different directorates. Ad hoc teams are swiftly set up to deal with specific issues, and then disbanded. The Treasury is less and less like a traditional bureaucratic organization and more and more like a merchant bank, able to put together teams of people with a range of skills to deal with specific tasks.

It cannot of course be totally fluid. A merchant bank can choose not to tender for business for which it is not equipped. In the Treasury, however, there are no bits of business that can be left undone. 'The minister's private office has to know where to send every piece of paper that comes into it to get it dealt with,' one official points out. This will always inhibit flexibility compared with private-sector organizations. But compared with the Treasury as it was, barriers are much lower.

Not everything recommended by the review has come about. One promise was that there would be a drive against the 'long-hours culture'. It is true that one senior official has managed to insist that he leaves each day at five to get his child from nursery, and this is accepted. But generally the lights burn as late as they ever did: in fact, later, given Mr Brown's demands and the reduction in the staff.

Another is the recommendation that staff be given time to play themselves into new jobs. This was illustrated by the case of Mr Heywood, the inventor, himself. Shortly after finishing the review, Mr Heywood was given a new and highly technical job as head of securities and markets policy. In it he had charge of the Treasury's interests in the Stock Exchange, other securities markets, derivatives exchanges and, by extension, derivatives. 'In public expenditure,' he observed, 'in the first few months when you are floundering around, as long as you say "no" you can't drop too many balls. In this area, it's quite difficult to do the job until you know what you are doing. There's a big entry threshold.'

When the person doing his future job suddenly quit for the private sector, Mr Heywood took over. His induction time: precisely half an afternoon. 'This is one area where the recommendations of the review that has not been taken forward with sufficient vigour,' he observes.

Treasury and Trésor

Anyone invited to lunch at the French Trésor would be well advised to accept. At the end of a meal there, in their magnificent offices in Bercy, a Parisian Canary Wharf, one recent British visitor counted sixty-eight varieties of cheese. The contrast with the Treasury canteen could not be sharper.

The Trésor used to share the British Treasury's austerity. It was housed in cramped quarters near the Louvre in the Rue de Rivoli. Its officials followed a vocation as monastic as those of the British Treasury.

The Trésor is part of a much larger ministry. In 1997, the incoming socialist government amalgamated what would in Britain be the Department of Trade and Industry and the Treasury into a single Ministère de l'Economie, des Finances et de l'Industrie.

It was also expected that it would abolish the Trésor. The Trésor covered only a small part of the work of the giant department: essentially, the management (and then privatization) of the state-owned industries, including the banks; most of France's European and international affairs; the national debt; and financial regulation. It had a reputation, however, that stretched beyond these areas, founded in its perceived quality; and backed by its privilege of reporting direct to the minister. Its protestations that it was merely the minister's servant had not convinced the socialists in opposition. Once in government, however, they rapidly discovered that the Trésor was an institution well worth having on your side.

What is it that gives the Trésor its clout? This can only be understood by also understanding the French Cabinet system. The French Cabinet is the small corps of officials who service each government minister directly, giving him his policy advice. Though you do not have to be of the same party as the minister to be in the Cabinet, you may well be; in any event many, even most, members of the Cabinet will move if the minister moves. Between Cabinet and minister, there are strong shared links; generally the top officials and their ministers will have been educated together. And typically, the minister will turn for his Cabinet staff to members of the Trésor, since he will know many of them personally, and understand that they are self-consciously the brightest and the best.

For the Trésor is unashamedly an elite institution. Only eight new recruits join it each year, four of them *énarques*, as graduates of France's famed Ecole Nationale de l'Administration are called. The hours are even longer than in the British Treasury: one official recalls that his wife calculated that on average he left the office at 10 p.m. 'If you left at eight, that was mid afternoon,' says a colleague.

The competition is fierce. There is only one director with three deputies. Only *énarques* ever get these jobs. Anyone over thirty-five is reckoned pretty old, and most officials will leave, for other plum jobs, by the age of forty-five. The power, however, is compensatingly great: a youngish official, for example, could find himself on the board of a big bank, effectively determining its policy. It is capable even of daring. This great institution in a country famous for its sense of *patrie* recently recruited a British Treasury official on secondment to help manage its national debt and present its macroeconomic policy to foreign investors.

Its officials act like the self-confident individualists they are. In the British Treasury, an official making a speech would check its wording with many colleagues to ensure that there was no nuance that appeared to contradict government policy. A French Trésor official would regard doing that as a slur on his own capacity to do his job. The British Treasury uses professionals – economists, lawyers – to work alongside administrators and advisers. The French Trésor expects its officials to have mastered legal and economic skills themselves. This self-reliance is reinforced by the fact that the Trésor reports directly to the department's most senior minister, with no intermediating junior ministers between them. They are instinctively less secretive than British Treasury officials.

That is not to say that the Trésor is perfect. Its reputation was damaged when France's state-owned banks started to run up huge losses when under its indirect management, and it is now as fervent for privatization as it used to be for French-style economic planning. Few women work at the Trésor. Its arrogance is not widely appreciated. It may not have love but it does have power, and it gives a share of that power to bright young people early in their careers. That is a lesson that the British Treasury is starting to learn.

Treasury exceptionalism

Britain, like France, is unusual in placing the responsibilities now held by Her Majesty's Treasury in one single institution. In most modern governments, responsibility is split. One ministry is responsible for economic policy, another is in charge of the public finances, certainly the spending of public money and usually the raising of the taxes to pay for it. America has a Treasury, but it also has a Bureau of Budget and Manpower. A similar pattern applies in Germany.

Britain is also unusual in keeping the numbers of advisers and administrators in its Treasury so low. 'When I compare our Treasury with those abroad, they have narrower spans of responsibility and more people, and as a result they can master the details of the job they are doing,' says one widely travelled official.

Treasuries in these countries understand the nature of the job they do and its importance to their governments. They make sure, within the limits imposed by discretion, that they are equipped to do it properly. Only in Britain, it seems, has professional austerity been taken so far as to undermine the institution itself.

This difference between the British Treasury and economic ministries elsewhere can cause confusion at European Union meetings. Many a British chancellor has been bemused to see his fellow economic ministers buzzing off to consult capitals on matters which he would not consider referring back. The explanation, however, is simple. Europe's economic ministers are usually of second rank at best. They carry little clout and cannot therefore take big decisions unilaterally. The British chancellor may sometimes be able to dominate them, but that does not mean that he is dominating their decisions. Moreover, they are frequently ministers from one party in a coalition government, and have therefore to consult their colleagues in other parties.

This British difference is long rooted in history. But proposals emerge quite regularly that we should go over to the continental model, or to something akin to it, by splitting the Treasury.

It actually happened once, in the 1960s, with Harold Wilson's creation of the Department of Economic Affairs under George Brown. It semi-happened during the brief life of the Civil Service Department. It nearly happened again under Lady Thatcher: 'We used to toy with the idea that we ought to have a ministry of the economy and a ministry of the budget which would have been a more aggressive promoter and would have been responsible for getting the most out of the budget. Ministers decided not to go in that direction,' says one senior Tory adviser, who rather wishes they had decided differently.

But the case for splitting the Treasury is today weaker than it has ever been. For today's Treasury is manifestly less powerful than the one which existed when Wilson came to power in 1964. It no longer controls monetary policy, which has been ceded to the Bank of England. Nobody thinks that the Treasury's cautious and anti-inflationary instincts are the chief obstacle to Britain's economic growth.

Those few people who would still split it are, rather, critical of its performance as a spending controller. They point out that, traditionally, the public-spending function of the Treasury has been subsidiary in status and power to the economic-management function. Spending has been determined more by the macroeconomic imperative of keeping totals down than by the microeconomic imperative of ensuring value for money. And, they claim, the Treasury was not very good at ensuring value for money. Certainly, the Treasury could stop impropriety and save candle-ends. But it did not seem to have any handle on what motivated departments, or on how to incentivize them to achieve value-for-money objectives.

In the late 1970s certainly, and the late 1980s probably, this was a powerful argument for splitting the Treasury. Freed of the dead hand of the economic policy wonks, so it was hoped, public-expenditure control could be put on a different basis.

But, as we shall see, the Treasury has gone a long way to meet this case. Departments have been given much more 'ownership' of their budgets, to use the fashionable phrase. They have incentives to save and incentives to achieve value for money. The Treasury has been given a more strategic role in determining totals for spending, combined with a more crusading role on value for money. It is more prepared to contemplate spending now in order to save later. It no longer tries to control everything in detail.

In any case, it is now unlikely that any prime minister would decide to split the Treasury. A strong Treasury is an instrument for tough times; and it is in tough times that a split Treasury might easily fail the nation.

While Gordon Brown remains at the Treasury, as when Kenneth Clarke was at the Treasury, a split is unthinkable whatever the arguments. Mr Brown is not a man to let real power in government go. But at any time the political obstacles to a split are immense. Splitting the Treasury, whatever its merits, seems like an idea whose time has gone.

Bigger and better?

The FER reduced the Treasury's numerical strength. Gordon Brown's activist agenda has taxed it. You sometimes feel that officials no longer have the detailed expertise they used to. 'We are skating on very thin ice in some areas,' says one senior Treasury official.

Open government is fashionable. But bureaucracy is not. To many people, the very idea that the Treasury is too small will seem risible. And certainly the present team believe that, with the possible exception of its international side, it is big enough to do its job.

Treasury officials always worked hard. They never had that much slack. True, they now have had to cope with an increased workload: more international work (especially European); more media work; more outside visits; and whole new areas such as financial regulation and privatization. But everybody in every senior job today works harder than their predecessors.

Due economy is a good thing; and so is delegation of responsibility. But the issue is whether too much is being asked of too few people.

The Treasury is an institution that believes in hair shirts. It prescribes them for everyone: for directors of companies, for workers in the private as well as the public sector; for doctors, for nurses, for dustmen; and it prescribes them for public spending. Austerity is not, at the Treasury, just a policy; it is a way of life.

The cost of the Treasury's nine hundred or so senior staff and their support totals around £60 million. The Treasury hates taking any one item of public expenditure as a percentage of the total, as it always looks small, but, nevertheless . . . £60 million is 0.002 per cent of public spending or 0.0007 per cent of GDP or around £1 a year for every man, woman and child in the country. You could double the Treasury's budget without anyone noticing the cost.

You would not want to double it. But if the Treasury is to do its job properly, if it is to be able to respond to crises as they arise, if it is to be able to do a bit of thinking ahead rather than just reacting, it needs more than the absolute minimum of staff. There is not much wrong with the present structure of the Treasury. But what is wrong could be put right by hiring just a few more high-quality staff.

There's a World Out There | 5

The Treasury is at last getting away from its tradition of purdah and connecting better with the outside world: industry, the Bank of England, academics.

'The Treasury is the only place in the world where, if you ring fifteen people, you will find thirteen of them at their desk.' This is one of those little sayings which you come across on your way round the Treasury. Once it was true. Is it still?

The Treasury was traditionally a self-referential organization, where contact with the world outside was kept to a minimum. 'They were so cut off,' moans one ex-special adviser. 'When Kenneth Clarke went on a mission to the Far East, he ended up accompanied by a bunch of American bankers, not British industrialists.' Certainly any town hall official who spent as much time behind his desk as the average Treasury official would be widely reckoned culpable.

The Treasury used to trot out a practised liturgy of reasons for its insulation. For example, there are the exigencies of the job. A top manager in the private sector will largely be in control of his own diary. A top mandarin at the Treasury is not. The demands of ministers are unpredictable. Parliament will not be kept waiting.

'You have to be available at fifteen minutes' notice however senior you are . . . If you go out into the world it's not like that. Senior managers can be out there talking to people,' one says.

Ministers aside, the pressures on time in senior jobs are intense. A lot of the work has to be done quickly. A department will typically dump a paper or a spending request on the Treasury at the last moment, hoping to bounce it through. Officials worry that, if they are not there, such tactics will succeed.

There is something in these arguments, but not a lot. It may suit senior officials to believe that they are indispensable, but of course they are not. In war, when the captain's dead and the lieutenant winged, the sergeant takes command. There are many Treasury Grade 5s who would relish being permanent secretary for the day. In truth, it is not ministers who would mind officials being away. It is the officials themselves, most of whom enjoy nothing so much as being in on things during a crisis.

Anyway, there is a day called Friday, when Parliament barely sits and most ministers set off for their constituencies. There are recesses, when most ministers will spend longer periods in their constituencies, and there are ministerial foreign visits. Officials need not actually be present to do the job. There are faxes, mobile phones and e-mail everywhere, which (except on matters of high secrecy) mean they can stay in touch with base.

Secrecy has been the second reason advanced for insulation. It is even less convincing. Of course, if Treasury officials were going to pop out to lunch at a clearing bank to tell them interest rates were about to go up, then secrecy would be at risk. But they are not. Discretion is part of every official's professionalism. Watch any competent Treasury performer, for example, in front of a parliamentary select committee of MPs and you will wonder that anyone can speak for so long and say so little.

Ministers have recognized the need for a change in Treasury behaviour and for greater openness. For many years, they and officials observed budget 'purdah', a period of about six weeks before the great day when they went out little and said nothing. Kenneth Clarke, who was not much enamoured of official rituals, simply abolished it. This has had no noticeable effect on the frequency of unauthorized budget leaks, which continued after purdah was abolished much as they had before.

Most officials privately welcome the greater openness with which they now function. And yet the legacy still remains, leaving all but the most confident inhibited from free-and-easy intercourse with the world outside the office.

Officials like to believe that they are on top of things. They would like others to think they are on top of things. However, this can present them with a dilemma when they meet the outside world. For they may be forced by secrecy to have to pretend not to know things which in fact they know perfectly well. It is not a comfortable position.

Suppose someone asks them a question to which they know the answer. Suppose, however, that the answer is that a Cabinet committee will the very next day decide the matter. This is a secret which officials may not reveal. But to stall may seem to show ignorance. It is therefore embarrassing. It is therefore tempting to stay in the office and avoid the embarrassment.

Treasury officials are also aware of a further danger of venturing forth: something economists call 'producer capture'. This is a term most used to describe what can go wrong in the relationship between big utility firms such as the gas and water companies and the regulators, OFGAS and OFWAT, who are supposed to police them. What happens is that the regulator spends so long in the company of these firms and their people that he comes to see the world through their eyes, and not, as he should, through the consumer's eyes.

This can apply to government officials too. The British Ministry of Agriculture, for example, is a committed supporter of the agricultural interests it is supposed to police. An allegation of this kind, however, would be damaging to the Treasury, whose institutional *raison d'être* is to protect the common weal against vested interests.

To Treasury man, the outside world is a dangerous place, full of people who want to grab the taxpayers' money or use the state's power for their own purposes. It is better to keep a clear head and avoid their blandishments.

But, in the words of one wise mandarin, the Treasury 'should try to distinguish between producer capture and recognizing that producers, too, have hearts. Without meaning to, the Treasury does things that are very harmful to producers, simply because it has never understood how these people tick.'

An element of secrecy is inevitable in Treasury work. Leak, for example, that cigarette prices are to double in the budget and see how many packs remain on the shelves next day. A good deal of information is 'market confidential'. If the Treasury broadcast the possible proceeds of some privatization or other, it would in effect set a limit to the price it would fetch. Nor is it ever likely that states will view with equanimity the putting into the public domain of negotiations between them.

More controversially, some at any rate of the advice given to ministers by officials should remain confidential. The Treasury has to look as if it knows what it is doing. If advice were published, and if with that it became clear that ministers often rejected that advice, the unity of its front to the world would crumble.

Total openness is not attainable; and if it were attainable it would not be desirable. The Treasury uses a more limited word for what it is trying to achieve: 'transparency', meaning that it should be open about the objectives of policy, and honest in assessing whether or not they are being achieved.

But there is good reason to think that the Treasury should be more open than it is. First, it no longer has control over the most market-sensitive decision of all: interest rates. That now lies with the Bank of England, which is open about its decisions only after they have been taken. The removal of this bit of policy much diminishes the risks of Treasury openness. The old fear, in any case exaggerated, that some official would accidentally signal a move in interest rates no longer applies.

Ultimately, it is easy to conclude that Treasury officials spend too little time in the world because they do not believe that it has much to teach them. 'The Treasury is very insular,' says one official. 'A lot of criticism passes us by.'

In particular, by its nature, the Treasury lives by economics. Ask a Treasury man the value of a bird singing in a tree and he will say, 'Whatever the public would pay for it to be there.' It therefore finds it difficult to deal with the arguments of those who do not share this world view. 'The Treasury is very bad at listening,' says a former official who has left to work for a pressure group. 'It doesn't understand people who don't think like it. The *Brent Spar* environmentalists were a classic example. The Treasury just could not grasp what they were banging on about.'

All this is true. It is, however, starting to change, as we shall see in this chapter. Indeed it has to.

Once upon a time, power worked through authority. Distance was part of its armoury; mystique central to its force. The Treasury was held in awe partly because it held itself aloof. The age of deference is gone; and that approach no longer works. The Treasury must be more open if it is to do its job.

The Treasury has to communicate, both internally and externally, to be effective. 'When you are outside the Treasury you tend to think that that must be where power lies. When you are there you feel much less confident because you feel uncomfortably aware that the levers you can pull are few,' says one very senior ex-official.

One important lever is the power to influence opinion. At the very least, you want to convince the outside world that you know what you are doing. They may then have the confidence to plan on the basis that you do. And you want to convince them too that your world view should be part of theirs: for example, that a successful industrialist is not one who maximizes government grants but one who innovates and competes.

Faith in the effectiveness of macroeconomic policy as a tool has faded. Its magic powers are gone and all that is looked for now is a more or less stable framework within which other policies can work. Instead, the emphasis is on microeconomic policy: on training and education for skills, combined with the encouragement of competition as the way of levering up productivity.

This new doctrine needs to be sold. Companies have to be convinced that their faults lie, not with a high pound or high interest rates, but with themselves. Competition has to be sustained against the usual producer lobbies. Training and education have to be sold to the companies that should provide it and to the people who need to undergo it. Government no longer holds all the levers. Other people do; often the most government can do is to persuade them to pull them.

Of course, the Treasury can use its traditional tools of communication to an extent: chancellor's speeches, budgets, spending white papers and other Treasury publications. There is a far greater output of such documents from the Treasury today than there was even five years ago; and the organization makes full use of the Internet.

But we no longer live in a paper world, where the written word is what counts. There is no substitute for getting out there and talking to people. The Treasury is now trying to do this, and it is to those efforts that we now turn.

Touring industry

Sir Terence Burns dealt with the office-bound culture in what, for the Treasury, was an unusual way. In 1992 he issued a decree that relevant officials should spend at least one day a month out of the office, visiting industry.

This decree was met with scepticism. As we have seen, the Treasury's instincts are against getting out and about. But industrial visits raised particular problems.

For a start who were they for? 'I can't see whom they are supposed to benefit, us or them,' said one official. 'It is sort of good public relations but most of the problems they ask about we do not have responsibility for. We are not in the business of deciding what bit of Liverpool gets what grant. That's for the Department of the Environment, Transport and the Regions or the Department of Trade and Industry.'

Then there were worries that industry would misunderstand. The relationship between companies and government is always ambiguous. Companies want things from government: grants, legislation and often protection from 'unfair' competition. At the same time, they want to be left alone. Government is blamed, for example, for 'red tape' and regulation, even though much of the latter, these days, emanates from the European Commission rather than from Whitehall.

In this debate, the Treasury took a fairly unambiguous position. It was in favour of competition, deregulation and eliminating subsidy. Nor was this simply the result of having Thatcherite ministers. Such thinking, which is common to most economists, infused the organization. If the incoming Labour government had gone for a much more interventionist industrial policy, as had its predecessors in the 1960s and 1970s, some of the most senior officials on the industry side of the Treasury would have resigned. (It didn't.)

If anyone was to deal with industry, so the Treasury had traditionally thought, it should be the relevant departments. 'They are exposed to producer lobbies,' a Treasury official explained. 'We are acting on behalf of the taxpayer and the consumer.'

There was a further difficulty. At the time the industrial visit programme was launched, what industry most wanted to see was a cut in interest rates. But within the ERM, and while inflation was being controlled after Britain's exit, interest rates could not be safely cut. The scope therefore for acrimony on industrial visits was obvious – and mandarins do not like acrimony.

There was something in all these concerns. But there was plenty to be said on the other side too. 'People in the Treasury get good at the jobs they are required to do: give ministers advice, point out the political mantraps. But they have never had to run a profit-and-loss account or understand a balance sheet. Some political decisions would go differently if the mandarins understood more of the problems businessmen face,' says one official.

The businessmen gained from meeting Treasury people too. Most of them held a crude view that the Treasury comprised bureaucratic pen-pushers. Such a view does not survive human contact. Treasury officials are clever. But they also have other characteristics to which business people could not fail to respond. Energy is one; you could not survive in Great George Street without stamina. Self-confidence is another. Besides, one should never underestimate the benefits to both sides in finding out that they were dealing with human beings, who had families and liked football. Stereotypes do not survive real contact, and the breakdown of these particular stereotypes had a generalized, if ill-defined, benefit.

'I remember a day in Yorkshire with Rachel Lomax [then a senior Treasury official] and it was great fun,' one participant recalls. 'Someone like Rachel who is very good impressed the hell out of them. Then we went out to explain the philosophy behind the budget. Large numbers of people turned up to hear the Treasury explanation. People thought that having it was terrific. Treasury officials may underestimate the impact they have.'

'Industrial visits were a creature of their time,' one who was involved in them recalls. 'We are talking about a period where discontent with economic policy was as high as it has ever been. There was certainly a feeling that the Treasury was sitting there without any knowledge of what its policies were doing to the real economy.'

'It's very difficult to turn round an impression like that, and I think it was reasonable to do one or two symbolic things.'

As missions go, it might not have been the most glorious. But all but the most hard-bitten Treasury sceptics would probably now concede that it was worth doing all the same.

Hitting the headlines

At his farewell party in 11 Downing Street, Lord Burns was gracious to the press. Several of Britain's heavyweight political and economic commentators were present: Peter Riddell of *The Times*, Philip Stephens of the *Financial Times*, William Keegan of the *Observer*. 'We've had our ups and downs over the years,' said Lord Burns, 'but this country is extremely fortunate in the quality of its economic commentary.'

There had certainly been downs. A decade earlier, Sir Terry had been observed in the same room in a fury with a particular correspondent and threatening dire retribution.

All governments at all times have split personalities where the press is concerned. Sometimes, they are the vital channel through which the government can transmit its message; sometimes, they are its irredeemable enemies. But in the Treasury, a department where a misplaced message can cost billions across the exchanges, the tension is even greater than in most other departments.

One Saturday afternoon in the 1980s, Number 10 Downing Street was proclaiming that the government would not raise interest rates to protect the pound, even if that meant it fell to below a pound to the dollar. Across the road in the Treasury, however, it had become clear that this line simply would not hold and that, whether the prime minister liked it or loathed it, interest rates would have to go up.

It was a confused picture, with authoritative information at a premium. When journalists sought to get hold of Robert Culpin, then the Treasury's press spokesman, they found that he was on his allotment. The duty press officer did not know what was going on. The confusion created chaos.

That has not been a problem under New Labour. Everyone would have known where to find Charlie Whelan, Gordon Brown's political press spokesperson for the government's first twenty months, on a Saturday afternoon – at the football.

Talking to him, you would be sure that he was reflecting the chancellor's position. You might not, however, be quite so sure that he was master of the nuances of the economics. If you were after economics you would refer, not to the chancellor's personal spin doctor, but to Peter Curwen. Peter Curwen was from the mould of the traditional Treasury senior press spokesman, highly capable and trusted, in so far as a man in that position ever can be, by journalists.

Still, for the chancellor to employ a personal as well as an official press spokesman was a big change. The prime minister's press secretary, it is true, has also often been a political appointee. But in Number 10 a broad brush is what is required. The Treasury, however, needs something more than that – an understanding of economic policy making. In consequence, press secretaries have been administrators on the way up. Robert Culpin, who has been an outstanding performer in every other Treasury job he has done, was succeeded by another high-flier, John Gieve. (Mr Gieve will unfairly be known as the one who didn't successfully work his tape recorder when the chancellor gave a controversial briefing and there was a dispute over what he had actually said.) Mr Gieve was followed by Gus O'Donnell, now the government's senior economic adviser, and Mr O'Donnell by Andrew Hudson, now in charge of health spending in the Treasury. Mr Hudson was followed by Ms Rutter before her contretemps with her employers and the emergence of the Whelan/Curwen double act.

The double act came to an end in January 1999. Mr Whelan, unfairly, came under suspicion of leaking against Peter Mandelson, the industry secretary, over a loan which the latter had taken from Mr Robinson to buy a house. Whatever the ins and outs of the affair, it soon became clear that Mr Whelan had become a story. That impeded his ability to do the job, and he resigned. The Treasury then returned to its more traditional arrangement, with the appointment of John Kingman, a young high-flier, to do the job.

In using high-flying general officials as press officers, rather than information specialists, the Treasury was unusual. Until recently at any rate, most departments appointed their press secretaries from the Government Information Service, a group of so-called specialist press officers. The Treasury, however, understood that the mysteries of economic policy might stretch most members of the GIS. Besides, it was felt unlikely that Treasury officials would willingly tell a mere press officer what was really going on. For the press office to know what was going on – essential if it was to do its job – it had to be headed by someone whom the Treasury respected.

The Treasury has also been unusual in the small size of its press office. The senior press spokesman aside, there were at the time of writing five full press officers. The Home Office had twenty-nine.

In principle, as we have seen, the Treasury is now seized of the importance of public presentation. Even legislation is not now done privately: in 1998, the Treasury published for comment its huge bill bringing in the new system for regulation of the financial services industry (see Chapter 12).

In practice, the Treasury goes through periods of greater and less great openness with the press, though around a rising trend. Typically, the Treasury starts feeling it is misunderstood, and puts out more information to try to prepare opinion. Then something goes wrong. A story rebounds; a leak goes too far; a chastening bout of internal recrimination takes places about who was responsible. Or Parliament gets on its high horse because it wasn't told first. The curtain comes down. But then the costs of silence again emerge. The episode is forgotten and the cycle restarts.

The Treasury is also less secretive about some things than others. It is, these days, far more open than it used to be about its macroeconomic strategy. This is because it realizes that this is no longer a matter under its control. Macroeconomic strategy can only work if the world out there believes it will work – particularly that bit of the world out there that comprises international financial markets. And, as we have seen, microeconomic policy needs constantly to be pushed by the Treasury.

However, on one subject the Treasury normally but inexplicably stays above the battle for public opinion: public spending. The regular public-spending battles in the government follow a consistent pattern. Departmental ministers try to show how painful cuts would be politically: if a penny more is taken off defence (for example), it will mean the end of great regiments. Ministers are said to be contemplating resigning, appealing to the Cabinet. Then, after the settlement is reached, all this changes. The defence minister is said to have won a triumph over the Treasury. In July 1998, George Robertson was said to have won cuts of 'only' £500 million defeating a Treasury bid for £2 billion. Ask for Treasury comment on any of this, and you will be met with silence.

To some extent this is excusable. The simplest way to get Mr Robertson to accept the cut in his budget is to allow him to claim that his budget has not been cut. But it has a major downside: that public support for public-spending restraint in general is undermined.

The Treasury profoundly believes that there is much waste in public spending. It thinks that more could be bought for less if it was bought wisely. It could produce a long list of sacred cows where, if ministers were willing, it could cut spending without hitting services, though at the cost of political controversy. But it never argues this case in public.

The public is therefore left with the impression that all cuts in spending will damage spending to which they are attached. According to the authoritative British social attitudes survey, 61 per cent want more spending on health, education and social benefits, even if it means higher taxes, compared with 5 per cent who want lower taxes even if it means lower spending. The public would also like taxes hypothecated to particular purposes, which is anathema to the Treasury.

The Treasury believes in the market place. There is a political market place too, however, where political actors are bidding for public sympathy. If the Treasury stays out of that market place, as it has chosen to up to now, it will ultimately pay a high price. If in the long run it is to succeed in keeping public spending under control, it will no longer be enough to operate in the corridors of Whitehall. It will need to convert public opinion to its perspective. Silence over public spending, though it may have served in the past, will no longer work for the Treasury in the future.

6 | Look, No Hands

A great change has taken place in thinking about economic policy, and the ability of the Treasury to manipulate the economy is now discounted. This chapter discusses the effect of that change on the work of the Treasury.

After 1991, the British economy enjoyed seven years of reasonably steady and non-inflationary economic recovery. It had almost come to be assumed that, come what may, next year's economy would be 2 per cent bigger than this year's economy which would be 2 per cent bigger than the year before that's. But the economic cycle has been about a long time, and wiser Treasury hands never assumed that growth was for ever. The summer of 1998 saw a number of events come together which threatened it: the Russian debt default, a financial crisis in the Far East and a sharp loss of confidence in equity markets. As successive surveys showed falling consumer confidence in Britain, the r-word, recession, was again to be heard.

The Treasury's chief response was to play down fears. In particular, it insisted, the chancellor's plans for public spending, unveiled in the Comprehensive Spending Review in the summer of 1998, were robust. What it notably did not do was to launch a new anti-recessionary policy, either by cutting taxes or by seeking to press the Bank of England to cut interest rates. It merely promised 'stable' policies which, it said, were the best way to avoid trouble. The Treasury, in other words, has got out of the job of steering the economy, though the Bank of England did its best to do what was needed by way of interest rate cuts. That is the most profound of all the changes in the Treasury in recent years.

The death of Keynes

For years – that is to say, roughly from the victory of Keynesian macroeconomics in the early 1940s to the advent of post-monetarism in the 1990s – the central function of the Treasury was to steer the economy. Keynesians, or at least their vulgar disciples in the world of practical policy, believed that economic variables such as growth, employment and inflation could be manipulated by the government.

At first fiscal policy – that is to say management of the gap between what the government raised in tax revenue and what it spent – was the main instrument. In the 1970s and 1980s, it lost its pre-eminence in favour of monetary policy, that is to say the level of interest rates. Fiscal policy remained important, though, because the theory was that the more the government borrowed, the higher interest rates would be.

Some outside critics believed that the Treasury was congenitally inclined to be restrictive: the phrase used was 'stop–go economics', where taxes were raised just as soon as the economy got a head of steam up. Such critics, led by Sir Samuel Brittan before he converted to monetarism, were in the ascendancy in the 1950s and early 1960s. Others believed that the Treasury – or at least its political bosses – were inclined to be too expansionist, in a way that risked inflation. Such people grew increasingly dominant into the 1970s and under their influence there was a sharp change to a deliberate policy of deflating the economy in the 1980s. But the whole period until the 1980s was dominated by the belief that these variables could be changed by the Treasury and that getting them right was the test of its abilities.

As the 1980s turned to the 1990s, the conventional wisdom took another twist. Economics became dominated by rational expectations theory and its aftermath. Broadly, rational expectations theory played down the ability of governments to manipulate anything. They could not do it, the theorists said, because markets had got wise to them.

For example, suppose that the government wanted to expand the economy. Suppose that its chosen instrument was to cut taxes without cutting spending. The first result would be an injection of spending power into the economy.

But this would not last. 'Ah ha,' market operators would say, 'it's expanding; and that means inflation will be right round the corner. We must demand higher interest rates to compensate us for that.' So interest rates would be forced up, choking off the increased demand.

This is of course a crude account of a theory of many subtleties. But it won through. By the time Gordon Brown became chancellor in 1997, the consensus was that the role of the Treasury in setting economic policy was important but diminished.

It had to set the framework. *Stability and Investment for the Long Term*, Mr Brown's economic and fiscal report of June 1998, set out what this required fiscally in the form of a 'Code for Fiscal Stability'. The government would observe the 'golden rule' that over the economic cycle it would borrow only to invest and not to fund current spending. It would abide too by the 'sustainable investment rule': net public debt as a proportion of GDP will be held over the economic cycle at a stable and prudent level.

Short-termism was out. 'The government's fiscal rules have been formulated to deliver economic stability. A key priority for the government is to operate fiscal policy in a way that meets these rules with a high degree of certainty,' said the report. 'It would be a serious mistake to divert fiscal policy away from this end in an attempt to manage short-term demand and inflationary pressures in the economy. Monetary policy is better suited to this task.'

Now, it is apparent that this greatly reduces the role of the Treasury. In the short-term management of the economy, it is monetary policy that matters. But the Treasury has lost monetary policy, which is now in the hands of the Bank of England.

True, Gus O'Donnell, the Treasury head of monetary policy, sits on the Monetary Policy Committee (MPC). He can speak but he cannot vote. And certainly he denies ever trying to twist its arms on decisions. 'Our role is not to say "on our reading of economic interest rates should do this or that,"' says one senior official, 'but to ensure coordination, for example with the government's overall fiscal stance. If we had a strong view about some aspect on which we had a comparative advantage – say, the state of public-sector finances – we might occasionally intervene. But otherwise, we try to resist, though sometimes we fail.'

There have been a few blips along the way. The MPC was designed to be a committee of economists, offering their best expert judgement on the appropriate level of interest rates. When, however, interest rates started to rise as the economy was strong through 1997 and early 1998, pressure on this from outside began to mount. Stories started appearing that the MPC was 'out of touch' with the real economy. The implication was that it should be stuffed with industrialists and trade unionists, whose aim was to increase short-run economic growth. That would have been fatal to the project.

Then there were problems because all nine members of the committee were not appointed from the start. Alan Budd, a member, had not yet left his previous job as the Treasury's chief economic adviser. The committee was split, between so-called 'hawks', in favour of bigger interest rate rises, and 'doves', who were opposed to them. The governor had an uncomfortable casting vote.

Things became easier when interest rates started to fall. It is harder to make stick the charge that they are falling too slowly than the charge that they are rising too fast. The governor resisted the temptation to be too tough by keeping interest rates up despite the slowing economy and so undershooting his inflation target. And the hawks-versus-doves argument was superseded by a much more interesting one: between activists, who believed in frequent small changes in interest rates, and pacifists, who wanted a more stable policy. The debate in the MPC was greatly improved. The Treasury's own verdict on this change at the beginning of 1999 was certainly 'so far, so good'.

There is a completely objective test of whether the policy is working: the inflationary expectations of the market. If you compare the yield on an index-linked gilt (i.e., one where you get compensated for inflation) and a non-index-linked gilt (i.e., one where you don't), you get an idea of what inflation the market expects. In early 1999, the gap was at 2.5 per cent, which is precisely the government's central inflation target. True, public expectations of inflation were not yet so low: they expected 4–4.5 per cent price rises, according to surveys. But this was not feeding through into wage demands, partly because of fears of recession. Independence is working – so far.

Some still wonder whether politicians will go on resisting the temptation to tamper with monetary policy. Suppose it is the run-up to an election. Suppose the government is in trouble; but suppose also that economic recovery and incipient inflation suggest that interest rates should go up. If a prime minister in those circumstances sought to intervene again, what would happen?

'Number 10 interference would be very dangerous if it re-emerged,' says one official. If it was overt, outsiders would react. They might speculate against the pound, or demand higher interest rates just as the government was trying to lower them. The elements of a traditional stabilization crisis could swiftly emerge.

But there are major disincentives to such developments. Prime minister and chancellor alike are deeply committed to stability: to the policy of giving monetary policy to the MPC and to three-year cycles of expenditure planning. To reverse all that would not only require them to eat many words. It would be a U-turn of historic proportions, and the record of U-turns, even from a limited election-winning point of view, is not good.

Giving monetary policy away is not an easy thing to do. But once you have done it, getting it back is even harder.

Macroeconomic policy after independence

The Treasury's macroeconomic job now is to achieve the budgetary aims of the policy: to set and raise the necessary taxes and to make sure they are not spent too freely or wastefully.

This is not as easy as it may sound. Public spending, as we shall see, always and everywhere threatens to get out of control. Tax revenues always and everywhere need to be protected against the political pressures to cut them and the lobbies for exemptions. A decent fist has to be made of both jobs if the Treasury is to fulfil even its new role.

The Treasury has more room for manoeuvre within this broad policy than meets the eye. A subtle view of rational expectations would hold that you can do things to affect economic outcomes so long as the market does not catch you at it. If you increase public investment, for example, while arguing convincingly that you are not, you get the advantages of the new public infrastructure without the disadvantage of higher interest rates. The brilliance of Gordon Brown's summer 1998 spending measures were that they did just that.

Meanwhile, the Treasury is giving greater priority to a job which it has long had but not long thought important: promoting microeconomic measures to improve economic performance. There is, for example, the whole area of welfare-to-work: changing the system of taxes and benefits to reduce incentives for people to remain on the dole and increasing incentives to get them into paid, productive labour. This could not simply be left to the Department of Social Security, which is more concerned with alleviating poverty than with work incentives.

Then there is competition policy, where the Treasury has to combat the natural instincts of departments such as transport, industry and agriculture to act as the arms in government of their client companies, and get them instead to promote competition. There is the regulation of privatized firms; deregulation generally; the promotion of free labour markets; the alleviation of employer costs; and of course privatization itself. The Treasury also fought a rearguard action against the potential ill-effects of the government's minimum wage. It sought to modify the recommendations of the independent Low Pay Commission so that the new level would be phased in and its impact on younger workers reduced.

In the pre-budget report in 1998, the Treasury pointed out a 'productivity gap' of 40 per cent with the US and 20 per cent with France and Germany. It highlighted low levels of investment in research and development in Britain. It proposed permanent increases in capital allowances for small businesses; changes to the tax treatment of venture capital, and possible changes to the structure of tax-advantaged employees' share-ownership schemes.

Much of this is detailed and unglamorous stuff. Much of it is also work where the Treasury does not hold the instruments of policy in its own hands. The Treasury can urge policies on departments but it cannot force them to adopt them: not at least unless they are of a magnitude which allows the chancellor and the Cabinet to intervene to force the hand of ministers who resist.

Those in the Treasury who promote microeconomic reform do not even have the clout that Treasury public-spending controllers possess. Spending controllers have the power, when push comes to shove, to say no. Microeconomic reformers have only limited tools at their disposal.

These policies have not been shown to work yet. Instinctively, the Treasury believes that Britain's underlying economy is now healthier. But there is little concrete evidence of this in growth rates. The Treasury recently decided that the potential growth of Britain's economy was around 2.25 per cent a year. Yet in the 1960s and 1970s it was widely thought that it should be put at 3 per cent or more.

You could argue that without microeconomic reform this rate would be still lower; or that it would be accompanied by higher unemployment; or that the economy would be unstable. But the hopes of the late 1980s that Britain's economy had been transformed – hopes which began with the politicians but infected all but the most hard-bitten Treasury officials – have largely been dashed.

Even if that were not so, this new work would lack the glamour of the old work. Once upon a time, Treasury top mandarins could see themselves as heroic heart surgeons, their skilled scalpels manipulating the most sensitive bits of the body politic to adjust the flow of blood around it. Now they are reduced to conducting BUPA check-ups, dispensing wise advice and making sure nothing too palpable has gone wrong. You could argue which in practice is the more valuable role – heart surgeons, after all, end up killing lots of patients. But you could hardly doubt where the glamour lies.

All this constitutes a big change; if it lasts, possibly the biggest since the Keynesian revolution itself. It is thus perhaps not surprising that the Treasury has not adjusted fully to it. The pecking order in the department remains largely unchanged. The brightest and best yearn to get their hands on fiscal policy – still widely regarded as the Treasury's core power – on budget making, and on monetary policy, despite the fact that the Treasury no longer controls it. Banking and industry are thought less glorious, but still enjoyable. Tax is regarded as less exciting, the job so far as may be of the Inland Revenue. Spending work remains more lowly rated; while personnel, pay, resource accounting and organization are outer Siberia.

This may be starting to shift. The quality of the top spending controllers has probably improved, though the middle grades remain patchy and their numbers small. Andrew Turnbull, the new permanent secretary, symbolizes the shift, for he is an ex-spending controller. As macroeconomic policy seems less important, so the Treasury interests itself more in microeconomic policy as the instrument to improve economic performance. But it will be some years yet before status and true importance in the Treasury are properly aligned.

The crystal ball

The area of Treasury work where the new consensus has changed things most is forecasting. When the economy was supposed to be steered by the Treasury, it was naturally of the highest importance that the road ahead should be adequately mapped. That is no longer the case.

Forecasting remains significant under the new economic dispensation. For example, if you do not know how unemployment is going to move, you have no good handle on the likely course of spending on unemployment benefit. But the mystique that used to attach to this area of Treasury work has peaked. Now it is a humdrum function, which matters, but matters less.

To outsiders, the Treasury is always incompetent, but the nature of its incompetence varies over time. For many years critics focused on its incompetence over forecasting. Treasury forecasters failed to spot upturns and downturns. The balance of payments yawed into deficit just when the Treasury said that surpluses were nigh, unemployment went up fast when it said it would rise slowly, and so on. Treasury forecasts supplanted weather forecasts as national sources of amusement.

However, the argy-bargy over the forecasts is now largely a thing of the past. The caravan has moved on. The critics have other targets.

It would be nice to record that this was because forecasting had improved. It would be nice if the Treasury was now able to say with certainty what was going to happen in the future. It would be nice but it would be wrong. Treasury forecasts go through good patches and bad patches. But there has probably not been any systematic improvement over the years.

'The results of Treasury forecasts over the last five years have not been good,' one senior adviser to the last Conservative government complained. Three main failures are cited: the failure to predict the timing of economic recovery from 1990 on; the failure to predict the risk of inflation from 1992 to 1995, following the devaluation of sterling; and the underestimate of government borrowing from 1990 to 1997.

The last particularly grates on former ministers. The forecast was defective in one main regard: that it severely overestimated tax revenues. According to one participant, 'I remember in 1992–3, the forecast of the public sector borrowing requirement changed by £7 billion in six weeks.' Though it may suit the Conservatives to say so, the early underestimate in part explains, if it does not excuse, their willingness to allow spending to rise so fast in 1992 and 1993.

But forecasting has become more difficult. The exercise has become intrinsically more complex. The British economy has become a more open economy. Key forecasting variables, for example interest rates, are shaped as much by international forces as by domestic forces, and that makes the job harder. Forecasting in one country is one thing. Forecasting globally is another.

Forecasting has also been complicated by changes in people's behaviour. For economic forecasters are not in fact like weather forecasters. They do not predict an objective phenomenon out there. Economic forecasters predict human behaviour, the effect of the sum of the behaviour of millions – indeed billions – of economic actors.

These actors may change their behaviour. In recent years they have. Once, financial markets were relatively relaxed about government deficits, since they were widely thought to help the economy pick up. Now they are relatively unrelaxed, since they are widely thought to make inflation pick up.

A final twist is that forecasts can themselves affect behaviour. If the Treasury says that the economy will turn down, then economic actors may believe that it will turn down, and act accordingly. The prophecy may be self-fulfilling. But it may be worse than that. Because of the forecast, everyone expects a downturn; because they expect a downturn, they produce less. The downturn is therefore sharper than expected. The forecast has proved to be the instrument of its own inaccuracy.

Another change has been that the Treasury forecasts have lost exclusivity. Once, they were by far the dominant forecasts of the economy. The only seriously quoted rival forecast came from the National Institute of Economic and Social Research (NIESR). Even NIESR forecasts were most prominent in the days before the Treasury forecasts were first published in the 1970s.

In the 1970s a host of rival forecasts emerged. One set, from the London Business School, was prepared by three young economists whom we have come across before in this book: Terry Burns, Alan Budd and Bill Robinson. The LBS was much quicker than the Treasury to take on new monetarist perspectives.

Forecasts then proliferated. There were few primary forecasts, i.e., forecasts which were built from the ground up. But there were lots of secondary forecasts, i.e., forecasts that pinched other people's equations and adapted them to the forecasters' own needs and perspectives. No serious City firm was respectable unless it had its own little model, giving its clients the hope (or at least the illusion) of being better informed than every other firms' clients. Weekly comparisons with other forecasts were made.

During the days when the Treasury ran its panel of independent forecasters (known as the 'wise men'), around forty forecasts were compared. (They are still monitored today.) Cynics thought that the seven-strong panel of forecasters was composed so as to include economists at both extremes – Patrick Minford as an extreme monetarist and Wynne Godley as a Keynesian. This meant that Treasury forecasts always looked as if they were in the middle of the bunch.

With this came the safety-in-numbers approach to forecasting. With some exceptions, the forecasts differed only in nuance. If they turned out wrong their authors could at least say that everyone else was wrong too. When, however, it was clear that other forecasters turned out to be at least as wrong as the Treasury, the Treasury's efforts seemed less pathetic. 'We have a good average record,' says one senior Treasury forecaster. And that from an official institution, which cannot take the risk of betting its bank on some particular economic fashion, is as much as it could ever hope to achieve.

Another even more damaging accusation was often levied at the Treasury forecasts. Ministers, so critics claimed, massaged them. They would intervene to insist that published figures were altered to show the success of government policies.

This criticism showed a misunderstanding of forecasting. It is not merely a technical exercise. It is not simply a question of feeding data to equations and publishing the results. Judgement is essential to forecasting, and forecasters apply judgement at every stage.

Ministers, naturally, have judgements to offer too. If, in the view of Treasury economists, the best forecast of public borrowing, the PSBR, lay between £10 billion and £12 billion, and if ministers said they felt strongly that £10 billion would be right, the Treasury would give weight to their views. After all, the public sector borrowing requirement measures the difference between two large numbers and is therefore inevitably forecastable only subject to wide margins of error. So within those margins, the forecast might be altered. Failing that, the accompanying gloss could be worded to reflect ministerial prejudices. Brave officials would leave a written record on the file when they changed wording for this reason. Less brave ones did not.

If, however, in the view of Treasury economists, the right forecast of the PSBR lay between £10 billion and £12 billion, and then ministers said that in their judgement it would be £2 billion, matters would be played out differently. Such a judgement would depart too far from those of the professional economists involved. If published, it would not only bring contempt on them but also tarnish the reputation of the institution for which they worked. So any attempt at such manipulation would be fought.

Officials invariably fight by fair means, i.e., by arguing their case. Where professional reputation is involved they do so with tenacity and courage. But everyone in the game knows that ultimately they could use other means. The scrupulous could resign, or threaten to resign. The less scrupulous could leak or threaten to leak to Parliament or the press. Ministers know that either would be more damaging to their political reputations than would an uncomfortable forecast. They dare not push their luck.

Gordon Brown has institutionalized this practical independence. The forecast is now audited by the National Audit Office, which, significantly, reports not to ministers but to Parliament. The accusations of political manipulation were always overdone. Today such manipulation would be impossible.

But the most important change reducing criticism of Treasury forecasts is simply this: they matter less. What has changed over the years is not the accuracy of forecasts. It is their importance.

At Keynesianism's height, the forecaster was king. In the 1960s, for example, when Harold Wilson's government was fiddling around with experiments in planning, forecasts were central to the project. The Treasury's were particularly so since the outside world believed that it had access to information that gave it an insight denied to all others. When a new government came to power it would wait with baited breath to 'open the books'. What it found it tended to believe.

Nobody believes this now. Britain in the 1960s and 1970s was still prisoner to a Keynesian orthodoxy which said that government, through fiscal policy, could 'fine-tune' the economy to ensure steady growth. Britain in the 1980s and 1990s was a prisoner to an alternative post-Keynesian orthodoxy which said that it could do no such thing. But of course, if it was powerless to fine-tune, the forecasts that told it how to fine-tune were powerless too.

So why do it? The question gets asked in the Treasury every couple of years. Kenneth Clarke in particular as chancellor asked it. A well-known and public sceptic about forecasts, he insisted that the Treasury consider 'outsourcing' its forecasts to the private sector. 'If I want macroeconomic forecasts,' he was heard to muse, 'I'll read the stockbrokers' circulars.'

'We have gone through the process many times of asking whether we should do it at all,' says one senior forecaster. 'But so far, the answer has always been affirmative.'

The Treasury could hardly do without any forecasting capacity. It has to be able to give the chancellor a view of what would happen to the economy if he (say) doubled taxes or halved spending. For this it needs some numbers. But in principle that is not decisive. For it requires only the most exiguous capacity: a personal computer, a secondary model, a routine mathematical exercise.

'We have to decide whether we become a spreadsheet forecaster. Either we do our own weather forecasting with our own balloons, or we listen to the radio,' says a senior forecaster.

So the question has been whether the Treasury should retain its role as a primary forecaster on a substantial scale. The Fundamental Expenditure Review considered the case in some detail – and concluded that it should.

'There is indeed no doubt that forecasting is a highly imprecise and uncertain business; indeed no one is more aware of the uncertainties involved than the forecasters themselves,' it concluded.

> However, we regard it as completely implausible that the Treasury would want (or be allowed by Parliament or the public) to eschew completely any attempt to predict the likely path of the economy over the period ahead. Forward economic projections or assumptions are clearly essential to the tasks of planning public expenditure, determining the appropriate levels of interest rates and so on. Indeed the Treasury would not be able to carry out any of its core macroeconomic responsibilities if it had no view of what was likely to happen to the economy in the future.

The FER also came down against outsourcing. The evidence suggested, it said, that there would be some loss of accuracy. There would be practical difficulties and a loss of control. And outsourcing the forecasting work would reduce the quality of economic advice provided by the Treasury in-house.

To Treasury economists this last is particularly important. Inchoately to cogitate about the state of the economy is one thing. To forecast it is quite another. It concentrates the mind. 'You are more likely to think coherently about the economy if you are trying to forecast it,' says one senior official.

There is one other factor. The Treasury has some information that is denied outside forecasters. Not much: with the greater openness of the government about statistics, most information is in the public domain. But here are a few bits and pieces of information – about the public sector's spending for example – where the Treasury inevitably knows things that others don't.

That is not to say that the amount of resources devoted to the Treasury forecast is right. The FER pointed out that the Treasury had 23.5 people working on its forecast, compared with Cambridge Econometrics's 22, the London Business School's 13.5 and the NIESR's 12.5. It said the Treasury should look again at best practice in other countries; that it should examine options for slimming the model from its current five hundred variables and make more use of the thirteen Grade 7 economists working on the model.

But even these figures exaggerate the Treasury numbers involved. Most of its people are not working full-time on the forecast. They spend much of their time analysing economic developments. No more than four or five officials are fully employed on modelling work.

Nor is the work given the glamour it once was. The forecast would once have been presented to ministers by the chief economic adviser. He would have been flanked by at least three officials of what today would be called director rank. Today, it will be presented by a single relatively junior official.

The forecasting team certainly does not seem extravagantly manned. A question remains whether the supply creates its own demand; whether, despite the recent reduction in reliance on forecasts, the numbers still cast a spell which those who study them are unable to resist.

A keen Treasury forecaster admits a problem. 'We have to make policy making less forecasting-dependent, so we don't base policy decisions on the belief that we can predict what is going to happen next year, let alone the year after,' he says. While forecasts are there, people will always be tempted to use them. The important thing is to have forecasts on tap, but never on top. And there the Treasury thinks it is now succeeding. 'The role of forecasting has diminished dramatically. It is not an issue any more,' says one senior official.

Objects of desire

The Treasury was, of course, officially indifferent to the approach of the 1997 general election. Internally, however, speculation as to the implications of a change of regime was at fever pitch. In particular, did Labour really mean it when it said it was pro-competition, pro-markets; anti-inflation and anti-fine-tuning? Or was this an election ploy? If they did not mean it, what would that imply for the Treasury? How was it to advise new ministers? Was activist macroeconomic policy, whose role had been so much diminished during the Tory years, about to make a comeback?

There was an easy bit to this and a difficult bit. The easy bit, according to one official, would be to deal with a clear change of objectives if the new government had one. 'If it is not to be permanently low inflation, what is it to be? We ought to be able to adapt the institution to the objectives.'

The more difficult bit would be if in conscience it had difficulty in believing that the new objectives were attainable. 'My current instruction is to deliver permanently low inflation,' another senior official said at the time. 'It could change to being one of permanently low unemployment. It's something I think about quite a lot. Suppose they say that what you must do is to bring unemployment down to a million. One would start asking to what extent this was feasible.'

It was an anxious period. 'We are put in an impossible position,' said another senior official. 'Constitutionally, we are not supposed to think about a change of government yet we are supposed to be able to operate with any government at any time.'

The Treasury would have liked to be closer to Mr Brown and his colleagues while they were still in opposition. Had this been possible, the Treasury would have been spared some anxiety.

Mr Brown and friends were not inflationists in economics. They understood the implications of globalism and free markets. Moreover, as young men they had seen a previous Labour government destroyed by its inability to get to grips soon enough with inflation. Their politics minded them to be tough from day one.

All this soon became clear. The Treasury's objectives under Mr Brown, set out in its 1998 annual report, were unimpeachable: 'to achieve long-term stability, maintaining sound public finances and open accountable and effective arrangements for delivering price stability'. And the Bank of England's newly granted independence was a guarantee of good behaviour. If the politicians in Number 11 stepped out of line, it would not merely be financial markets which punished them. The bank itself could do so directly by raising interest rates.

Nor did Mr Brown have anything very new to suggest by way of instruments to manipulate the economy. There was, for example, to be no return to a general incomes policy, though restraint over public-sector pay was to emerge as a strong theme of early Brownism.

There was one important change to the Treasury's objectives under Mr Brown. For the first time in some years the government added a distributional objective, focused on helping poorer people. The Conservative government had broadly appeared to be indifferent to the effects of its policies on social and economic equality. To Mr Brown, in particular, such matters were central.

Otherwise, however, and to an extent that previous generations would hardly have believed, the politics has gone out of macro-economic policy. Between a Conservative chancellor, such as Kenneth

Clarke and a Labour chancellor, such as Gordon Brown, there are real and fundamental differences over policy. But they do not have any real and fundamental difference about macroeconomic policy.

The strength of the union

There is only one macroeconomic issue on which the government's position was very different from that of its predecessor: European Monetary Union. 'The government is committed in principle to joining a successful single currency provided that the economic benefits are clear and unambiguous,' Mr Brown's Economic and Fiscal Strategy report declared.

For the Tories, the economic substance of EMU had inevitably taken second place to political realities. On the one hand, a majority in the party was opposed to EMU, not just on economic but on constitutional grounds. It was seen as a threat to British sovereignty. On the other hand, Kenneth Clarke, the chancellor, was a strong pro-European, and John Major judged that he could not afford to lose him. The result was that the government suffered that peculiarly nasty injury that befalls those who seek to straddle a barbed wire fence.

For the incoming Labour government, the inner-party politics mattered much less. Both Tony Blair and Gordon Brown were (by British political standards) pro-Europeans. A motley crew of sceptics remained on the backbenches, but they had little backing in the party at large, including among the trade unions. Mr Blair and Mr Brown did have to worry about public opinion and the emotional attachment there to the pound sterling. It was committed to a referendum before EMU entry, and there was no gain and much damage to be had from a referendum which was lost.

In general, this was not conducted as an argument over economics. The economic arguments seemed to the politicians, as they seem to most uncommitted economists, finely balanced. It was an argument over politics.

Mr Blair and Mr Brown became politically active at a time when Europe was again one of the hottest issues in politics. At that time Labour embraced withdrawal from the EU, and they saw that as folly. They also saw as folly Lady Thatcher's one-woman anti-EU posturings.

But to make a break with this past was not altogether easy. True, Labour opposition to Europe had largely evaporated. But pro-Europeanism was still a politically problematical stance. Mr Blair in particular worried about the Murdoch press, whose New Labour sympathies clashed with a visceral anti-Europeanism. Mr Brown struggled to combine his personal enthusiasm for entry with the imperative of remaining more or less in line with the prime minister.

The result was something of a mixed message in the early days of the government. Sometimes it was reported to be contemplating early entry. Sometimes it wasn't. Sometimes, Mr Blair and Mr Brown were said to agree. Sometimes they were said to be at loggerheads. For Treasury advisers – and briefers – it was not an easy time.

For the Treasury, of course, economics did come first. But the economics of EMU were not easy either. The Treasury in general has been Eurosceptical in the proper sense of the word: that is to say, it has been sceptical of exaggerated claims of Europe's likely positive effects on the British economy. Equally, it is under no illusions about economic sovereignty.

Sovereignty, in a world of global markets, was not like virginity, something you had or did not have. You could have more or less of it, and only within narrow limits. EMU might restrict British freedom over monetary policy (though the Brown strategy document insisted that freedom over taxing and spending would remain). But as Britain had restricted sovereignty anyway, that hardly mattered. What mattered was the results.

British officials could see some benefits from EMU membership: better integrated capital markets, strong guarantees of free trade within the EU and, perhaps, a powerful mechanism to hold British politicians in check if ever they got another attack of spendingitis. But they could also see one powerful disbenefit.

Britain's economic cycle was out of sync with Europe's. Britain had gone into recession sooner, and emerged quicker. That meant that Britain's interest rates were out of sync with Europe's. EMU entry would involve a more or less common European interest rate, which might or might not be appropriate for British conditions. As EMU began in January 1999, British interest rates were three percentage points higher than European interest rates – and it was not clear that the two could be aligned without risking inflationary pressures in Britain.

There was another psychological point to weigh. ERM ejection had, as we have seen, left scars on the Treasury. That, however, involved only withdrawal from the Exchange Rate Mechanism, where you still have your own currency. With a common currency, the difficulties would be multiplied.

Suppose unemployment in Italy multiplied; suppose at the same time, Britain was growing at an unsustainable rate. The crisis could be resolved in various ways. Italians could migrate en masse to Britain; this might not prove popular. Or EU resources could be channelled to Italy; this would prove expensive. But if ministers would not contemplate either, what was to be done? What under EMU was the alternative?

One rule of British official life is: always leave room for the big back-out. It was a rule that had been ignored in the case of ERM entry, with devastating consequences. Now again, in the case of joining EMU, it was not remotely clear what the back-out would be. No Treasury official could contemplate such a situation with equanimity. Before the election, those at the top had reached the conclusion that they could not advise any new government to join immediately.

And later? Mr Brown remains instinctively in favour of entry. Mr Blair, although equally cautious politically, is no less enthusiastic in principle.

The Treasury will be sceptical at its peril. If the venture is undertaken and fails, Mr Brown would be unlikely to remain chancellor. But it will avail the official Treasury nothing to say: 'We warned you.' The likelihood is that the Treasury's future is a European future – and we shall return to the implications of that in Chapter 13.

Budget Secrets | 7

The budget used to dominate Treasury life. No longer: but it remains more
important than many suppose.

The very word 'budget' has its origins in a joke. A joke more than
250 years old in fact; it derives from the wallet or *bougette* used by
Robert Walpole as chancellor in the 1730s to hold his papers about
his financial plans for the year ahead.

The wallet, later to become a box, became the budget. The traditional budget day photograph featured the chancellor leaving 11
Downing Street for the Commons holding his budget box aloft. As
spin-doctoring proliferated, his wife might also be introduced into
the shot. This tradition did not survive the arrival of Gordon Brown
in the job. He had a brand-new budget box made by four apprentices
in Rosyth in Scotland and included them in the picture. 'New Labour
equals new jobs for young people.'

The press is also starting a new tradition: that of describing each
budget as 'boring'. Even the liveliest package is liable to attract this
epithet.

One reason for this is budget pre-leaking. In 1947, Hugh Dalton
had to resign as chancellor after leaking a few titbits from his speech
to the evening paper as he was entering the chamber. The newspaper,
even in those days of hot-metal typesetting, was able to carry the
story before he sat down. No modern chancellor would have stayed
long in office if he had followed Dalton's example by resigning for
leaking.

It would be hard to prevent informed speculation about the content of a modern budget in any case. The scene has been transformed with the coming of the Institute for Fiscal Studies' green budget ('green' as in provisional, not as in 'environmental'). The green budget represented the Institute's experts' guess at what the chancellor might do. As it was working on the basis of the same facts as he was, it usually proved to be uncomfortably close to the real thing.

In any case no sensible chancellor would want his budget to come as a complete surprise. No doubt from the point of view of the watching punters, surprise would often suit the chancellor, particularly where he was being less rapacious than they expected. But the chancellor has to consider a second audience: that in the financial markets, who may hold his fate in their hands. And with them, surprise is risky. If, for example, he disappointed their expectations as to the tax increases he would impose, or cut spending less than they wanted, they might punish him by pushing up interest rates or pushing down sterling, or both.

The prudent modern chancellor therefore primes their expectations with judicious leaks as to his intentions. He gives careful thought as to how best to manage them so that what comes out on the day is invariably a bit better than they expected.

The conventional wisdom has it that those budgets that play well on the day look bad with the hindsight of history and vice versa. This is doubtful, though it has served to comfort many chancellors who wake up to a bad press. In so far as it is true, it shows only that most people like handouts and dislike higher taxes. In general, chancellors, for obvious political reasons, err on the side of taxing too little, and it follows that their give-aways look less juicy in retrospect.

No chancellor today dares court a bad press or view a bad market reception with equanimity. Both the press and the markets will be prepared in advance. If the result is that the package, when it comes, seems boring, that is a price well worth paying.

The other reason that budgets seem boring is to do with the

decline of macroeconomic fine tuning (see Chapter 6). The traditional budget was carefully examined as to whether it was pumping money into the economy (to promote growth) or taking it out (to fight inflation). It would be otiose to repeat here the reasons why that sort of thinking has gone out of fashion. But nowadays there is far less focus on the macroeconomic stance of the budget.

Globalism too makes for boring budgets. The fiscal stance of a single medium-size economic power is no longer of great importance. The chancellor's budget decision is a relatively minor force acting on the economy compared with the performance of the rest of the world and its impact on British imports and exports.

With this change has gone another: the decline in the number of budgets. In the 1960s and 1970s, budgets proliferated. Every March came the real thing. But there were often one or more 'mini-budgets' in between them. Sterling would go into crisis, or the balance of payments would go into deficit; and the chancellor would reach for some new fiscal measure to put things right.

Indirect taxes could in those days be raised without a budget through the regulator, a special power given to the chancellor by Parliament. They often were.

There were also credit controls. Credit was not the free-and-easy thing it is today. It mainly took the form of 'hire purchase', a loan whereby the consumer did not properly own the goods until it had been paid back. The chancellor could and did regulate the economy by stiffening the terms under which hire-purchase arrangements could be made, for example, by increasing the size of the compulsory deposit.

Academic opinion differs as to whether this fiddling about made no difference, or actively destabilized the economy; but no one now maintains that it did much good. In an open economy such as today's, it is even less likely that such policies would work.

Anyway, they are no longer necessary. With floating exchange rates and capital flows to fund the balance of payments, countries can run balance of payments deficits for years. No one worries about them, unless their essential credit-worthiness comes into question. So mini-budgets are a thing of the past.

Indeed, one bold experiment of recent years went in precisely the opposite direction. An attempt was made to consolidate all the Treasury's important decisions of the year into a single budget: the unified budget.

This was first recommended by an Institute for Fiscal Studies Committee chaired by Lord Armstrong in 1978 (*Budgeting Reform in the UK*, IFS, 1980). In 1992, Norman Lamont announced that he was going to put it into force. No longer would there be a first set of announcements, about the government's spending plans, in the autumn and a second set, about revenues, the budget, in the spring. For according to Treasury doctrine, revenues should determine spending rather than vice versa. A system under which spending was announced before taxing went in precisely the reverse order.

In any case, it seemed obviously artificial to separate decisions on spending from decisions on the revenue to finance it. Putting the two together would, Mr Lamont thought, have practical advantages too. It would strengthen his hand. When Cabinet colleagues demanded to be allowed to spend more, he would be able to crush them with the thought of the higher taxes that that would require, and their impact on the government's supporters.

The Treasury, it has to be said, was never a wholehearted convert to the unified budget. For one thing, it raised practical difficulties. The separation of spending and taxes might be hard to justify in theory; in practice, it helped with the organization of the workload. Spending could be decided in outline by Cabinet in July. Detailed negotiations would follow in August and September. The government could then announce its spending plans in November. That would clear the decks for a crescendo in work on the budget in the following March. When, however, the whole process came to a head together, at a date between the old autumn statement and the old budget, all the work had to be done at once. The Treasury never buckles, but it blanched.

The Treasury had a more fundamental reservation. Many an old hand was particularly worried that the new system would have one effect that would be deeply damaging to the institution. It would, they argued, put taxes 'into commission'.

What that meant was that taxes would no longer be decided by the Treasury alone. They would become a subject of collective discussion, decision even, by Cabinet.

For the Treasury, 'into commission' has the ring of 'hung by the neck until you are dead'. The Treasury realizes its weakness in dealing with departments over public spending. It is heavily outnumbered. The overall total is for the Cabinet formally to decide. The Treasury can threaten, cajole and wheedle but it cannot ultimately veto.

That is not true of tax. Tax is for the chancellor alone. He will of course tell the prime minister what he plans. He will also consult individual ministers on individual taxes which affect their department; indeed they may be responsible for the detail of some of those taxes. But by tradition he only tells the Cabinet the content of his proposals on the day he announces them to Parliament, when it is far too late for them to do other than applaud them.

The Treasury's fear was that this might end with the unified budget. Colleagues would seek to spend. The chancellor would warn them of the dire tax consequences. They would demand that he spelt these out. He would name a number of terrible taxes he would raise. They would respond by suggesting other less terrible taxes he could raise: not income tax, which is painful, but, say, company profits tax, which isn't. Soon the country's economy would be run by departmental ministers whose interests were in funding as much spending as they could. The result would be woe and ruin.

This fear was probably exaggerated. The unified budget did not last long, but there was no noticeable sign of a shift of the kind the Treasury feared during its brief life.

In any event, Gordon Brown was not going to take the risk. He announced in opposition that Labour would do away with the unified budget. It would instead produce a green budget in advance of the real thing, giving a notion of where its thinking was going.

The unified budget was rendered formally redundant, in any case, by Labour's changes in the way government spending was set. First, totals were frozen at the levels planned by the Tories for the government's first two years in power. Then a three-year plan was announced. As the annual spending round had gone, so the need for an annual budget unifying tax and spending was reduced.

There was a political advantage to this change too. Gordon Brown was not satisfied with making one big announcement a year to Parliament. To put his case across, he wants at least two big parliamentary occasions a year. He also wants to make sure that neither of them coincides with the Queen's speech. And he argues that, by avoiding any autumn pronouncements, he is enabled to make final budget decisions on tax levels as late as possible, when all the necessary information is to hand.

By early 1999, Mr Brown had comfortably exceeded his target of two major parliamentary events a year. So far he had managed one every 3.4 months. But the Treasury hopes for a somewhat slower pace from now on.

The new pattern is for a pre-budget report in the autumn, which is an opportunity to restate the government's economic strategy. It is followed by the budget itself, in the early spring, which concentrates on taxes.

There has also been a change in philosophy on taxes with the change of government. The Conservative view of the tax system was essentially that it should be passive. The idea was to create a level playing field, which did not artificially boost one form of activity over another. They wanted low taxes. And they wanted fiscal neutrality. That meant keeping marginal tax rates as low as possible; broadening the tax base; and closing loopholes. They preferred taxes on spending to taxes on income; and they wanted to simplify and deregulate the tax system.

Mr Brown's approach is philosophically different. First, he wants an active economic policy, particularly in job creation. Hence the 10p lower rate of income tax announced in the 1999 budget to encourage people to take jobs. Meanwhile, there has been a detailed review of tax and benefits and a new welfare-to-work programme.

Labour wants to encourage enterprise and productivity. So, for example, capital gains tax has been reformed to encourage people to hold shares for longer. Labour is making positive efforts to encourage saving, especially by lower-paid people. Hence, Individual Savings Accounts (ISAs) and stakeholder pensions. And there is a new emphasis on fairness: for example, Mr Brown cut VAT on domestic fuel and power, on the grounds this bore hard on the poor, and imposed the windfall tax on the privatized utilities, on the grounds that this would penalize 'fat cats'.

This emphasis requires different things of the Treasury. For what is 'fair'? To answer that question, it needs to spend much more time on fact-based policy analysis and on statistical modelling of tax policy, particularly of its distributional consequences.

The making of the budget

Even today, budget-making is still a huge operation for the Treasury. Like the painting of the Forth Bridge, it never stops.

Various elements have to be coordinated. The macroeconomic forecasts have to be made. They are integrated with the proposals on taxing and spending. Indeed, projections of tax revenues now make up a substantial part of the Treasury's forecasting model. Detailed tax policies have to be constructed and their yield estimated; present spending has to be estimated, together with future projections.

This coordination exercise is not confined to the Treasury. The Inland Revenue, a Treasury satrapy with its own traditions and mores, is intimately involved. So is Customs and Excise (see below). The social security benefits agencies have to be involved. So do individual departments on particular proposals. The Treasury has to seek views from outside interests on some proposals, because it lacks the detailed expertise to consider them properly inside. Many of the budget 'leaks' that appear each year originate from such consultations.

The Treasury draws up each year lists of representations on particular tax changes. The most important lobbyists may get to see a minister. Less important lobbyists will see officials, or be confined to written representations. Long lists of budget 'runners' are drawn up. They are assessed against various criteria. Would they help women? Would they do anything for the environment? Gradually they are whittled down to shortlists of the most attractive proposals.

All of the Treasury's junior ministers have tax responsibilities; all of course work under Gordon Brown's strategic direction. Dawn Primarolo, when financial secretary, bore the bulk of the burden. Patricia Hewitt, the economic secretary at the time, was given a special brief for environmental taxes, and was also in charge of the Treasury's review of the law on taxes on charities. Barbara Roche, the next financial secretary, coped with small companies because of the experience in this field she had garnered when at the Department of Trade and Industry. They were helped by the special advisers; Chris Wales in particular, who was with Arthur Andersen, an accountancy firm, is regarded by the Treasury as a high-grade expert in the field.

Preparations for the day are intense. When the chancellor's speech is out, a huge pile of budget documents is circulated to the press and the City. These vary from the Red Book, setting out the main themes and measures, to detailed press releases on specific taxes. Many are prepared by individual departments, but the Treasury has to coordinate them. It also has to prepare the budget brief, a huge volume containing 'lines to take' for each issue raised by the budget. A full version is given to Treasury ministers. A bowdlerized one goes to all ministers in the government.

Within the Treasury, a small team does editing of budget documents. A pocket guide is prepared: quarter of a million copies were circulated in 1998, many of them to schools.

Sometimes changes have to be made late in the day. And there is the perpetual fear of unauthorized leaks. In 1996, a disgruntled employee of the government's printers passed a set of the documents to the *Daily Mirror*.

The Treasury may not prepare every bit of the budget but it has various important functions to perform. It may, for example, look over a number of Inland Revenue proposals for the taxation of small businesses, in themselves insignificant, but banded together forming a small-business package. 'We have to define what our comparative advantage in the construction of the budget is,' says one official. 'We see the tax system as a whole. We can bring out the interconnections.'

The day of the budget is one of great tension. The government has an overwhelming advantage over the opposition. By tradition, the budget speech is not heckled in the House. The leader of the opposition, who replies to it, gets only minutes' notice as to its content. The chancellor gets a five-minute ministerial broadcast to present his proposals to the nation. Officials are locked in with the BBC, in particular helping with charts and interpretation.

But the budget still has to fly. There is a premium in clever tricks for the chancellor's speech: an apparent hint of income tax rises to come, only for it not to happen, for example.

The Treasury courts the press. Journalists are locked in a room at the Treasury to study the documents and then their questions are answered by a senior official. Again, the government enjoys a tremendous advantage. Full budget documents are often not available until five o'clock; newspaper first editions may have to be complete soon after seven. To conduct serious critical analysis is hard, given the amount of the material published by the chancellor and the tightness of the deadline.

Often, next day, the Treasury will follow up with a morning press briefing aimed at correcting any 'misconceptions' that may have sneaked through. Traditionally, the chancellor and his senior officials then give lunch to senior journalists on *The Economist*, though this is another tradition which Mr Brown appears to be holding in abeyance.

Even that is not the end of it. A week's debate on the budget follows in the Commons: though departments other than the Treasury will shoulder part of the burden, Treasury ministers are much involved. And that is the start of a much longer parliamentary process: debating the Finance Bill. Though again the Treasury delegates much of this work, it has to keep an overall grip. On rare occasions, one of its specific revenue proposals falls and a frantic search has to be mounted for something to replace it.

The Inland Revenue and the Customs

The Treasury is used to working by getting other people to do what it wants done. That is certainly true of tax, where a large part of the job falls to Her Majesty's Customs, and the Inland Revenue, to carry out.

The position of these two bodies is slightly unusual. Formally, they are separate departments under the chancellor. Like the other Next Steps agencies around Whitehall, they enjoy considerable operational independence in delivering a programme agreed with their parent departments. But Customs and the Inland Revenue have even more independence than the other agencies. Their chairmen have considerable statutory powers of their own. On some matters, they have an arm's-length relationship with ministers: for example, ministers cannot get to see details of individual tax cases even if they want to. One Treasury chief secretary was told the outcome of a case involving Customs, in which he had been involved as a lawyer, the night before it became public. He was lucky to get even that much notice.

Britain is unusual in having two separate agencies like these. The two, however, have quite different cultures. The Customs' tradition is dominated by the duty men: successors to the hardy types who used to fight smugglers with guns and dogs – and are still today doing much the same thing, seeking drugs. Somewhat oddly, into this set-up has been pitchforked a quite different kind of tax, value-added tax. But the heart of the Customs is collecting duty. Aided by some well-planned fly-on-the-wall documentaries, it has a high reputation. The Customs is generally reckoned much less prone to corruption than the police.

Such popularity is foreign to the Inland Revenue. This is a department *contra mundi*. It has no friends and its ethos is not to care. It sees it as its duty to collect the revenue, come what may. If you are rich and fail to pay your taxes, the Revenue will not be keen to get you sent to prison, so long as you pay up, penalties and all. If you evade duty, however, the Customs will not be content to get its money. It will want you to pay the full criminal penalties.

The dividing line between the two agencies and the Treasury on tax policy is not all that clear. Both have a policy input. In the average finance bill, the Inland Revenue and the Customs will be responsible for 90 per cent of the policy decisions, for example, on anti-avoidance measures. As a rule of thumb, four of these involve the Revenue for every one involving Customs.

Moreover, the detail of tax policy is decided by them. If the chancellor asks, 'Could I [as opposed to 'should I?'] abolish capital gains tax indexation,' the advice comes from the Revenue.

The two departments employ more than sixty thousand people between them. Most of these, it is true, will be involved in collecting taxes or customs dues, but six hundred will be working on policy. In the Treasury's tax policy division, there are just nineteen civil servants.

The Inland Revenue has had some intellectually distinguished people because it is very powerful. However, in some areas the Treasury has a comparative intellectual advantage. Bright young economists are more likely to want to join the Treasury than the Revenue departments because the Treasury is where economic power lies.

The Customs has its comparative advantages too. It is more plugged into Europe than the Revenue. This goes back to the negotiation of the EU's VAT directives, which were negotiated by Valerie Strachan, at the time of writing its chief executive. It is also used to cooperating with Europe to stop smuggling and scams.

Outnumbered, and in many ways, outknowledged, by the two agencies, the Treasury has to be strategic. It concerns itself with the three ps: policy, programme and presentation.

The Treasury regards itself as the 'think-tank' on tax. Its job is to look at policy in the round, and to see where taxes might be the way to deliver it. For example, in 'welfare-to-work', the incentive effects of taxes are central, and it is the Treasury's job to propose changes to make them contribute to its objectives.

When new taxes are being considered, the Treasury will try to work them up a little before sending them to the Inland Revenue or Customs for consideration. Those two departments have a reputation for being better at saying why things won't work than at suggesting ways in which they could work – a negativism that has driven some past ministers to distraction. So, for example, when the Labour government came in committed to a windfall tax on the privatized utilities, the Treasury completed the basic design of the tax, before sending it to the Revenue to work out the fine detail.

It is also the job of the Treasury to make sure budget bits coalesce and do not contradict one another. They must chase things with the two departments pre-budget to make sure they happen. They also have a feedback role. Because they share a building with ministers, they are more likely than Revenue or Customs officials to know the politicians' minds.

Finally, presentation is very important with tax. Witness the Treasury's success in introducing changes to Advance Corporation Tax, which hit pension funds hard, without the industry spotting it in time to do anything about it. The Treasury reckons that it is good at presentation.

Environmental taxes: a case study

Environmental taxation is the nearest thing to fashionable taxation as you will ever see. Even so, if you open the pre-budget report, published in November 1998, you cannot but be struck by the sheer amount of space that is given to environmental matters.

Ten of the document's 132 pages are devoted to them. Two pages go on a summary of Lord Marshall's report on business use of energy. Detailed accounts are included of the 'auto-oil programme' on fuel quality, the specification of ultra-low sulphur diesel and aggregates taxes. The Treasury has a whole high-powered team working on nothing else.

Here, on the face of things, is a huge departure for the Treasury. This area of policy would have hardly been heard of ten years ago. It started of course under the Tories, but was given a new impetus with the arrival of the Labour government. In July 1997 the Treasury put out a statement of intent on environmental taxation, stating its principles: 'just as work should be encouraged through the tax system, environmental pollution should be discouraged'.

Its methods of working are new Treasury too. Perhaps the biggest change is in openness, both within Whitehall and outside.

Until quite recently, other departments were not allowed near the Treasury's tax responsibilities. The Treasury feared that, if once they got involved, their ministers would start to usurp the chancellor's tax prerogatives. It worried that departments would be an influence for the bad, designing taxes, for example, to favour industries which came within their sponsorship rather than for the general weal.

But the Treasury came to see that such attitudes were self-defeating. The Department of Transport, Environment and the Regions, for example, has vastly more people working on transport than the Treasury, and so knows much more about the detail. The Treasury alone could not get things right with car or fuel taxes. So it has abandoned its old solitude. It has learnt to tap into the expertise of the DTER, naturally while keeping the ultimate decisions to itself.

The same is true of consultation with outside interests. Again, outside interests know more. Again, the Treasury is not as fearful as it used to be that giving details in advance will merely spark opposition and avoidance measures. Greater openness pays dividends. And it can lead to substantial improvements: the landfill tax, for example, benefited from exceptions introduced as a result of outside consultation.

Environmental taxation is a field in which the old ethos of the Treasury is highly relevant in a new policy area. For example, the Treasury has long preferred to use economic instruments to persuade people to fulfil their social obligations rather than using regulation. Environmental taxation does this. The Treasury is always on the lookout for taxes which will be relatively painless. Environmental taxes, because they have benefits besides revenue yield, fit the bill.

The Treasury is a sceptical department in the best sense of that word. It is not taken in by general propositions or broad principles. It wants to see what they would mean in practice, in hard evidential terms. And that is particularly important where the environment is concerned.

Take, for example, the reduction of carbon dioxide in the atmosphere. Everyone agrees that is desirable. And so environmentalists tend to want tougher emission standards for new cars to cut it.

This is the sort of policy about which the Treasury rightly asks hard questions. Suppose the cost of those standards forces up the price of new cars. Suppose that means that people keep their old gas-guzzlers longer. Would that really help the environment?

It was the Treasury that spotted a crucial flaw in the emissions argument. The new cars would have to be built in new factories. In the course of building both the factories and the cars themselves, CO_2 would be emitted. The Treasury calculated that it would take fourteen years before the gain from the lower emissions on the new efficient cars made up for the loss from the emissions produced in building them. This is evidence-based policy making, the new Treasury buzzword reflecting the desire of ministers and officials alike to see proper analysis before going ahead with new initiatives.

Environmental taxation may now be passing its peak. The Treasury is inclined to think that most of the water has now been drawn from the environmental tax well. 'We must be near the bottom when the top of the environmental group's agenda is a tax on peat, which would yield just £10 million a year,' one official says.

Recently, German Greenpeace activists visited the Treasury to discuss one particular form of environmental pollution. Officials carefully explained that the costs of dealing with it one way would exceed the benefits. 'You don't understand,' said one German. 'For us, it's like throwing away sweet papers on the street. You just don't do it.' That German would not get a job at the Treasury.

8 | The Abominable No-men

The Treasury fights an instinctive war to keep public spending down. This is for reasons rooted in politics and economics.

Year in, year out, the reason most people hate the Treasury is because it is hard on public spending. To those in need – and still more to the pressure groups who claim to represent them – it is immoral. How can the Treasury deny more resources where the ill effects of the lack of them are so palpable? To other supplicants, it is irrational. How can the Treasury alone fail to see that putting more money into infrastructure would expand the economy and that the investment would pay for itself? How dare it seek to limit the use of private capital for public purposes? How can it resist projects, for example new computers in government, where a little spending today will bring big savings tomorrow?

These are real arguments; and deserve a more considered reply than the Treasury sometimes gives them. However, the Treasury is unlikely to change its stance. This chapter seeks to explain why.

Economics plays a part in its thinking. While most normal people think state spending is too low, most economists think it is too high. Economists worry about incentives, and fear that excessive taxation will destroy the dynamism of the economy.

But Treasury hostility to spending builds on narrow economic arguments so that they turn into a broad institutional philosophy. Faced with a spending proposal, 'no' is still the safe answer. Though Treasury opposition to more spending is perhaps more nuanced than it was, say, in the 1980s, a pro-spending Treasury is still impossible to imagine.

The economics of public spending

Common sense dictates that there has to be some limit to the proportion of the nation's wealth which is devoted to public expenditure. If, *reductio ad absurdum*, services such as health, education and welfare consumed the whole of output, then everyone not on welfare would starve to death. 'It is patently obvious that it is the Treasury's job to control public spending. It is inconceivable that we could have a government with absolutely no objective for public expenditure,' says one senior official.

The question is therefore not whether public spending has in some sense to be limited. It is what that limit should be and how it should be set.

Over the past quarter of a century, thinking not only in Britain but globally has shifted against state spending. Some economists argue that public spending should be cut in absolute terms. Others, without going so far, would like to see its rate of growth reduced. Some want it held constant as a share of GDP. Others would like its share of GDP reduced. Few now would argue that the economy would be better served if public spending's share of the national cake increased.

The desire to cut public spending has been a constant theme in Britain's recent political economy. What have not been constant are the arguments used to back cuts.

From 1974 to 1979, Denis Healey struggled to persuade a recalcitrant Cabinet to cut back on public spending. Partly he used (as all chancellors do) a purely political argument; that, other things being equal, the more his colleagues spent, the more he would have to raise in taxes. Partly Mr (now Lord) Healey used a confidence argument. Whatever the Cabinet thought about spending, international opinion was against it. It was particularly against it when it was financed not by taxes but by borrowing.

At first, Mr Healey argued for cuts in order to stop the international financial community intervening in Britain's economy. Then, when they did intervene, in the form of the International Monetary Fund mission of the winter of 1976–7, he argued for more cuts to satisfy them.

Two other fashionable arguments against public spending were deployed, and adopted by Treasury apologists for cuts. One was the thesis developed by two economists, Roger Bacon and Walter Eltis, in an influential book, *Britain's Economic Prospects*. They argued that public spending displaced private. In particular, if the public sector drew too heavily on the nation's stock of saving, then the private sector would have less of it. The result would be lower investment and, in the long term, lower economic growth.

Another reason put forward was related to inflation. Workers, it was argued, wanted a higher standard of living every year. Suppose, however, the government instead pre-empted the resources that could provide that, by increasing its own spending. Workers would be denied an increase in their real wages. They would try to satisfy their demands by seeking higher and higher increases in nominal wages, the cash in their wage packets. This would bust any incomes policy and lead to an inflationary wage–price spiral.

Under Lady Thatcher less was heard of this argument, since inflation was supposed to depend on the supply of money, not on wages. However, the Bacon–Eltis line got a new lease of life once monetarism became the lodestone for the conduct of economic policy.

The supply of money was limited under monetarism. Public spending and private investment were competing for that limited supply. On the one hand, the Treasury would be borrowing to fund public borrowing. On the other, private firms would be borrowing to finance investment. Unless public borrowing was checked, the result of this competition would force up interest rates. The state could afford to pay, since it had pretty well unlimited tax revenues at its disposal. Private firms could not, since they had to make profits. The result would be lower private investment.

Other arguments against state spending grew more insistent. One, as we have seen, related to incentives. The more of the pay packet that was taken by the state, it was argued, the less incentive there was for people to try to earn more. This was particularly true of rich people, who could *in extremis* leave the country and work somewhere where taxes were lower.

The so-called Laffer Curve, an American import, enjoyed a brief vogue. It purported to demonstrate that lower tax rates on the rich actually increased revenue by removing evasion and disincentive effects. The government therefore brought down the top rate of tax on rich people from a peak of 98 per cent in the 1970s to 40 per cent in the 1990s. But Laffer was wrong: the tax cuts did not increase revenue. And, with less raised in tax, there was less in the public purse and spending had to be cut to compensate.

Another criticism of state spending was based on international comparisons. In the 1990s, it was widely argued that there was a correlation between levels of state spending in different countries and their rates of growth. So, for example, the Asian tiger economies, which on the whole restricted public spending to around 20 per cent of national income, grew faster than European economies where the state spent 40–50 per cent of national income. It remains to be seen how much more is heard of this argument in the wake of the Asian economic crisis of 1997.

These and other arguments have generated a full and lively economics literature – see, for an interesting discussion, David Heald's *Public Expenditure* (Martin Robertson, 1983). The Treasury is quite capable of using all these arguments, choosing whichever seems most powerful or fashionable at any point in time. But, in truth, it is open to doubt how far its hostility to public spending really is based on a judicious weighing of the arguments. The Treasury's tendency to lean against public spending is instinctual rather than intellectual. It is based on long experience and collective knowledge, going back far before economic science was developed. Spend too much, tax too little – that way, history shows, lies peril.

The government that came to office in 1997 was explicitly opposed to tax-and-spend. Nevertheless it did not share the knee-jerk anti-spending reactions of its predecessors. By forcing the Treasury to think more clearly and rationally about the arguments and the trade-offs, the new government has moved the argument on.

Deconstructing spending

A first and obvious defect with the arguments against public spending is that they treat all spending as if it was a single homogenous lump. For example, capital spending, on things such as roads, could in principle increase the national wealth. Yet it is lumped together with current expenditure on things like unemployment benefit which transfer income from one lot of people (the employed) to another lot (the unemployed) without increasing overall wealth.

Spending financed by borrowing is different from spending financed out of taxes. Spending undertaken by the state is different from spending by and partially financed by local authorities.

And different forms of spending make different demands on the nation's resources. If the state decides to hire an extra teacher, it has to pay that teacher. The resources to do so have to come from somewhere. If, on the other hand, it decides to increase welfare benefits, the recipient has more to spend but the person who pays the taxes to pay for the benefits has less; a transfer has taken place, but there is no greater demand on the nation's resources.

If, to take a third case, the nation decides to nationalize the railways, all that happens is that one asset (the rail business) moves from private hands to public hands and another (the money) moves the other way. The economic effects of the two kinds of transaction – spending on goods and services and spending to change the ownership of assets – are entirely different.

Not surprisingly in these circumstances, the definition of what constitutes public spending also varies over time. Self-financed local government spending (i.e., council spending financed from the rates or council tax) has sometimes been included in the control total for public spending and sometimes not. Receipts from privatization are sometimes scored as negative public spending. Sometimes, they are ignored. And so on.

If the Treasury's opposition to public spending was based solely on economic arguments, these distinctions would figure prominently. It might, for example, still be hostile to welfare spending as a drain on resources. But it might be enthusiastic for investment in infrastructure. Careful distinctions would be drawn between different kinds of spending, and different attitudes taken towards them, depending on their likely economic effects.

Some traces of that kind of thinking are now creeping in. For example, in the Comprehensive Spending Review of 1998, the Treasury was enthusiastic for a large increase in spending on science. It was willing to contemplate higher pay for teachers in return for better performance. It has sought reform of the European Union's Common Agricultural Policy which would increase its cash costs, but would mean much lower prices for consumers and a big gain in resources for Britain.

A number of devices have been enlisted. One is 'Challenge Funding', where the money goes to whoever, in a given field, comes up with the most exciting plan for using it. Another is the Capital Modernization Fund, set up in the wake of the Comprehensive Spending Review, to encourage sensible capital investment.

But this kind of thing does not come naturally or easily. You cannot spend long in the company of Treasury officials without knowing that, their frequent disclaimers notwithstanding, you are amid a tribe professionally and institutionally reluctant to spend public money.

In the course of preparing this book, I interviewed around a dozen Treasury officials concerned with spending. Each was asked: has there ever been an occasion where you have argued the case for spending more on something that you control? Only one official said yes. Virginia Bottomley, then the health secretary, had been making the most tremendous fuss about her budget. That was par for the course, and left the Treasury largely unmoved. But this official was particularly sensitive to the virtues of providing respite for carers looking after people unable to care for themselves – something of which, as it happened, the official had personal experience. A small sum here, it was felt, could help placate the marauding minister and do some good beside. The proposal was agreed by ministers: 'I thought, "That's rather nice,"' said the official concerned.

Yet in principle lots of interviewees should have said yes. 'Under all governments, the Treasury is likely to find itself from time to time advocating higher expenditure on some things. For example, in the 1970s we produced regular reports for Denis Healey showing that the most effective way to cut spending on social security was to do something about poverty,' said one senior official.

After the departure of Lady Thatcher in 1990, the government collectively became less hostile to public spending. First, one chancellor, Norman Lamont, came up with the idea of bribing the electorate with its own money in the run-up to the 1992 election. (It worked.) His successor, Kenneth Clarke, was not an anti-spending ideologue. His Fundamental Expenditure Review (to be sharply distinguished, of course, from Gordon Brown's Comprehensive Spending Review) delineated clearly the Treasury's responsibilities for promoting economic growth. Even before Mr Brown arrived, it accepted that on occasion there were overwhelming arguments for more state spending in particular areas – a concept which Kenneth Clarke was more open to than most of his predecessors.

One official is responsible for coordinating the Treasury's annual survey of public spending and putting it together with the general economic principle underlying the budget. One idea was that good schemes for more public spending to increase growth – perhaps, for example, more spending on education – should get a more favourable wind. 'The idea is that we create a certain amount of creative tension. We are responsible for delivering the overall total; we say, "We must get spending down for the good of the economy," but people come back to us and say, "Yes, but surely we need to spend more on training,"' said one official.

The argument seems compelling, indeed overwhelming. Yet not all officials think it will work. Spending hawks in the Treasury find the new willingness to contemplate more spending 'odd'.

'Things were simpler under the old Treasury rule of just cutting. Otherwise it is not clear who is responsible for what.' In this official's view there is a traditional and well-established division of responsibilities in Whitehall. Proposals to spend more come from departments. The Treasury's job is to examine them, and to resist them. 'We are not supposed to be running an employment policy in the Treasury. That is what the education and employment department is supposed to be for,' said another official.

Nor is there any doubt as to the Treasury's prime motivation. One phrase recurs in almost every interview with spending controllers: 'We are the taxpayers' representative in government.' Each department has its client group, wanting more spent. Left to themselves, they would spend without limit. It is the Treasury's job to resist such pressure.

Three catchphrases follow from this vocation: economy, efficiency and effectiveness. Economy speaks for itself: crudely, everything should be done as cheaply as possible. Efficiency means the avoidance of waste, but also that the ratio of benefits to costs is as high as it can be. Effectiveness, a rather more complex concept, means that the policy should be properly designed, with clear objectives and, where possible, measurable outcomes.

Even strictly applied, however, these phrases need not imply a general hostility to spending. In principle there should be many projects, which meet all three criteria. Why then is the Treasury invariably found opposing them? Here, we have to enter the ways of the Treasury mind.

The last of the small spenders

To the outsider, and even the departmental insider, the Treasury may seem all-powerful. The Treasury itself, however, is aware of the weaknesses of its position.

It is outnumbered in Cabinet. The chancellor can only really rely on the support of the chief secretary, a fellow Treasury minister. Also in recent years a Cabinet minister, the chief secretary is the minister charged with controlling spending.

The chancellor can usually sort-of rely on the support of the prime minister, since if he has lost that support, he cannot long remain chancellor. Only sort-of, however, for every prime minister is prone to his or her own spending enthusiasms. Some also like to buy off truculent colleagues with the chancellor's money.

The chancellor can hope to win over non-departmental ministers, largely by threatening huge tax increases if he does not get his way. But the bulk of the Cabinet comprises spending ministers, under pressure to find more money for their own departmental purposes. A majority for restraint is never assured.

Moreover, despite its power, the Treasury does sometimes lose control over public spending. It lost it totally in 1974–5, when a weak government with a small majority sought to spend its way out of difficulties: public spending rose by around 5 per cent a year in real terms. It happened again in the run-up to the 1992 election, again with a rise in real spending of nearly 5 per cent in election year.

Though the Treasury has been successful in restraining public spending recently, this has been in a uniquely favourable set of circumstances. In particular, the economy has been strong (which reduces upward pressure on social security spending); inflation has been low (which helps contain the costs of government); and the public-sector unions have been cowed and quiescent (ditto). The institution has not been around for a thousand years, however, without knowing how transient such factors can prove.

To departments, it may seem that the Treasury holds all the cards. They cannot spend more without its imprimatur. The Treasury has to approve the estimates which are submitted to Parliament and, at least formally, voted upon. The chief accounting officer of the department, the permanent secretary, will be personally accountable to the Commons for any spending not covered by estimates.

The Treasury, however, is more aware of its weaknesses. For a start there is its size. Take the health budget, which absorbs around £45 billion, or 5 per cent of the nation's income. The Treasury has a single official at the moderately senior Grade 5 level, who is also responsible for overseeing expenditure on personal social services. His total staff when interviewed was fourteen: the senior ones were two Grade 7s (i.e., high-fliers in their late twenties or early thirties), an accountant and an operational researcher working on health outputs.

The next chapter discusses how the Treasury tries to do the job properly when it is so outnumbered, and the new techniques which it is evolving to help it to do so. But inevitably, the Treasury will know far less about the detail of its subject than the departments it monitors. Inevitably therefore it will be driven back towards general prohibition as a substitute for detailed assessment.

Because it is less well informed than departments, it cultivates a generalized suspicion as part substitute for detailed scrutiny. This has led it to cast a well-tutored and cynical eye over departments' wheezes to get round spending limits.

Departments are adept at playing the public-spending game. This year, they seek a special payment to a tiny number of aged disabled servicemen: who could say no? Except that the Treasury realizes that next year they will come back arguing that there is an anomaly between aged disabled servicemen and equally disabled younger servicemen which must be eliminated; and the year after that that the level of disability necessary to qualify for benefit has been set unfairly high; and the year after that that perhaps it would be fairer all round to give an allowance to all ex-servicemen. The Treasury would not long survive without a keen eye for the thin end of wedges.

Departments too are good at coming up with bumper wheezes for spending more without spending more. One ancient chestnut, now, however, in danger of coming back into favour, is hypothecation. It may be out of the question to spend more of the taxpayers' money on roads. But how about putting the receipts of parking tickets into roads? That would not be more spending at all, would it? This argument seems to have been partly accepted by the government. John Prescott has won the right to allow councils to spend the money they raise from charges on motoring to improve public transport.

In each individual case, hypothecation looks attractive. In the round, however, it has the potential to prove disastrous. By the time revenue has been hypothecated slice by slice in this way, the Treasury would have none left to pay for services for which no one wants hypothecation, such as defence.

Another ancient chestnut coming back into fashion is the use of private money for public purposes. Public spending, say its proponents, is not public spending at all so long as the private sector finances it. So if the Department of Transport wants to build a road, that is OK so long as it raises the money from the private sector. It is only not OK if it raises it through the Treasury via a government bond.

This again is a seductive argument. But there are persuasive counter-arguments. The private borrowing will cost more than public borrowing would have. The money may be raised privately but it will have to be paid back out of the public revenue. A bad project is a bad project however funded, and the government's record in choosing to back bad projects is lamentable.

The Treasury had a set of rules, the Ryrie Rules, designed to say what was allowable as privately financed spending outside the public-spending totals, and what was not. But the Tories became enthusiastic for spending more without raising public spending. Labour took up the idea and ran with it. The Ryrie Rules have become gradually eroded under the banner of the Private Finance Initiative (see pp. 199–202).

Another characteristic predisposes the Treasury to restraint on spending: its understanding of the limitations on government. It would be a caricature to portray the Treasury as a redoubt of free-market liberals. Indeed, in recent years, Treasury free-marketeers have tended to leave, pursuing their own free-market interests by seeking the vast salaries on offer from the City of London. Those who remain tend to have a firm grasp of public purpose and public service.

However, the Treasury has also learnt from its own long experience of trying to improve Britain's economy. Through the post-war years politicians indulged in increasing intervention through planning and macroeconomic stimulus in an attempt to improve performance. They did so with the acquiescence, with varying degrees of enthusiasm, of Treasury officials.

These efforts failed. Such improvement as there has been in Britain's performance came after this era, when chancellors contented themselves with setting the broad parameters of economic policy; to sorting out those areas, such as education, where only government could do anything; and leaving the rest to the free market.

'One reason we are all in favour of markets is because we are all rather modest about what government can achieve,' said one young official. 'A Treasury instinct is to ask: how do we know that consumers would not value it more if we just gave them the money?'

The Treasury also has a detached view of what motivates spending departments. They understand that departmental officials are under the lash from their ministers, who want to spend more. Equally important, however, they are under pressure from interest groups. From one viewpoint, the health service can be seen as a miraculous institution, purveying care to rich and poor on the basis of need. From another, it can be seen as a doctors' and nurses' monopoly preservation society, whereby poor practice and rotten value for money are defended under the heading 'clinical freedom' and consultants' status is a way of rendering inviolable their Friday afternoon round of golf. 'The Department of Health does have patients at heart but it also has the interests of producers at heart,' one official pointed out. 'Grommets for children's ears don't help them, but they do provide a living to many consultants.'

Finally, the Treasury knows that it has a role to play as scapegoat. Richard Parry, Christopher Hood and Oliver James ('Reinventing the Treasury', *Public Administration*, Autumn 1997) recall the famous law firm of Spenlow and Jorkins in Charles Dickens's *David Copperfield*. Mr Jorkins was in fact a sleeping partner. However, Mr Spenlow made him out to be an ogre, implacably hostile to the incurring of expenditure by the business. He, Spenlow, would of course be delighted to oblige a suppliant, but Mr Jorkins would not have it. Thus Spenlow preserved both his firm's tight budgets and his good relations with all and sundry. Similarly, 'the Treasury would not wear it' enables departments to see off those wanting more spending, without endangering their good relationships.

But still a big spender

The Treasury therefore brings to spending control a professional devotion to the interests of the taxpayer, an instinctive suspicion of the motivation of departments and an economic predisposition towards free markets. Given all this, the puzzle may not be so much that the Treasury is so mean. It is that there has been, despite the Treasury, an upward trend in the ratio of public spending to GDP. Though that now appears to have been halted, it is too soon to be sure: 'A trend is a trend is a trend, but the question is: will it bend?'

There are compelling reasons for thinking that public spending will tend to rise as a proportion of national output over time, whether or not that is truly in the national interest. Public-choice theory was first popularized in the United States. It seeks to explain why budgets constantly tend to expand. Bureaucrats seek to maximize their empires. The benefits of an item of expenditure to an individual may be very great, but the cost of that item, spread over all taxpayers, is very small: it is only when many such expenditures are added together that the spending totals leap. Taxpayers may want more spending because it benefits them, hoping the while that the burden will fall on other taxpayers. Politicians are subject to electoral cycles, which incentivize them to spend more as elections approach. That way, spending levels are gradually ratcheted up.

Above all, there is the effect of rising public expectations for public services. The public immediately perceive the advantages of better services. It tends less readily to perceive that taxes will have to go up to pay for them.

Meanwhile there are certain economic forces that tend to drive up the costs of public spending. Public services tend to be labour-intensive. It is easy to see how you substitute a machine for a person in a car-making plant, less easy on a hospital ward. So productivity is harder to increase in hospitals than in car plants. However, nurses' wages in the long term are likely to go up at least as much as car makers' wages. The result is a rise in the real costs of hospitals. This phenomenon is known to economists as the 'relative price effect' and will always tend to mean higher public spending without necessarily also meaning improved services.

Public services tend to be 'luxury goods', at least in the economists' definition of that phrase: i.e., goods on which people want to spend a higher proportion of their income as they get richer. Certainly this is true for health services. The better life gets, the more people value health and longevity. It is largely true of education, which becomes more necessary to employability and also more attractive in itself. As these are (after social security) respectively the second and third biggest individual departmental budgets in Britain, the pressure for more money for them is always on.

Tax expenditures

In the long term, a rise in public spending is intrinsic and inevitable in a society such as our own. Many would think it a good thing. In the face of this, the Treasury faces a labour of Sisyphus to keep spending under reasonable control. No wonder it takes a philosophically sceptical view of its merits. And it is evidence of its recent power that, despite all the forces tending to push public spending up, its share of national output has now remained broadly constant for twenty years.

What the Treasury does not on the whole do is to seek to make huge and radical cuts in public spending, rather than just honing its growth. This meant in the Thatcher years that it was the constant butt of criticism from the right, which believed real cuts to be not only desirable but achievable.

The Treasury is not, despite Tory suspicions to the contrary, soft on public spending. It does not have a secret agenda to boost the size of the bureaucracy or to keep taxes up. No, the reason the Treasury tends not to mount a wholesale assault on public spending is that it does not believe it would be politically practicable.

An example may help. Treasury man, brooding in his bath, might note the runaway increase in public spending on the police in the 1980s and early 1990s. Since conventional public-spending restraints had failed here, he might contemplate something more radical.

Is there, for example, any intrinsic reason why police services should be supplied by the public sector? They were once semi-private, until the arrival of the Peelers in the nineteenth century. Many policing services are carried out privately: for example, security guarding of premises, where the numbers employed actually exceed the number of police.

Much police work is involved in the protection of private property, against theft, vandalism and so on. But the benefits of private property go to private individuals. So why should not those individuals pay the cost of protecting it?

Then there is the question of value for money. In police services, huge increases in gross expenditure on the police have not brought obvious public benefits. Crime seems to depend on other factors, such as the number of young people of criminal age, and the type of drugs they are taking. Despite spending on the police, crime has gone on up.

Moreover public spending on the police does not primarily benefit the public. It primarily benefits the police. There are more of them. They are better off.

Finally, police services largely benefit middle-class people, who have more to protect and are more successful in persuading the police to attend to their needs. Police tend to treat many working-class areas, for example the run-down council estates, as no-go areas. If, however, the middle classes are the ones who gain from a strong police force, surely the middle classes are the ones who should pay for it privately.

So our Treasury official might brood as the bathwater lapped over him. But once the towel was safely wrapped around him – or at least once he got to work – such idle speculation would be cast aside.

Treasury officials would be quite capable of arguing the case for privatizing the police. Equally, they would not generally bother to do so. This is because the Treasury as an institution resists the temptation to push too hard against political boundaries. It is unwilling to fight battles it is not reasonably confident of winning. It therefore has an instinctive preference for gradualist solutions.

There are a variety of reasons for this disposition. One is wholly sensible: the need to preserve the power of the chancellor. For a chancellor to be powerful, he must be believed to be powerful. Defeat not only hurts at the time. It reduces the stock of power held by the chancellor for future battles.

Radical solutions can only be pursued by those prepared to invest large energies in them. They involve huge risks. A chancellor who really did want to privatize the police would have to overcome, in turn, the likely resistance of the home secretary, the instinctive hostility of most of his Cabinet colleagues, prime ministerial caution and parliamentary uproar. Unless provoked by crisis, it is an unattractive course, and not one Treasury officials are likely to recommend their boss to pursue.

It has other drawbacks too. First, it runs up against the limitations on the Treasury's knowledge. Though Treasury officials could draw up a plausible case in outline for privatizing the police, the administrative and legislative details are far beyond its capacities. Such a proposition would likely be devilled by the detail, which a hostile Whitehall beyond its walls could use to sabotage the proposal.

Secondly, radical policy thinking is time-consuming. Absorbed day to day by the need to do what must be done, the Treasury manages its time by avoiding idle speculation.

'Think the unthinkable? It would come down to whether that was a rational use of resources. I don't want to waste my time on things that are politically not on,' said one official.

'There was once a suggestion that companies should sponsor the armed forces so that, say, Sony of Japan could sponsor a regimental badge. I didn't think it was worth spending time on in working hours.'

But it is not just a matter of politics. Treasury officials are also leery of big changes for reasons born of long experience of government.

In theory every item of government expenditure should be constantly looked at. Is this value for money? Is it still needed? Could it be done cheaper, better? Should it be privatized?

Such thinking often tempts politicians. Politicians are squeezed between the voters' dislike of taxes and their demands for more and better public services. In this uncomfortable position, they always think there is some buried crock of money out there. A review of everything will surely uncover that crock. So they order root-and-branch reviews, beginning with Edward Heath's Programme Analysis and Review when he was prime minister in 1970–74, Mr Clarke's Fundamental Expenditure Review and going on with (though inevitably not ending with) Gordon Brown's Comprehensive Spending Review of 1997–8.

This sort of exercise was viewed sceptically by the greatest book ever on British public administration: Hugh Heclo and Aaron Wildavsky's *The Private Government of Public Money*. Programme analysis and reviews (PARs) set loose all the forces of bureaucratic and political resistance to change. Because every policy is being reviewed, they allow departments to cry that their most sensitive programmes are at risk: 'shroud-waving' as the jargon calls it, on an unparalleled scale. As a result, concluded Wildavsky and Heclo, 'PAR threatens to become a recipe for do-nothingism.' It remains to be seen if the latest Comprehensive Spending Review exercise will prove more effective.

One Treasury official concerned with welfare approaches the subject with an opinion born of experience. 'I've watched attempts at radical change. I have a jaundiced view. You can't just turn the system on its head, you have to slide it there. If you get it wrong or do it too quickly, you finish up not only hurting a lot of people, but costing a lot of money shoring things up.'

Those Treasury officials who pressed hard for the Child Support Agency as a means of getting fathers to pick up bills for child care at present falling on the state would have done well to heed such wise words before dashing ahead.

9 | Control over Spending

The demise of the Public Expenditure Survey Committee (PESC), the old system for controlling public spending, was inevitable. But will Gordon Brown's new system fare any better?

With Gordon Brown, the style of his announcements has always been a study all of its own. A former television producer, Mr Brown made his name in opposition as much for his mastery of the presentational arts as for his economic prowess. And so he continued into office. Before his great performances he seemed, like so many great actors, tense and brooding. During them, he often flirts with danger. Only after does the force of what he has done fully strike home.

Pre-trailed public-spending cuts may, for example, turn out to be accompanied by disguised increases in public spending. Mr Brown's trumpeted two-year spending freeze was softened, when his first budget was unveiled, with more money for education and health, and some sleight-of-hand increases for local authorities. Well-signalled higher taxes here – for example the windfall tax on utilities profits – are offset by lower taxes there, for example on low-paid workers.

Journalists, being journalists, find it hard to reject the original spin. As Jill Rutter, briefly Mr Brown's official press spokesman, told the Social Market Foundation, 'It is easy to see why journalists succumb. After all, the first hit usually feels good. You beat others to the headline. Your editor is happy.' Critical faculties are sometimes suspended.

Financial markets are reassured by newspapers repeating that the chancellor has been tough. The Iron Chancellor's reputation is boosted. Meanwhile, however, taxpayers and service beneficiaries, who perhaps had expected to be hit, are cheered by the unexpected bounty.

Mr Brown's announcement in June 1998 of his revolution in the way governments control their spending broke new ground in his public-relations technique. The papers were primed in advance with stories which promised a new regime for fiscal responsibility, including the 'golden rule' that government should not in the long term borrow more than it invested in public infrastructure. That was the hard-man side of the policy. Nevertheless the advance stories also signalled increased state investment. That was the soft side of the story. But much of this had long been policy; and it was reported somewhat wearily. No journalist got hold of the real and dramatic story: that Mr Brown had decided on huge changes in the apparatus governing the control of public expenditure that had dominated Whitehall life for thirty years.

The rise and fall of PESC

The acronym 'PESC' has never meant much to Whitehall outsiders. Spelling it out – 'Public Expenditure Survey Committee' – doesn't help much either. Yet within the Whitehall village, PESC was for years the most important single determinant of what went on: the stuff of official wheeling and dealing, the focus of ministerial hopes and fears, and ultimately, the most significant influence on what individual citizens did or did not get by way of public services. The annual public expenditure round was Whitehall's equivalent of the seasons, the governing rhythm of its life.

PESC began with the 1961 report of the Plowden Committee. Under it, the government would review its spending annually. It would not, however, confine itself to the year ahead. Instead, plans would be produced and agreed for a period five years ahead.

Planning would not take place in cash. It would be conducted in real terms, that is to say, in terms of the quantity of public services provided. If prices rose, more cash would be needed to pay for it, but it was assumed that the cash would be available. After all, tax revenue would be expected to go up as prices and earnings went up.

Though this was not in the published version of Plowden, the annual review of spending would be conducted by a Cabinet committee of senior ministers. These were to be Platonic ministers, those without departmental spending axes to grind. They would consider major spending proposals against each other within overall limits agreed by Cabinet. 'Public expenditure decisions,' said Plowden, 'should never be taken without consideration of (*a*) what the country can afford over a period of years having regard to prospective resources and (*b*) the relative importance of one kind of expenditure against another' – though in a masterly understatement it added that 'this may appear to be self-evident but in administrative (and, we would hazard the opinion, in political) terms it is not easy to carry out.'

Still the attempt was made. In retrospect, PESC, as originally conceived, was the high water mark of central planning in government. For that proportion of the economy disposed of by the public sector it was central planning of practically Stalinist proportions. Hundreds of billions of pounds would be allocated and spent according to the orders of a tiny band of ministers, serviced by a huge and objective civil service machine.

To the rational mind such a system had many advantages. It reduced short-termism. Departments would have to think ahead, including thinking about the long-term costs of new policies. It confronted priorities. Ministers collectively would decide what in their thinking came first and what therefore were lower priorities. It embodied policy analysis. In determining their priorities, ministers would have available the most expert advice on policy and its consequences. PESC was, said its defenders, the most sophisticated system of policy planning anywhere in the world. PESC seemed so rational indeed that it survived vicissitudes that would have destroyed lesser creations.

From the start, ministers irritatingly refused to behave as the system said they should. They were supposed to weigh priorities against the government's objectives. Instead, and despite the role of the non-departmental ministers, they continued to argue departmental cases, and even politics. Even the Cabinet, it turned out, could not always be relied on to behave rationally, responding instead to powerful appeals from powerful figures in its midst.

Various attempts were made to combat this. Edward Heath, prime minister from 1970 to 1974, introduced two additions. The Central Policy Review Staff (CPRS) under Lord Rothschild was set up to advise the Cabinet collectively on strategy. Programme analysis and reviews (PARs) were introduced so each bit of spending was looked at in detail to see if it was achieving its objectives.

Neither was successful. After a brief spell of glory, the CPRS went into decline. It was always unrealistic to suppose that it could genuinely brief the whole Cabinet. Most ministers were too busy arguing their own corner to be bothered with what the young think-tankers, however brilliant, were proposing.

While Mr Heath was there to back them up they had some sway. But his successors were not so keen. The CPRS was first used by them mainly for one-off inquiries into knotty problems (for example, the choice of nuclear power station technology). It was increasingly detached from the central debate. During the Labour government's last 'winter of discontent', with an election looming, its contribution was a paper on alcohol policy, recommending higher taxes. Its abolition shortly afterwards by Margaret Thatcher, after the leak of its alarmist thoughts on public spending, was not widely regretted. By then too PARs, which had generated paper mountains and not much else, were also gone.

Later on, new devices were employed to hone priorities. It was increasingly felt in the 1980s and 1990s that too much was being negotiated bilaterally between individual ministers and the chief secretary to the Treasury. A first attempt to deal with this was the so-called Star Chamber of non-departmental ministers to adjudicate on bids, chaired by the deputy prime minister, Lord Whitelaw. But bilateralism persisted. In the later years of John Major an attempt was made to revive the role of non-departmental ministers in the form of EDX, another Cabinet committee. This time, it was to be chaired by the chancellor, rather than a semi-detached minister. It was to act even more like a true Star Chamber, passing down arbitrary verdicts on ministers who appeared before it.

The Treasury had high hopes of EDX. 'It may seem like a transfer of power away from the Treasury to hand decisions to a group of ministers,' said one senior official. 'But we vet all the papers. We have two ministers on the committee. Departmental ministers have an hour to make their pitch, but there is then no further carry on. They can go up to six weeks without hearing; and then they learn the verdict.'

Even better, appeals to the full Cabinet got short shrift. Because the total of spending was already fixed, more for one minister meant less for another. Few ministers were so altruistic as to lay down their political lives for their colleagues.

The EDX years were comparatively good ones for public-expenditure control. Helped by a benign macroeconomic climate – good growth, more jobs and low inflation – expenditure figures came in more or less to plan. Still, its initial good effects began to wear off in the later years of the Tory government. One of the committee's heavyweights, Michael Howard, the home secretary, was increasingly preoccupied with getting money for his own department to build endless prisons. With the end of the annual PESC round under Mr Brown, the role of EDX was further diminished.

Sometimes, PESC did not work because the targets were set too high or failed to stick. But the other great vulnerability of the PESC system was less that it set unrealistic targets as that it was easily blown off course by unexpected changes in economic circumstances.

In the 1970s, the problem was inflation. PESC was designed to plan spending in real terms: inflation was ignored. In 1974–5, inflation was running at around 30 per cent a year. Yet PESC gave government departments no incentive to resist inflation. Big pay increases for public-sector workers, for example, were compensated for by big increases in public-sector budgets.

The result in 1976 was the introduction of cash limits. Spending would henceforward be determined by the cash available. If costs rose, departments would have to make compensatory savings. This was temporarily an effective remedy, indeed arguably too effective. In 1977–8, while departments were learning to use the new system, cash limits bit more deeply than intended into spending. More indeed was cut than through all the agonizing rounds of cuts forced by Denis Healey, the chancellor, in the Cabinet in 1975–6.

Under the 1979 Tory government, for a while, cash was king. Real spending totals were suppressed altogether before eventually being restored alongside cash limits.

But in the Tory years, PESC proved inadequate in the face of another kind of economic problem. It was vulnerable not only to inflation but to changes in economic activity.

When the economy slows down, more people are unemployed and claim social security. So public spending tends to rise.

Keynesians argued that this was a good thing. It injects purchasing power into the economy and thus gets it moving again. Monetarists argued that it was a bad thing. It tends to lead to increases in government borrowing during recessions, which in turn tend to push up interest rates and impede recovery. In the real world of the 1980s, it was the latter view that predominated. PESC planning was thus continually undermined by higher unemployment, necessitating cuts in spending outside the PESC planning process.

PESC, then, went through four main phases. The first, from 1969 to 1976, involved planning in real terms only – which led to cash spending spiralling out of control. That was superseded with the coming first of cash limits, and then attempts to plan spending in cash alone. That too ended in disaster, with minor fluctuations in inflation mattering more to the true level of public spending than the decisions of Cabinet. Then the Star Chamber was introduced, chaired by a senior non-departmental minister, to adjudicate claims. But in time, and after the departure of Lord Whitelaw, its first distinguished chairman, the Star Chamber lost its authority and effectiveness. EDX, a version of Star Chamber with the chancellor in the chair, was more successful and (as we shall see) survives.

That cannot be said for the PESC system itself. For Mr Brown's dramatic announcement was that, for now at any rate, the day of the annual public-spending round is over. EDX's role of presiding over that process is therefore redundant.

Four defects did for PESC. One was its ambition. It was machinery of huge complexity. The sheer logistics of keeping a track on the figures and where they were leading were daunting. As with all such complex systems they could be made to work only by informal mechanisms and tacit adjustments which, however, undermined the logic of the whole construction.

A related difficulty was that PESC sought to reconcile multiple objectives, without, however, ever making them explicit. 'No one knows,' say Hugh Heclo and Aaron Wildavsky (op. cit.), 'how to design a single, consistent budget process that would meet the three criteria normally expected of public spending – that is, to relate spending directly to economic resources, to use spending to meet policy objectives and vary spending inversely with economic ups and downs.' In practice, the PESC world turned into one of ad hoc adjustment and crisis intervention, particularly in times of economic instability.

Then there was PESC's inflexibility. Planning five years ahead is inevitably vulnerable to economic ups and downs. Even three years, as in the system's last days, is stretching things. In good years the system might have sufficient elastic to cope. It always incorporated, for example, a 'contingency reserve', which was effectively money in the chancellor's back pocket. But in bad years, that is to say years of internal or external economic shocks, the plan was always liable to collapse.

A fourth weakness was its unworldliness. It treated both bureaucrats and ministers as if they were purely rational animals, pursuing the wider national weal. But that is only part of the truth about these species. As well as the wider policies, bureaucrats also have their own objectives: growing empires, satisfying clients, pleasing bosses and advancing careers. (The next chapter deals with these and how the Treasury copes with them.)

All this is true in spades of ministers. Ministers do of course have an interest in the collective weal. At the higher level, and contrary to popular cynicism, most top politicians have a strong sense of public duty. At a lower level, they also have an interest in the re-election of the government of which they are members. Governments which waste taxpayers' money may be presumed to be less likely to win elections than governments which do not. So ministers have some incentive to align their policies and priorities with those of voters. Strong prime ministers with the support of strong chancellors will urge this on their colleagues. Some may even sack ministers who allow self-interest to outweigh collective interest.

But self-interest always lurks. A minister who does not fight for cash will be criticized for it. Chris Smith, the culture secretary, found this to his cost in June 1998, when a Commons committee chaired by Gerald Kaufman, a party colleague, pilloried him for failing to fight hard enough for booty for the arts. A minister who sacrifices his budget to the chancellor's will rarely prosper. Some of Mrs Thatcher's ministers, either from conviction or to suck up to the boss, sought to offer cuts rather than being forced to make them. Their careers were thereby shortened. The poll tax might not have been a failure if Nicholas Ridley, the environment secretary, had fought for more funds to lubricate its introduction instead of accepting a tough Treasury-imposed settlement.

A minister who fails to win his public expenditure battles will find himself impotent. Nearly all changes of policy turn out to require more spending, at least in the short run. Without room in their budgets, ministers are reduced to stasis.

Politics, like boxing, is a hard game. Prime ministers may think they respect colleagues who put their own interests behind them to fall in line with theirs, but with such altruism soon goes a reputation for weakness. Chancellors are delighted when ministers fail to fight against cuts, but they do not generally think more highly of the individual colleague who has failed to come out of his corner. Likewise other departmental ministers, pleased though they are that their colleagues' weakness means more for them, are not nevertheless disposed to admire their concessions. The eager cutter ends up the subject of scorn in the press and pity among his colleagues.

Meanwhile departmental bureaucrats despair of ministers who cannot win their battles (which, from the bureaucrats' point of view, is largely what ministers are there for). The civil servants' ability to knife weak ministers without of course ever appearing publicly disloyal is one of the secret wonders of Britain's system of government.

The theory therefore was of a Cabinet collectively deciding on and disposing of public spending according to its priorities and principles. The reality was that politics ruled. PESC was in many ways a noble creation. It was a system which a rational society composed of rational men and women could rationally embrace. But the gulf between the theory of PESC and the reality of PESC was always wide and the system therefore always vulnerable.

Such relics of PESC as survive will be transformed beyond recognition by the Brown reforms. The question is: will the new system fare better than the old?

Gordon's world

The official Treasury adopts its usual approach to the new system: of claiming for it both change and continuity. On the one hand, much of it is not new but an evolution of what went before. On the other hand, much is new and, as a means of controlling expenditure, superior. But the outsider will notice more the shock of the new.

The original impetus behind the reforms was political. Tony Blair in opposition and the modernist wing of the Labour party were convinced that its 'tax-and-spend' image was in large part responsible for its eighteen years out of power. People might say, when asked by pollsters, that they wanted more public spending even if this meant higher taxes. But in the privacy of the ballot box, their actions belied their declarations. They voted for low-tax parties. So Mr Blair determined that Labour would be one such.

To this Gordon Brown added an important economic dimension. In a global economy, with free international financial markets, 'tax-and-spend', even if desirable, was not possible. It would inevitably lead to a crisis of the currency; or a loss of foreign investment; or an exodus of entrepreneurial talent. The modern nation state, in other words, is severely constrained in its choice of mix of public and private use of its resources. Chancellorial freedom was largely a myth.

The first feature of his new regime was to put in place a lasting framework for fiscal policy. This was the bit emphasized in the original briefing on the Brown reforms, but largely downplayed as familiar. In the words of the chancellor's Mansion House speech on 11 June 1997, it meant 'sustainable public finances ... a balanced current budget combined with a prudent approach to public debt'. Following a two-year freeze on public spending, current spending would rise by 2.25 per cent in real terms over the remainder of the parliament, lower than the average 3 per cent of recent history.

Current and capital spending would be properly separated out in planning public spending. No longer would ministers' spending on schools, roads and hospitals be indiscriminately added up with spending on benefits and current public services. Moreover, Mr Brown, to the Treasury's pleasure, wanted to end the bias of the system in favour of current spending. Under successive Conservative governments, governmental capital spending had been cut to pay rising social security bills. To put food on the table, the leaky roof was ignored. However, this was not viable in the long term and the costs of a crumbling infrastructure were there for all to see.

Mr Brown determined to reverse this. Government capital spending was to be doubled towards 1.5 per cent of GDP. (Mr Brown insisted on christening this an 'Investing in Britain' fund.) The Public Finance Initiative, launched by the Tories as a way of financing public projects from private funds, was to be further developed.

Within this framework – and this was the most radical change – the annual cycle of public expenditure review was abolished. During the first two years, departments were supposed to have completed comprehensive spending reviews of everything they did. They would then be given figures based on those reviews which would set out what they might spend for the next three years.

'The Comprehensive Spending Review was the mother of all public expenditure surveys,' says one senior official. 'Though it was recognizably of the same family as the old reviews, it was on a different scale.'

The thinking behind it was more subtle tactically than was publicly divulged at the time. The Treasury's great worry when Labour was elected was that all its fine words in opposition on tax-and-spend would come to naught. New ministers would be determined to spend more in their departments and would thus overwhelm the Treasury. So the chancellor reaffirmed his opposition policy of a two-year freeze on spending while everything was reviewed. The idea was to stop other departments spending in the first twelve months. With the ruling that there would be no more money, and that the next eighteen months would be devoted to a fundamental spending review, would-be spenders were stopped in their tracks.

This tactic succeeded beyond the Treasury's wildest dreams. Under the leadership of Mr Blair and Mr Brown, shadow ministers had become accustomed to obeying orders and to sticking to the hard line against spending pledges. When Labour came into office, it took most ministers some time to shed their habit of obedience.

Labour had been in office for the best part of a year before the bids started flowing in. 'It was tough. I don't know what odds Ken Clarke would have given against sticking to his plans for two years,' says one observer. It meant that departments could not simply get more money, so they had to spend their time on devising plausible long-term policies.

The second objective was that the spending plan, when it emerged, should be affordable for its three-year term. With the downturn of the economy towards the end of 1998, as we have seen, doubts were cast on this. The Treasury always accepted, however, that if a recession took hold, rather more borrowing would be required – and it regarded this as perfectly sensible. The main determinant as to whether it holds is whether social security expenditure, notoriously prone to exceeding target, can be contained. But early signs were that it was at last being confined within its limits. One of Brown's devices, using a tax credit to replace social security spending for working families, cuts public spending too.

The main thing that would blow the plans out of the water would be a resurgence of inflation, pushing up public-sector costs. And that is not on the cards.

The third objective was that spending should reflect the new government's priorities, to shift money from other programmes into education and health. And again that happened, with 5 per cent a year growth built in for both. In the long term, it remains to be seen if such relatively rapid growth is compatible with affordable levels of public spending. 'The cuckoo in the nest is growing,' says one observer.

But for the time being, it should, temporary crises notwithstanding, allow a genuine improvement in both health and education services.

The review was a good deal less successful in bringing about genuine innovative policy making. At best it was a curate's egg.

Some innovative things went on. For example, thanks to Jack Straw, the government took an overall look at the criminal justice system, which had never been looked at in that way before. 'SureStart' for pre-nursery-school children in deprived areas is one example of many initiatives in education, though the Treasury is not yet sure they have been successfully brought together. The Education Department, contrary to its traditions, has now embraced output targets and objective measurement for schools. The defence settlement, though the Ministry of Defence claimed a great victory, is viewed with quiet satisfaction in the Treasury, and Health, apart from pay, has moved in ways that please it.

On the other hand, the review did not penetrate deep into John Prescott's bailiwick, the Department of Transport, Environment and the Regions. And, more seriously, it barely touched welfare.

Welfare was an example, perhaps, of the Treasury being too good at its job of cutting spending. Officials there were amazed and delighted in 1997 when Harriet Harman decided to press on with the cuts in single-parent benefits inherited from the Tories. They did not see it as their job to warn of the danger that they would not go through. Though the cuts were forced on the parliamentary Labour party, they were forced on it at a great cost. 'Never again' was the message learnt by the government. So the DSS was effectively deleted from review and taken over by a welfare group led by the prime minister.

That was suboptimal. Tony Blair's strength lies in strategic direction, not minute policy formulation. But minute policy formulation is what social security reform requires. Moreover, the government didn't really know what radical reform meant. Mr Blair had thought it meant what Frank Field, initially his welfare reform minister, said it meant: that is to say, much right-wing rhetoric about individual responsibility and privatization. In practice, however, it turned out that what Mr Field wanted was universal welfare benefits, which would have meant huge increases in spending. And that, for Mr Blair as much as for the Treasury, was out.

Question marks remain too about the wider strategy. Is there too little left in the locker if new political initiatives are required later in the parliament, perhaps because the government's political fortunes need restoring? The Comprehensive Spending Review allocated all resources in advance. This is the diametric opposite of Mr Clarke's strategy, which was to keep a large contingency reserve which he could release for spectacular new announcements year after year.

The contingency reserve now agreed for the CSR is small: only £1.5 billion in year one, £2 billion in year two and £2.5 billion in year three. This wouldn't pay for many BSE crises, let alone for many bold new initiatives. The Treasury has watched with admiration the government's genius for announcing the same policy several times over, in such a way that the press report it as brand new. But it remains to be seen how long the trick will last. The hope is that the CSR will last until the next review starts, two years into it, in the year 2000. But that, as officials are aware, is getting close to election time. The pressures to spend may be back.

More fundamentally perhaps, the CSR was a triumph for a strong prime minister and a strong chancellor, working together. Nothing illustrates this more clearly than the brutality of its execution. The two just called in ministers and told them how much they were getting. There was no appeal. But Mr Blair and Mr Brown could do that because they were strong. If that strength erodes, so could the CSR system.

However, for departments, the toughness of the CSR overall was made up for by specific compensations. They gained new freedoms. Annual budgeting went. No longer would there be a great rush to spend at the end of one year; or alternatively a total freeze until a new year with a new budget began. Treasury dictation over budgeting conventions went too. No longer would assumptions of likely changes in pay and prices be centrally propagated. Departments would have to decide for themselves.

The move away from annual budgeting is not universal. Spending on some programmes, for example social security, is not primarily determined by departmental policies. It depends more on the state of the economy, rising in bad times, falling in good. For these programmes the annual cycle will remain. But for the major discretionary programmes, the change is a big one, which will knock forward into big changes in the way departments organize and plan.

The Brown plan contained other important announcements. Gone was Labour's opposition to privatization. In 1997, Mr Brown published a 'Domesday book' of state-owned assets, identifying everything the government owned from its wine cellar to the roads. Now, he promised to raise £1 billion a year selling off central government's assets, with a further £2.25 billion from local government. Air Traffic Control would go, and there would be 'a broader partnership with the private sector' in the Horse Race Totalizator Board. The money will be used to finance Mr Brown's investment plans. 'We will realize the value of what we do not need to invest in what we do need,' he told MPs.

Further ahead, the government plans another reform for the year 2000: the introduction of resource accounting and budgeting (RAB). Under the old PESC system, capital spending was curiously dealt with. The Department of Health, say, would fight like hell for the money to build a new hospital. The cost was then taken to fall in a single year. The running costs would be spread. Under resource accounting and budgeting, the approach will be more aligned to that which a private company would follow. The cost of the hospital will be spread over its life.

Mr Brown claimed that his system would eliminate vote-buying rises in public spending. 'Of course politicians enjoy winning elections,' he said at the Mansion House. 'From my own admittedly limited experience I find that I like winning elections. But I have to say that our fiscal rules have been specifically designed to preclude party political manipulation of the public finances for electoral purposes.'

Problem solved? Maybe. Ingenious politicians can often find ways round the restrictions they have imposed on themselves; and Mr Brown, a formidable exponent of the various techniques open to chancellors to disguise extra spending, has yet to show that he can resist temptation.

Which raises the wider question: to what extent will the public expenditure system, as reformed by Mr Brown, resolve the problems of PESC? Has the government now licked the problem of setting aggregate public spending and then keeping it down? Is this a permanent revolution, or merely another stumbling forward that fundamentally changes nothing?

It is far too early to say. For one thing, systems operate in practice very differently from how they operate on paper. The story of government is the story of unintended consequences as much as of intended consequences, but it will inevitably be some years before the unintended consequences of the Brown reforms are clear. They still have to be worked up in detail and put into practice. In retrospect, their success or failure will no doubt seem predictable. Predicting it in advance is very much harder.

Good management of the economy – and good luck with the economy – will be important to the outcome too. At the time when the new system was introduced, the British economy had enjoyed seven years of steady growth and relatively low levels of inflation. Perhaps that will be the future; perhaps at the end of the millennium Britain really has discovered the elusive way of achieving stable economic growth for ever. But perhaps such a view will come to seem in time hopelessly hubristic. There could be shocks from the outside world (for example, a financial collapse in Asia knocking on through America to Britain). Nor can it be taken for granted that a stable framework of monetary and fiscal policy, even if it is maintained, will continue to deliver growth without inflation. Declaring the end of history is often the signal for history to reassert itself.

Nonetheless, even now, it is worth looking back at the failures of the old system, and asking whether the new system should do better. Certainly, the new system should prove rather less complex than the one it replaces. The numbers still have to be done, the figures forecast and their implications assessed. But they do not have to be done in full and according to a set timetable every year. There is a greater degree of fluidity now, which should reduce complexity.

It is true that to a degree complexity for the Treasury will be replaced by complexity for individual departments. Departments will now have to do things – for example deciding precisely how much to allow for inflation – that have in the past been done for them.

There is perhaps here an analogy with a company that goes into outsourcing. The job still has to be done. But it is reasonable to expect that it will be done better by a contractor who knows his bit of the business, who owns it and has to make it work, than if it is done in-house. Simplified tasks are on the whole done better and that could prove an advantage of the new system.

In some regards, it should also prove rather more flexible. The partial demise of annual budgeting will remove one of the principal faults of the old system. Departments will no longer spend as much time trying to fit their programmes to rigid annual timetables. There may be less wasteful stop–start in government, which would be a huge gain.

Against that, a three-year plan remains. Indeed part of the virtue of the new system is supposed to lie in its inflexibility; set targets, no election hikes, no wriggle room for ministers or bureaucrats: in short proper, implacable control.

If all goes well with the economy, this may prove fine. It is when it fails to deliver that the real test comes. For its ability in the long term to survive the worldliness of politics remains open to question.

At the moment, conditions for it are uniquely favourable. Mr Blair's government at the moment has a strong centre. Mr Brown is part of that centre. Mr Blair and Mr Brown are pulling together. So far, therefore, most ministers have not dared to kick against the traces. Despite all the pressures, the zero-growth limit on spending in the government's first years has held because ministers have feared the wrath of Messrs Blair and Brown more than the wrath of their clients.

The test will come only in adversity. Economic adversity will produce pressures for a more expansionist policy. Political adversity will produce pressures for the lubricating hand of more spending. Moreover, if ministers collectively start to lose their confidence that they are going to be re-elected, they may look more to their individual reputations. There will be the postmodernizer leadership contest to think about. In such circumstances, many might again return to their instincts, and seek to spend.

Systems can be better or worse; but at the end of the day, they are only systems. History does not suggest that even the best of them can be robust against the realities of politics and power. Mr Brown has launched his new system at a uniquely auspicious time: when the government is popular and its policies are perceived to be working. Public-spending control in good times, however, is a relative doddle. The test will come only when (if?) the bad times roll.

10 | Control and Self-control

Much of the Treasury's control of spending depends on individual negotiations with other departments. How does this work?

The language of public-expenditure control is the language of war. Treasury officials tell their ministers that they are 'having a battle' to defeat the spenders. Departments are 'displaying their bleeding stumps', i.e., going on about the politically sensitive programmes they are likely to have to cut. Nevertheless, Treasury ministers may be advised to 'keep their powder dry' by not moving too swiftly to cut them back. Their arguments can always be 'blown out of the water' at a later stage. Sometimes they may be advised to accept a 'tactical retreat'; at others, to make sure that they 'maintain the high ground' in the argument; or, that their interests are best served by 'trench warfare'. No wonder relations between the Treasury and spending departments are not always harmonious.

Appropriately, relations with the Ministry of Defence are particularly inclined to be talked about in such warlike terms. In defence circles, 'Treasury-dictated cuts' are regarded as Britain's next worst enemy after Slobodan Milosovic.

The defence of Britain is an enormous business. The Ministry of Defence spends £23 billion a year; it employs 335,000 people and spends nearly 2.7 per cent of GDP.

Occasionally, of course, the MoD has to fight a real war, but the biggest battle it fights most years is with the Treasury. Not since Henry V at Agincourt has any army fought against such apparently overwhelming odds as the Chancellor's does against the military hordes. The Treasury team responsible for defence non-procurement spending, in the 1990s, numbered just fifteen. This included clerks, secretaries and bag-carriers.

Defence spending absorbs the time of a single Treasury middle-rank official. The director-level official who used to be in charge has gone, and even at the middle level, what used to be two people's jobs is now reduced to one.

Superficially at least you would expect defence's tanks to roll straight across Great George Street's defences. Yet they have not. Defence is one of a number of departments (they also include Trade and Industry) where state spending has been falling: down by roughly a quarter in real terms between 1990–91 and 1996–7.

Treasury officials would not claim all the credit for that. Objective circumstances were primarily responsible. Even the Ministry of Defence was unable to maintain that the end of the Cold War should make no difference to how much it was allowed to spend.

The cut was primarily determined at Cabinet level. However much Tory ministers might be predisposed to strong defence, they could see that, in these circumstances, there were more attractive ways to spend the taxpayers' money. However much Labour ministers might be predisposed to cut defence, they dared not risk being thought to be risking Britain's security.

It would be naive to expect the MoD to surrender without at any rate a rearguard action. The MoD could (and did) argue that the more complex post-Cold-War world required more if different forces – for rapid reaction, for peace-keeping, for fighting terrorism and so on.

Moreover, for the Cabinet to decree cuts is one thing. Actually to deliver them on the ground is another. Sending people to die is one of the things that the Ministry of Defence does, but it finds sacking fine soldiers, sailors and airmen an acutely painful business.

When therefore each year the Cabinet had concluded its discussions, when the MoD's budget was set and the broad outlines of

Britain's defence strategy agreed, a job remained to be done. To contain spending from then on was for the tiny defence force in the Treasury. That spending came down was their victory.

How is it done? The last chapter concentrated on the macro-level determination of public spending and the way things are resolved at the highest political level. This chapter looks at the worm's-eye view. It tries to show how spending is controlled day by day, week by week through the year.

The aims of control

In a typical conglomerate company, the operating divisions will be given a great deal of practical freedom. Normally, they will be set their individual budgets and told what they can invest. But from then on it is up to them to do the job, subject only to the duty to supply head office with regular information and meet their profit targets. The corporate trend has been to run down central controls, reduce central planning and give ever greater freedom to the company's operational units.

Why does the Treasury not proceed in exactly the same way? Why does it not simply give departments their individual budgets, as determined by the Cabinet, and let them get on with the job of maximizing what they can get out of them? If, after all, departments knew they were playing with their own money, instead of the Treasury's, they would have stronger incentives to use it to the best effect.

As Jon Stern has pointed out (in Dan Corry, ed., *Public Expenditure*, Institute for Public Policy Research, 1997), there are some obvious ways in which government differs from private firms, which makes such a technique inappropriate. In private companies, the heads of subsidiaries are in principle subordinate to the main company. If they fail, they can be sacked. Government, however, is a collective undertaking. The Treasury cannot sack individual departmental heads at either the political or the official level. Head office in a company can do something about a business unit that is failing. It can downsize it, sell it, shut it. The Treasury does not have these options. It is not possible to declare the Department of Education and Employment closed on grounds of overspending.

Moreover, in government there is a more important integrative function to be performed. The heads of division of a private company may grumble that they are being asked to show an 25 per cent return on capital while another division has to show 20 per cent. But companies are about profits, not fairness; and the anomaly is tolerated. In government, however, one minister will hardly tolerate it if one department is being lightly treated while another is being strictly limited. The Treasury has to be seen to apply an even-handed discipline to all.

Just giving departments a budget and letting them get on with it is therefore not an option – however much some spending departments would like it to be one. Should the Treasury therefore go to the other end of the spectrum, whereby it controls every penny that the government spends?

The controlling art

'Gentlemen,' wrote the Duke of Wellington,

> while marching to Portugal to a position which commands the approach to Madrid and the French forces, my officers have been diligently complying with your requests . . . We have enumerated our saddles, bridles, tents and tent poles and all manner of sundry items for which HMG hold me accountable . . .
>
> Each item and every farthing has been accounted for with two regrettable exceptions, for which I beg your indulgence. Unfortunately . . . one shilling and ninepence remains unaccountable for in one infantry battalion's petty cash and there has been hideous confusion as to the number of jars of raspberry jam issued

to one cavalry regiment during a sandstorm in western Spain . . .

So that I may better understand why I am dragging an army over these barren plains, I construe that perforce it must be one of two alternative duties . . . I shall pursue either one . . . but I cannot do both.

1. to train an army of uniformed British clerks in Spain for the benefit of the British accountants and copyboys in London, or perchance
2. to see to it that the forces of Napoleon are driven out of Spain [quoted by Sir Nick Monck in Corry, ed., *Public Expenditure*, op. cit.].

There was a time when the Treasury's instinct was for total control. Once it had wrested budgeting from individual departments, it used its new powers to enforce a strict and literal economy. 'Saving candle-ends' neatly summarized the Treasury approach to economy.

Such an approach was perhaps feasible in a Victorian economy, where in any event public expenditure as a share of GDP stood at under 10 per cent. It is clearly not possible today.

The Treasury has plenty of powers. No department can undertake a new policy involving expenditure without the Treasury's consent. Nor can it submit a paper to the Cabinet or to any of the committees of the Cabinet without submitting it to the Treasury first. Individual items of expenditure also require Treasury approval as soon as they exceed a certain level: no more than £10,000 in some cases.

These powers do not, however, run to a unilateral veto over departmental spending. In theory at least all spending is agreed between each department and the Treasury. It is for the department and its minister to defend their budget against their outside critics. In practice, however, so far as the formalities go, the Treasury holds the whip hand. If matters cannot be resolved at official level, they can be referred to ministerial level, where would-be spenders have a hard task.

Yet these formal powers alone do not explain how the job is done. Back to the MoD, where we have already noted the vast discrepancy in the resources available to the two departments. If in reality the Treasury sought to scrutinize every penny that the MoD spent, both departments would grind to a halt. The Treasury would be overwhelmed by paperwork. The MoD would be paralysed by delayed decisions. In the real world, therefore, a process is required which makes the rules work and delivers the outcomes, but which does not require the detailed appraisal of everything.

Here lies the art of Treasury management. It involves many subtle techniques.

The Treasury has to ask the right questions to show what expenditure is justified and what is not. It has to do so in a way that increasingly teaches the MoD itself to ask the questions as to whether it is justified or not.

'Why do we have more officers per plane than, say, the French? How quickly can we put thirty thousand men in the field and do we have to do it that quickly? How much are our stocks of military stores costing us? Indeed, do we know what our stocks are costing us?' These are the questions that flow naturally from the Treasury official in charge of defence spending.

But within such a huge budget, there are other constraints on what the Treasury can really look at. 'I literally cannot afford to have one of my staff spending two months getting to the bottom of something that is worth only a couple of million quid a year,' says the same official. He regards it as the MoD's job, not his job, to know the answers. 'I sometimes think too many of my own resources are being drawn on by the MoD to do things they should do for themselves. I want to get them to do more and more of them,' he says.

Scrutiny will vary by area. For example, there are some areas where you would expect the interests of a department to diverge from the interests of the public whom it is supposed to serve. One is the pay and rations of its own staff. The military is not particularly well paid by comparison with people of equivalent calibre outside service life. But it has its own way of adding to its perks and prerogatives.

'When at the end of the year I find that there are still three £0.5 million flats in Mayfair, when generals have bigger offices than ministers . . . but I wouldn't want to overplay the anecdotes. When there are people yomping down a track preparing to be shot at, there are limits to how much you can talk about better outputs. Let's just say that there are areas like military pay and allowances where there is creative tension in our relationship,' says one Treasury official.

There are individual small items which the Treasury will watch. These are areas that are sensitive politically. In the case of defence, service land is one. The public understandably notices that the Ministry of Defence reserves large and beautiful tracts of Britain to itself. They suspect that it does so because it likes flying noisy planes over them and does not see why it should be prevented from doing so by so frivolous a consideration as people's enjoyment of their leisure. So successive reviews of military land holdings have cut down the amount of land the MoD holds.

Gold-plating of equipment is another. Once a piece of equipment is approved in principle, the temptation is to add extra bits and pieces even though they would not be justified on their merits.

Such things are liable to be picked up by the press. They may surface in Parliament. They are embarrassing to ministers. Although in principle it is the department's job to defend what it has done, if too much of this kind of thing starts happening, then confidence in the effectiveness of Treasury control will be lost. It follows, therefore, that the good controller will devote attention to digging out such weeds before they spread.

Mostly the Treasury will concentrate on the big items. Even here, however, it does not like to see itself in the business of vetoing. Rather, it prefers to think it can help to find ways of doing what needs to be done more cheaply and more effectively.

Sticking with defence, an example comes in the field of procurement. Here a battle has waged for many years. The MoD likes to buy equipment designed specifically for its own purposes. It prefers to do so from British suppliers, whom it thinks it can rely on. These objectives chime with its patriotic instincts. They also can win it the support of employment ministers (who want more jobs) and industry ministers (who want more industry). And there is always the argument that other countries do it, so Britain must too.

This quaint nationalism does not impress the Treasury. As an economic ministry, it is instinctively pro-free trade and on the whole believes you should buy what you need where you can get it cheapest. Moreover, it understands that the best can be the enemy of the good. If you can buy a tank that does 95 per cent of what you want at 50 per cent of the cost from America, then that is what you should do. The Treasury has lost more of this battle than it has won: the MoD has proved adept, and the Treasury hopeless, at log-rolling support for its case. But it is an example of how the Treasury seeks to focus its efforts on value-for-money, rather than seeking simply to veto MoD projects.

Change of control

There is, as we have seen, a spectrum of ways in which the Treasury could control departmental spending: from total control to freedom within their budgets. As has been argued above, total freedom is not an option that is appropriate to government. Departments can dream of a world where they have total liberty: they are unlikely ever to live in it. Indeed, when in 1998 Gordon Brown decided to give them more power to determine their own budgeting assumptions, the prevailing mood around Whitehall was not of joy but of panic, like a grumbling teenager who wakes up in the morning to find that mum and dad really have left home.

However, the clear trend of recent years has been one of a substantial move along the spectrum. The Treasury as an institution is trying to cut down on the amount of detailed spending control it imposes, and to concentrate instead on helping departments to do the job for themselves.

There are powerful intellectual reasons for this. In recent years, thinking has blossomed on what is known as the 'new public management'. This challenges the old Stalinist ways of running public institutions. It says instead that public managers, like private managers, respond to incentives. If, for example, they know that the Treasury will seize back for itself any savings they may make, they will not bother. If they can keep those savings to improve services, they will.

New public managers say that big organizations tend to have built-in inefficiencies. They therefore favour devolving departmental work to functional agencies doing particular tasks according to guidelines agreed with the department, and making them accountable for delivering on those tasks. New public managers believe in empowering staff at a lower level to take decisions and make the best use of resources.

New public managers do not believe that the state should do everything itself. Instead, they favour purchaser–contractor relationships, where the state buys in the services from profit-making private providers.

This philosophy has been largely adopted by the New Labour government in general, and by Gordon Brown in particular. The Treasury may have been moving that way before Mr Brown arrived, but he has given the change a strong impetus.

The New Public Management required change at the Treasury. If departments were contracting out, if they were empowering their staff, if they were devolving to agencies, old-style central control was clearly impossible.

Meanwhile, another quite separate reason for a change of style of control emerged. In the course of the Fundamental Expenditure Review, the Treasury went out to departments and asked them what they thought of its control methods. The answer shocked it.

Naturally, they had not expected everything to be sweetness and light. Saying 'no' is never a passport to amity. A degree of friction, officials in the Treasury knew, was part of the job.

But what it found was nevertheless surprising. At a philosophical level, departments were perfectly well able to accept Treasury control. They knew that expenditure in total had to be limited. They understood Treasury perspectives both on overall priorities and on economy, efficiency and effectiveness. These were no serfs burning to be free, for they understood the role the masters played.

What grated was not the substance but the style. The same adjectives came round and round again when departments were asked what they thought of the Treasury: aggressive, rude, arrogant . . .

'When they write asking for more money, it would be best if we just said, "Sorry, no, haven't got any this year,"' says one Treasury official. 'Instead we wrote them a five-page letter tearing their proposal to shreds.'

Sir Alan Bailey was once the Treasury's top official on the spending side, before becoming permanent secretary at the old Department of Transport. 'It is a common observation among permanent secretaries that the fiercest critics of excessive intervention by the Treasury tend to be those with previous Treasury experience,' he has said. And he accused his former colleagues of a lack of sensitivity towards departmental difficulties. 'It is difficult for people in the Treasury to realize how sheltered they are from the constant pressures of public accountability, to which those in spending departments are exposed,' he pointed out (in Corry, ed., op. cit.). He might also have mentioned the Treasury's immunity to the pressures on those who actually deliver public services on the ground.

The Treasury can live with unpopularity. What was increasingly borne home on the FER team, however, was that this relationship was dysfunctional. In the short run the Treasury could bully departments into doing its will. In the long run, it was fostering a confrontational culture. Life being life, departments would find ways of thwarting the Treasury. Even where they did not, in the clash between the two, the public weal was in danger of being lost from sight.

The review produced a number of proposals to counteract this. It recommended cutting substantially the amount of Treasury second-guessing of departmental proposals. The Treasury would try instead to lead by setting rules; for example, on the appropriate return on public investment or on the procedures for deciding whether private capital could be brought in. To improve the standard of these rules, microeconomists, who had previously worked as a group separately from the administrators, were bedded out in the spending control teams. Meanwhile, the number of Treasury staff on the public expenditure side was cut.

'The most effective people in the Treasury on the public expenditure side are not the abominable no-men,' says one senior official of the reformed system. 'Nobody controls public expenditure just by sitting here saying no. What you have to do is to try to create systems which give people more of an incentive to contain costs and get rid of systems that give people positive incentives to inflate them.

'The Treasury won't control spending well by hectoring people in departments who are doing the job. But if you go along and say to a department, "It's striking that your central headquarters is twice the size of that department's when your aggregate spending is the same and the number of people you employ is the same," you can cause the department to ask questions. They need to check their processes against other departments, to benchmark.

'If we spend less time on casework, we will be able to do more of this and in the long term we will have more chance of controlling public expenditure. I am not proposing that we give up controls that matter in exchange for nothing.'

Hitting targets

In December 1998, Britain was bombing the Gulf. The government was entering the weeks which saw the departures of Peter Mandelson, the industry secretary, Geoffrey Robinson, a Treasury minister and Charlie Whelan, the Chancellor's press secretary. Anyway, Christmas was coming and the media were in no mood to notice the sombre. The Treasury document, *Public Services for the Future – Modernization, Reform, Accountability*, received scarcely any attention.

It was an important landmark nevertheless. For what Public Service Agreements represent is a deal between government departments and the public, brokered through the Treasury. The deal is: pay your taxes, and we will deliver what you want.

For years, the idea that public-sector outputs could be measured would have seemed ridiculous. Education; good health; defence: how could you quantify such things? Instead of output measures, the government used input measures. If education spending went up, then, it assumed, so did the quality of education. The fact that this money might be wasted, or simply seeping into unjustified pay increases or achieving objectives other than those sought by ministers barely occurred.

The Tory government started to reform this. For example, it introduced league tables for schools based on exam performance. The idea was that schools should be accountable for what they achieved. It was also thought that targets would encourage better performance. Failing schools would try harder. Successful schools would strive to preserve their positions. And so on.

A lot of this was crude stuff. Targets for outputs are tricky things. They can create brand-new distortions of their own.

For example, the Labour government set itself the target of reducing class sizes to 30 or less. That means that a small rural school with 31 pupils will have to have two teachers, each teaching 15.5 pupils. So it will enjoy a highly favourable teacher–pupil ratio. Meanwhile a school in a tough inner-city area next door may not get any more money, because it has 29 pupils to the teacher.

If you have noticed an increasing number of police cars racing round with their sirens blaring, you are probably right. The reason is not, in all probability, more crime needing more urgent attention. It is that the time between being called and attending the scene of a crime is a measure of police efficiency. Hence every call is a rush call.

Such problems are more generally understood than they used to be. Indicators and targets are getting more sophisticated. In education, for example, the drive is on to express them in terms of improvements in standards achieved, rather than as absolute levels. This is to reflect the fact that some schools have intakes from lower socioeconomic groups and could not therefore hope to match schools drawn from the middle classes.

That process reached its peak with *Public Services for the Future*. Here, department by department, were set out their objectives. They existed even for those departments where it was hard to measure outputs directly. For example, the Ministry of Defence was enjoined to ensure that 'by April 2001, the number of personnel in Armed Forces fully matches that required to carry out their tasks: Royal Navy/Royal Marines at 98 per cent of requirement; Army at 95 per cent of requirement; Royal Air Force at 100 per cent of requirement'.

Education was a department that had long resisted targeting, which it instinctively regarded as somehow contrary to the ideals of a liberal education system. Its Public Service Agreement was therefore startling. It commits to, for example, 'an increase in the proportion of those aged eleven meeting the standard of numeracy for that age (level 4 in the KS2 test) from 62 to 75 per cent by 2002'.

There was even a start to an end to departmental compartmentaliz-ation. Three sets of targets did not refer to individual departments. For the criminal justice system, for action against illegal drugs and for help for families with young children through Sure Start – all of which involved input from more than one department – cross-departmental public-service agreements were published. In other cases, departments produced joint targets in areas where they needed to work side by side.

This is a recognition of a serious limitation to the target approach. Targets apply not just to individual departments but to units within them; they are highly specific and are designed to be met. On the other hand, understanding is dawning that policy cannot be dealt with in individual boxes. The new movement is for 'joined-up government', that is government which organizes itself to deal with complex objectives which cut across individual departments.

In social organization, the market is not enough. We need communities too. In governmental organization, specific targeting is not enough. We also need cross-cutting organization and objectives.

'Little regard has been had to the consequences of one organization's actions on another, or of the potential for a better collective outcome by working collaboratively, even where this has meant not maximizing one's own outputs,' Sir Andrew Turnbull, the Treasury's new permanent secretary, told administrators in an important speech in December 1998. 'We have become increasingly conscious of the fact that life, people and families are cussed, problems do not fall into neat boxes but have a tendancy to interact and accumulate. There is now a greater recognition of the need to bring a multi-disciplinary approach to solutions and a greater sensitivity to the benefits of collaboration.'

A loss of control?

The change away from central Treasury control and towards giving departments responsibility for meeting targets is far from complete. Hard experience has taught the Treasury caution. New notions come and go in the world outside, but government has to roll on. The new world may seem exciting but it has to be shown to work: and in particular to deliver spending control in practice. 'There would be a real risk of loss of control over public expenditure if we got carried away by our own rhetoric,' says one senior official. 'I would not expect us to get carried away by our own rhetoric.'

There are institutional reasons to suppose that the process will not go too far. Higher-level Treasury civil servants like the new method of control. But at a lower level, there are lots of less elevated civil servants who are quite capable of administering old-style control but not intellectually up to new-style control. Old habits will probably die harder than the Treasury's top mandarins hope.

You can imagine all sorts of ways in which old-style control could be reborn. Departments may learn to manipulate the new methods to their high-spending ends. Or the new methods may allow through individual dubious projects which then become causes célèbres. The press may splutter and the Public Accounts Committee may chunter and the Treasury may be forced once more to strengthen its grip. Finally, we could go through what has not for some time faced the Treasury: a recession, perhaps accompanied by inflation leading to soaring spending on benefits and a public-expenditure crisis. In those circumstances, sophisticated control will be forgotten, and all hands will seize whatever sharp cutting instruments are to hand.

Whatever the future holds, there is room even now for concern about the reduced numbers of spending controllers. The new methods, it is true, are less resource-intensive than the old, and therefore should need fewer people. However, you could equally argue that the Treasury employed too few people on spending before the change. Great George Street has, as we have seen, a hairshirt mentality, and a conviction that cutting yourself is the key to cutting others. This is doubtless admirable, but not necessarily sensible.

Testimony on whether the Treasury was sufficiently resourced on spending control before the change is conflicting. 'When I arrived,' says one official, who joined the Treasury from a spending department, 'I was gobsmacked at how many senior officials there were and how little they had to do. The job was infinitely smaller than the one I had come from. People were competing for interesting work: it created unhappiness and lack of security.' But other officials report a completely different picture: of long and arduous hours and insufficient resources to do the job properly. In truth the picture seems to have varied from area to area depending on how much detailed project control the officials shadowing each individual department chose to exercise.

The shortage of resources became more obvious with the change of government. The Tories had been in power for eighteen years. Kenneth Clarke, the chancellor, had been a minister in most of the important Whitehall departments, and had his own clear priorities. An incoming government, however eager, would take time to brief and to get up to speed.

The Labour opposition was already talking about big changes in public spending. It was signalling a desire to shift resources substantially to health and education from other programmes. It wanted to tackle the 'wicked issues', that is to say, problems such as social exclusion that involved more than one government department. It had high ambitions for its welfare-to-work programme. And it wanted to do all these things while freezing public spending for its first two years in office.

This was a formidable agenda. If it was to work, it was bound to require a substantial Treasury input. The government had barely taken office when it announced the launch of its Comprehensive Spending Review, which would examine everything that government was spending from the bottom up. The question then became: was the Treasury, reduced in numbers as it was, powered up to do the job? And certainly there were soon indications that ministers were not entirely satisfied that it was.

One failure was that the Treasury, in some areas, lacked knowledge. 'The Treasury is very good at quick reactions. If you ask for a paper on a subject by Friday you will get it, and it will be a reasonable stab at the problem. But it is less good at looking at things in depth,' says one official.

A second, related criticism is that the system, and the degree to which individuals are stretched, impedes the asking of fundamental questions. In their anxiety to keep count of the trees, hard-pressed officials have no time for the wood. It is no good expecting the Treasury to be like some academic think-tank. It thrives on the adrenalin of decisions. It has not proved easy to persuade its officials to find time to think long-term and in depth, and it probably never will be easy.

Pam Meadows is a former civil servant turned outside policy analyst and she embraces this criticism. 'No one says "Do we need an army?",' she writes (in Corry, ed., op. cit.). 'They ask whether we should buy one type of tank or another, or even one type of shell or another.' In other words, the big questions do not get asked.

The Treasury denies this; indeed defence spending is an area where, so it claims, fundamental questions *were* asked in the most recent review. In any case, it points out, expenditure control is not an exercise for philosophers. It is for practical men and women who get the job done.

Pensions policy – a case study in Treasury control

In December 1998, the government published its long-awaited new policy for pensions, 'Partnership in Pensions'. The signature at the top was that of Alastair Darling, not because he had been (as he was) chief secretary to the Treasury but as secretary of state for Social Security. It was, of course, also the collective policy of the government. But it was also – to an extent which only insiders would recognize – a policy which owed much to the thinking of Her Majesty's Treasury.

The document gave no comfort to those in the Labour party who had lobbied for a higher basic state pension; the state pension would continue to be tied to prices, and thus fall as a percentage of average earnings. Nor did it reflect the views of those experts in social policy who had argued for a pension to top up the basic state pension for everybody. Though new 'stakeholder' pensions were created for some people who did not have pensions now, membership was voluntary. Indeed the existing state top-up pension, SERPS, was in time to be run down, except for poor people. Though there was to be some extra state spending in the short run, for the long run the purse strings were firmly held. The only substantial concession to pensioners was that there would be a guaranteed minimum amount that every pensioner would get, and this, unlike the basic state pension, would rise in line with earnings.

That the official Treasury should be concerned to keep down state spending on pensions is no surprise. Other Treasuries, in France, in Germany and in the United States, have found their budgets threatened by pensions, as the ratio of workers to the retired falls. In Britain, the demographics are less severe, but generosity to pensioners would still require penalties for taxpayers.

State pensions are very expensive. Broadly speaking, social security accounts for one third of government spending. Of this third, half goes on pensions – £32 billion on the basic pension and £3 billion on SERPS. The elderly also get another £7 billion in income support, the money paid to poor people on a means-tested basis; and another £7 billion goes to older people in housing benefit. Other bits of social security spending may also go to older people: for example, some of the Disabled Living Allowance. All that means that the Treasury keeps a careful eye on pensions.

The Treasury's direct interest in pensions focuses on public spending. But it also has an indirect interest, in its role as economics ministry. The first concerns the tax implications of pensions policy. Under the British system (and subject to certain limits) you do not pay tax on any income that you put into a pension. When the pension is due, however, you have at some stage to buy an annuity with your fund, and that annuity is taxable. There is one exception: you are allowed to take a certain amount of your fund as a tax-free lump sum; this is an anomaly which is, however, so popular with the public that no chancellor has dared to touch it. That apart, the system seems a fair way of avoiding taxing the same money twice.

However, the Treasury – and still more the Inland Revenue – always worries when there are chunks of income that are not taxed. The danger is twofold. First, people may use the precedent to argue that other chunks of income should not be taxed. If money you put into a pension is tax-free, should it also be tax-free if you use it, for example, to insure your life? Secondly, people may try to find ways of avoiding tax on their eventual pension. For example, it is often argued that people should be allowed to use their pension to fund their long-term care if they fall sick, without paying tax on the benefits. Whatever the logic of this, it would be costly to the revenue.

But there is an even more fundamental pensions issue than this for the Treasury. Pensions policy does not only affect the state's finances. It may impact directly on the economy. For example, if employers were forced to pay high contributions into a compulsory employees' pension scheme, that would push up the cost of labour. It might make British goods less competitive abroad, and it might destroy jobs.

Pensions policy can have effects on the mobility of labour. Some employers offer defined-benefits pensions: that is to say, your pension will be guaranteed to provide you with a certain proportion of what you were earning at work. Others offer money-purchase pensions: that is to say, your pension will depend on the value of your contributions when you come to retire. Defined-benefit schemes tend to give employees an incentive to stay with one employer so as to be sure of their benefits. Contributions-based pensions are portable, with the pension fund being carried around from job to job. The Treasury believes that contributions-based pensions are better for labour mobility, which, they think, is important to economic growth.

Then, there is the issue of funding. State pensions are now funded on a pay-as-you-go basis. That means that today's taxpayers pay for the pensions now being drawn. Private pensions are paid out of self-contained pension funds. But however they are funded, the resources consumed by pensioners have to be taken from the resources of the working population.

Some argue that all pensions should be funded. Taxpayers today should not only pay for today's pensions but should also create a fund out of which their own pensions will be paid. This will only work, however, if the fund is invested in such a way as to create more wealth in the future, out of which the pensions can be paid when they are due.

Whether, in fact, making people save more for pensions now will mean we are richer in the future is a moot point. Some economists think that, if you make people save more for pensions now, they will save less for other things. Some doubt that higher savings now would lead to higher income in the future anyway. The relationship between higher savings and investment and higher rates of economic growth is disputed. Some think it depends on what form the savings take. If they are private savings, then private investors will use them profitably to create more productive capacity. But is this true of a state pensions scheme, where the government may just spend the extra savings itself without adding to production?

This is the briefest summary of a highly complex argument. But it is enough to show that the Treasury's interest in pensions policy goes much wider than just its implications for state spending. It extends to its whole interest in the performance of the economy. Pensions, therefore, could not conceivably be left to be settled by the Department of Social Security on its own; the Treasury has to take a close interest in pensions policy as a whole.

The pensions review that preceded 'Partnership in Pensions' was therefore of consuming interest to the Treasury. Admittedly, it was not in control of the process, but in the early days of the review, a great deal of work was done in preparing papers on policy and the

Treasury was closely involved in this. The decisions, however, were made by ministers.

At first, the process was a shambolic one. Senior ministers had many issues on their plates, and focusing on pensions was not one of them. In any case, the government was divided, with Harriet Harman, the social security secretary, at war with Frank Field, the welfare reform minister. The chief secretary at the Treasury at the time, Alastair Darling, did some work with John Denham, then a bright junior minister at Social Security.

But progress was at best patchy. Only in 1998 did things start to take shape, in a small informal group run by the prime minister. And here the Treasury was directly represented by the chancellor. Various options were killed off – for example, that of a compulsorily funded but privately run second pension scheme, which had been favoured by Mr Field. Final decisions were not taken until very close to publication – and it only went to the formal Cabinet Committee on Welfare Reform for endorsement at the very last moment.

The politics of pensions were obviously important to the outcome. Ministers were nervous about the politics of compulsion. They thought that compulsory pensions contributions might be seen as just another tax, and therefore a breach of their policy of avoiding tax-and-spend.

But equally important was long-standing Treasury doctrine. The Treasury did not like SERPS, which is expensive. Under the proposals, SERPS was rejigged in the short run to make it more attractive to poorer people. In the long run, however, SERPS will not be attractive to better-off people, who are likely to do much better investing in their private or occupational pensions. So there will be a shift from state to private spending on pensions.

Where state money is involved, the Treasury wants to see it concentrated on those who need it most. Thus, it is instinctively in favour of means-testing, which concentrates state support on the poor. The new guaranteed minimum pension has precisely this effect.

It is a top-up of the basic pension for those without other income.

Here, Treasury officials did not entirely get their way. They would have liked to make sure that even this form of help for the poor did not rise too quickly, by guaranteeing no more than that it would rise in line with prices. But ministers decided that, having rejected bigger rises in the basic pension, they should at least appear to be generous to poorer pensioners. So Gordon Brown ensured that minimum pensioner incomes were guaranteed to rise at least as fast as earnings.

In theory, Treasury officials might construct a case for going even further towards concentrating pensions policy on the worst-off. The basic state pension goes to everyone. If it was abolished, the money at present going to better-off pensioners with adequate pensions of their own would then be saved, and it could be used to pay either for higher pensions for the poor or for the relief of taxes. Or it could be subject to a means test.

But, according to one senior official, this was 'the dog that never barked in the night'. Whatever the theoretical arguments for getting rid of the basic state pension, it is politically sacrosanct.

The Treasury reckons it has done well to subject the basic state pension to a slow euthanasia. As it rises only in line with prices, it will gradually provide a smaller and smaller share of retirement incomes.

Even means-testing it would be hard politically, without being particularly lucrative. Calculations for the review showed that even a tough means test, to take it from richer pensioners, would only save the state some £3 billion a year. For that, no politician was likely to take the risk. As for straightforward abolition, that would for now be suicide for any government which tried it.

One day, twenty years hence, the state pension may seem so small that its abolition becomes possible. Now, however, abolition is a non-starter. Treasury officials being Treasury officials, they do not waste time thinking about non-starters.

11 | Old Dog, New Tricks

The Treasury has been at the forefront of a number of Whitehall initiatives: privatization, public–private partnerships and resource cost accounting and devolution.

To the outsider, the Treasury can seem an unchanging place, where every argument under the sun has risen and set. To the insider, stasis and change contend. Within a context of an unchanging broad philosophy, policies and techniques come and go. This chapter deals with three new policy areas which have come to the fore since the mid-1980s.

Selling the family silver

Gordon Brown's June 1998 public spending announcements shocked a few Labour backbenchers. But a decade earlier he would have struck his whole party dumb. He announced a programme of public investment. Then he came to how it was to be paid for. The answer, it turned out, was a new programme of privatization.

Mr Brown did not precisely put it this way. One of his qualities is an ability to dress up New Labour thinking in Old Labour language. In this language, wherever possible, privatization became 'public–private partnership'.

The Tote is an example. The Tote is a publicly owned body which enjoys among other things a monopoly of on-course pool betting on horse racing, and runs a chain of betting shops. The Conservatives on several occasions shaped up to privatize it. However, racing politics is Byzantine, and change hard to achieve. Besides, many Tories preferred that the Tote's profits should go, as they do, to subsidize racing, than that they should disappear into the Exchequer's maw.

Mr Brown in opposition decided to privatize it. He then leaked his plans. This was not because he had studied its particular circumstances in detail. Mr Brown is not a racing man. Rather, the Tories had discovered a gap between what he said he would spend and what his taxes would raise. The proceeds of selling the Tote would help bridge that gap.

His plans came under fire from Robin Cook, the shadow foreign secretary and racing's staunchest ally in the Labour Party. Mr Cook's stock was then high, and Mr Brown went quiet about his plans.

But Mr Cook was less strong by 1998, as a side-effect of the break-up of his marriage. Mr Brown did a deal over Tote privatization with Jack Straw, the home secretary, who was formally responsible in government for the Tote, the details of which were not disclosed to officials.

Mr Brown's words did not seem very threatening. He announced that the government would 'consider how to extend the existing public–private partnership in the Tote into a broader partnership with the private sector'. The existing public–private partnership consisted of a company jointly owned by the Tote and bookmakers to supply terminals which took Tote bets in bookmakers' shops, and it was relatively small beer. So an extension of the partnership did not sound very far-reaching. However, the next morning's papers reported, with remarkable unanimity, 'government to sell Tote'. The journalists concerned did not make this up.

Other sales included the National Air Traffic Services and the Royal Mint. At least £2.75 billion a year was to be raised by local authorities from selling surplus lands. When, a few weeks later, the government announced its defence plans, there too were plans to raise £2 billion for new spending by selling surplus assets.

The chancellor's statement finally resolved any Treasury doubts as to what New Labour's attitude to privatization would be. Before the election, this had been one of the most debated subjects within the Treasury.

Labour's manifesto was noticeably reticent on the subject; so were the policy documents produced in opposition. But Labour spokesmen had not been notably silent. From the very first big privatizations of the early 1980s, they had laid into every single proposal. Public assets were being sold. They were being sold cheap. 'Fat cats' were reaping huge rewards from privatized utilities. Mr Brown himself proposed (and later implemented) a 'windfall tax' on the alleged excess profits made by the privatized utilities.

At the same time, it was obvious that Labour's true intentions were rather different from its rhetoric. It clearly could not afford to promise to renationalize everything that had been denationalized. A long battle was fought inside the Labour party over the most controversial of the Tory privatizations, that of British Rail. The trade unions, backed by the left and Old Labour, wanted a return to public ownership. Mr Blair and Mr Brown resisted. In the end, a formula was adopted which suggested some public stake. After the election, little more was heard of this.

'It's a very interesting question what a government of a different hue would do with the privatizations I've got in train, if you'll excuse the pun,' said one Treasury official before the election. 'Would it freeze it? Put it into reverse? At what cost? They are biding their time.'

What they would do about existing privatizations was a moot question. Future privatizations were even more moot. Could the party really, after all it had said, go ahead with selling off public assets? How could it do so when those assets most easily identified and sold had already gone? Even if the chancellor wanted to, could he get it through the prime minister, the Cabinet and Parliament? The brains of Britain's great political administrators were stretched.

Had they known Mr Blair or Mr Brown personally, they might have had fewer doubts. The prime minister was no softee on public organizations. He after all was the one who had ditched Clause Four of Labour's 1918 constitution, the one that committed the party to public ownership of everything. And Mr Brown was driven by his desire to push up public investment without adding to public spending. Asset sales, which count against public borrowing, helped him to do so.

The first earnest of the new government's intent came in November 1997. Alastair Darling, then the Treasury's chief secretary, produced his National Asset Register, listing the assets held by the government. It was exhaustive.

The Cabinet Office said that it had no plans to sell its collection of silver candlesticks, its silver cutlery or its magnificent Asprey silver plate. However, the publication of the register caused commentators to resurrect the gibe of Harold Macmillan, a former Tory prime minister, against Margaret Thatcher's privatization: that she was selling off the family silver to pay the butler's wages. When Treasury officials put a *sotto voce* £300 billion valuation on the collection, suspicions grew.

Admittedly many assets were not valued. This was partly because of the speed of compilation of the register, pushed through by the Treasury in just six months. It was also because the government did not want to give potential buyers commercially sensitive information. And there are some things the government collectively was not yet ready to sell: most of the Foreign Office's collection of magnificent embassies and fine residences, for example, though Mr Brown cast an envious eye over them. He would return to those later.

Yet the great breakthrough of the asset register is that, for the first time, departments were given an incentive to dispose of surplus assets. The idea is that the proceeds will no longer simply disappear into the Treasury's maw. Departments will be able to keep £100 million of what they realize from each single sale and up to 3 per cent of their budgets in total, so long as they spend it on capital items, not current.

The intake of breath among Treasury old hands was audible. This was a dangerous precedent. The Treasury likes to seize back any savings from individual departments for the public purse generally. Moreover, this approach could distort priorities. The Ministry of Defence, for example, which is awash with things it does not need, could flog them to pay for newer non-necessities. The Department of Social Security, however, which is awash with claims it cannot afford to pay, has little to sell – though it has done a peculiar sell-and-lease-back deal on its peeling social security offices.

Those of a macroeconomic bent breathed in even more sharply. It is true that selling an asset to pay for capital spending is financially neutral. But it is not economically neutral. For new capital spending, on roads, hospitals and so on, draws on real resources on the economy. If, for example, the existing schools were all leased to the private sector and the proceeds spent on new ones, there would be huge new demands on the construction industry, which could overheat. The proceeds of sales could not therefore just be appropriated for more spending – as Nigel Lawson, the chancellor who was most responsible for privatization, had understood.

'Since 1986, we have not done privatizations for proceed reasons,' said one Treasury official before Mr Brown's intentions became obvious. 'Nigel would have had a fit if he thought we were looking at things in that way.'

Under Mr Lawson, the purposes of privatization had been quite other. He believed as an article of faith that the businesses would be more efficiently run, at less cost to the taxpayer, and to the advantage of the consumer, if they were in private hands. This would be so even if they remained regulated monopolies; though if they could be subjected to competition too, so much the better.

The Treasury, it has to be said, was rather slow to grasp the potential scale of the benefits of privatization. Privatization was initially a politically led phenomenon. At the time they were launched, the most senior Treasury officials were not much concerned with such microeconomic policies. They were immersed in what the Treasury in those days regarded as the big stuff, the search for a viable fiscal and monetary policy for the economy as a whole.

Privatization was not an entirely new idea. Edward Heath's government from 1970 to 1974, for example, had dabbled with it, forcing nationalized industries to sell off bits of their operations which were non-essential. A big battle had taken place over, of all things, gas showrooms. But the conventional wisdom remained that utilities were natural monopolies, and that natural monopolies could not be entrusted to private firms, however tightly they might be regulated. In any case, since capitalism's dynamism stemmed from competition and there could be no competition in such industries, there was no point in selling them.

This argument was defective in two ways. First, it was wrong about what was a natural monopoly. In fact, in all sorts of industries, competition has been introduced – in telephone services and gas supply for example. To be fair, this has only become possible relatively recently, as computers make it possible for different companies to share the telephone lines and pipelines on agreed terms.

Consumers have benefited greatly. The Treasury cottoned on to this eventually – though gas was initially sold as a monopoly, electricity wasn't – but it was not quick to do so.

Secondly, it has become clear that even in regulated monopolies, privatization usually improves company performance. This is because managers become focused on their share price. If it falls, they may be taken over and lose their jobs. If it rises, they may make fortunes from share option schemes. The old nationalized industry managers were only motivated by the public-service spirit. Managers in privatized firms have more concrete incentives to perform.

In defence of the Treasury, it was not alone in being slow to grasp these notions. Indeed, though behind ministers, it was ahead of the conventional wisdom. And once it had grasped them, it displayed an enthusiasm for privatization which went beyond the usual official commitment. Here was an organization whose philosophy was to represent the consumer and the taxpayer. Here was an opportunity to put that into practice. It was seized.

The Treasury organization of privatization is felt by some to have been defective. True, a central point collected information on privatization and served as a repository of Treasury wisdom on the subject. True, the Treasury was involved in each case. But individual departments did most of the work. It would have gone against the Treasury grain to set up a big enough unit to cope with that work – but some think it might have been more efficient and a more economical way of building up a collective corpus of privatization knowledge.

In so far as the Treasury did get involved, it was through those bits of the Treasury that usually dealt day to day with individual departments rather than centrally. Errors were made in consequence. Not enough competition was introduced, especially in the early days. Some businesses were sold too cheap. Regulation was sometimes too lax, especially when established by those departments which were inclined to the producer rather than the consumer view of the world. And a lot of merchant bankers walked off with excessive fees.

'The Treasury should have established a semi-permanent, self-reviewing team of people who would have done all the main privatizations, with people seconded from the sponsor departments,' says one official in retrospect. 'We failed to spot the arguments for doing it differently.'

Privatization has nevertheless to be accounted a policy success. The Treasury indeed has many innovations in privatization techniques on its escutcheon. It pioneered many of the ways of introducing competition in what were previously thought of as natural monopolies. It discovered new ways of handling the tactics of sales so as to maximize revenues. After early rip-offs, it found ways of driving down the fees of advisers. 'People travel the world to come and ask us how to do it,' says one official. 'And we don't even charge for our advice.'

The private finance of public projects

If you board a new Northern Line Underground train, enjoy your journey: it has not been paid for out of your taxes. The same is true if you cross the Severn on the new bridge, though you will have to pay a toll to get into Wales. Increasingly, the capital to build your children's swish new school or your mother's smart hospital has not come from the state's coffers either. Private finance of public projects, which for so long seemed nothing more than an endlessly discussed idea, is now producing results on the ground.

The Private Finance Initiative (PFI) was launched in 1992. It brought together various tentative schemes to use the private sector to design, build and/or fund public projects. Miraculously, it seemed, a way had been found by the Treasury to improve public services without increasing public spending. In the hands of the assumed-to-be efficient private sector, moreover, cost overruns and delays would be a thing of the past.

The reason this had not happened earlier was the same as the reason it happened in the 1990s: the Treasury. The Treasury is concerned with keeping public spending down. It is always on the lookout for the cunning devices invented by government departments and their ilk for circumventing such restraints. Using private money to pay for public projects seemed one such.

Such projects increased demand in the economy, just as surely as direct public spending increased demand. Moreover, the notion that such projects came free was a simple illusion. True, the public sector avoided the up-front costs, which fell on the private contractor. But the private contractor had to be repaid. Sometimes, as in the case of the Tube, the revenue might come from the fare box. At other times, as in the health service, it would have to come from taxes.

Moreover, private money came dearer than public money. The Treasury can borrow cheap, since governments are perceived to be unlikely to default on their debts. Private firms cannot borrow so cheaply. Efficiencies aside, the total costs of a project when it is privately financed, compared with those of an identical project which is publicly financed, are bound to be higher.

The Treasury had traditionally imposed strict limits on public use of private money. Under the Ryrie Rules, named after Bill Ryrie, the Treasury second permanent secretary who wrote them, it was easier to get camels through eyes of needles than private–public projects past Treasury scrutiny. For example, private finance could only be used if it could be shown to be cheaper than funding the same project from public money. This was so even if there was no public money available, so that the alternative to private finance in practice was delaying or ditching the project altogether.

Ministers, of course, disliked these rules. The Tory governments were on the lookout for ways round their own spending restraints. They were aware that they had cut government capital spending sharply in their attempts to cut total spending. It is relatively easy to cancel a new hospital before anyone has got used to having it around; it is relatively difficult to cut things which people are already enjoying. So the brunt of cuts in public expenditure, time and time again, fell on capital projects.

Ministers had therefore been pressing for a relaxation in the rules. But they ran into tough opposition in Great George Street. 'When the ideas were first mooted, there was quite a lot of resistance,' says one Treasury official. 'The great fear was that this was little more than creative accounting. We would ruin the public finances by building up lots of liabilities that would come back and hit us.'

In theory, what is required for a project to qualify under the PFI was for the risk to be borne by the private sector. In practice, the rule is often bent. For example, private finance for one social security computer was justified on the grounds that the contract said that if it was used for fewer cases, the contractor would get less money. He was therefore bearing the risk of a decline in the number of social security claimants. Not everyone regarded that as a sensible definition of risk.

By 1998 the Treasury was claiming that private finance had 'delivered' £9 billion of projects since 1992. Such figures should be taken with a pinch of salt: what precisely qualifies as a private finance project, for example, is much argued over, and 'delivered' is one of those Whitehall weasel words that defies efforts at precise definition. 'PFI hasn't happened yet,' says one former official. 'You find that when there is a genuine risk transfer, the private sector isn't interested.' But there is no denying the potential if and when all the parties have got their act together.

In so far as PFI does take off, some in the Treasury still think that future generations will pay a high price for it. 'We can only have a boom in private finance once. We are building up liabilities and, assuming ministers want a given level of tax, other projects in the future will have to be displaced,' says one official.

But other officials are genuine enthusiasts. It is not, they say, that they have gone soft on spending. Rather, they have invented a new way of buying more for less. 'We transfer a bundle of risk to the private sector, whose return is dependent on delivering the output we want. The efficiency gains are at least one order of magnitude greater than the extra cost of capital,' says one convert.

'We haven't presented the PFI very well,' one senior economist admits. 'The flavour is that it's about off-balance-sheet finance. What it should be about is the transfer of management. The economist's perspective has been to push the value-for-money aspects. The only case for allowing a bit of off-balance-sheet financing was to give it a bit of momentum, to get some steam into the thing.'

The Treasury does not itself plan such projects. It does, however, run a panel to advise on the initiative. The panel has been through ups and downs. At its worst, it was chaired by Sir Alastair Morton, whose forthright manner almost gave the whole idea a bad name. His successor, Alastair Ross Goobey, was a former Conservative political adviser and did not long survive the change of government. Now the task force is effectively run by Adrian Montague, an expert on global finance from Kleinwort Benson, an investment banking firm.

The Treasury has taken a firm grip. For example, it found that private-sector providers were running poor-value conferences to educate would-be private partners in the initiative. So it began to run its own. Though proposals come from departments, the Treasury has been proselytizing amongst them as to what is required. It has become tougher with private providers who seek to get away with cosy deals free of scrutiny by negotiating privately on the grounds that the facts were commercial secrets. 'It will have to become accepted that the price of doing business with the public sector is that contracts will be subject to openness requirements,' the Cabinet Office said publicly in May 1998.

The Cabinet at first seemed to think that any private finance projects would come on top of the old public finance projects. The Treasury managed to persuade ministers that this – 'additionality' in the jargon – went too far, and that private finance should in part at least be a substitute for public finance. They also got a grip on phoney schemes. 'We call the lie whenever we see projects that are put forward on a lease finance basis and force them to go forward to tender on a risk transfer basis,' says one official. In other words, the PFI is not just a way of using public money instead of private money; it is a way of offloading risk.

'The Public Finance Initiative is a middle way between traditional public procurement and full privatization,' says one official. 'It is challenging public-sector managers to procure in new ways.'

A question of resources

Resource cost accounting: these are words which cause the eyes to glaze over. Of the items that make up the Treasury revolution of recent years, resource cost accounting is the least well known: for train-spotters, for anoraks. Yet some Treasury insiders believe that, of all the recent reforms, this is the one that will have the most lasting effect.

Its essence is not very complicated. Before resource cost accounting, the Treasury kept the books on the crudest possible basis, known as accruals accounting. All that mattered was how much cash the government spent in a given year. It made no difference to the accounts whether that cash went on current spending – on things it used up – or on capital spending that would yield benefits for years.

Even sillier, everything depended on when the cash moved. If the Home Office stocked up on paper this year, the whole cost of it fell in this year's public accounts. There might at the end of the year be a stock of paper left, so that the Home Office did not have to buy any more next year. But instead of part of the cost falling in this year's accounts and part in next's, the whole lot was loaded upfront. It was a bizarre way to manage.

It created huge distortions. At a macro level, a fierce fight could take place between a department and the Treasury over some one-off item of capital spending. If it was finally approved, the whole cost fell in the year of its building. Thereafter it became a free good.

So suppose the Department of Health battled for a new hospital. The Treasury would resist this great lump of expenditure, explaining (to its own satisfaction) how an existing hospital could do the job. But eventually it might lose the argument and the hospital would go ahead.

If that happened, the whole cost of building the hospital would fall in the year it was built. No allowance would be made for the fact that it would have to be staffed and run from year to year. Still less would any account be taken of the fact it would gradually wear out and have itself to be replaced. Depreciation of capital, absolutely fundamental to private-sector company accounting, was foreign to the Treasury's accounts.

It led to lunacies. For example the government would try very hard not to pay its bills one year because, if it left them to next year, it would come off next year's budget. (In the public sector everyone always thinks next year will be easier in budgetary terms, though it rarely is.) When you paid became as important as what you paid. 'The health service used to get by by not paying its bills,' one Treasury official says. 'This did not show up in its accounts because they were cash accounts. Now it will.'

With courtier's tact, the Treasury gives the credit for good ideas to its ministers. Reading the official account of resource cost accounting (*Resource Accounting and Budgeting*, Her Majesty's Treasury, January 1998) you could easily come away with the impression that it was Gordon Brown's invention. It 'supports the delivery of three key government commitments: a new fiscal framework, the first-ever national asset register and the Comprehensive Spending Review', it says.

In fact, it goes well back into the Tory years. Its launch took place in 1993. It was a copy of what had been done in New Zealand, in many ways the pioneer of public-service reform, where it was implemented between 1989 and 1993. America, Spain, Sweden, Iceland and Finland have also gone down the same path.

The idea may be simple. Implementing it is not. Andrew Likierman, the charming ex-London Business School professor who is in charge, works hard even by the standards of a hard-working department. Even so, the first accounts will be published only in 1999–2000. It will be 2001–2 before, subject to Parliament's approval, resource accounts replace the existing appropriation accounts as the principal financial reporting system covering departments and their satellite bodies.

Resource cost accounting is intimately linked to the Treasury's drive for efficiency. Departments will be expected to report systematically on what their spending is achieving. For example, the Department of Health will have to produce detailed justification for its investment in hospitals and clinics, saying what it will achieve in terms of numbers treated and health improvements.

Resource cost accounting does not in itself guarantee rationality in government. Nothing can. Resource cost accounting does, however, make rationality in government possible, if that turns out to be what ministers and their officials sincerely want. To see if they do, we shall have to wait into the next millennium.

Devolution

In the 1970s, when devolution to Scotland and Wales last entered a government's legislative agenda, the Treasury was against it, root and branch. It feared the break-up of the United Kingdom, and the loss to the Exchequer of Scottish oil revenues. And even if devolution did not lead to the break-up of the kingdom, officials thought, it could be damaging, with the Scots seeking to put up public spending just as the Treasury was seeking to cut it.

The attitude towards devolution in the years 1997–9 was much more relaxed. Partly this was because the Treasury recognized it could do nothing about it. Scots opinion was settled against the status quo. Labour was committed to change. It would have been a waste of time and effort to play the Platonic Guardian, issuing warnings against the consequences. So the Treasury didn't.

Of course, long term, devolution could have important implications for the Treasury. If, for example, the kingdom was to divide, there might be serious issues for economic confidence both in Scotland and in the rest of the country. There would also be serious practical issues to confront. What share, for example, of the national debt should be allocated to Scotland and what retained by everyone else? At what interest rate? But the Treasury is confident in its ability to react fast. For it to happen, the Scottish National Party would have first to win an election; and then to win support for independence at a referendum. This, officials think, would give them time to devise their strategy for dealing with it.

Short of that, the Treasury's approach to devolution has been to treat it, as much as possible, as business as usual. At the moment, Scotland, Wales and Northern Ireland appear to receive higher shares of public spending than they should get on a needs basis. They automatically receive a guaranteed share of increases in spending strictly reflecting their relative population, and not those needs under the Barnett Formula (see pp. 245–6). But the government announced early in the devolution process that Barnett would stay. The Treasury might have taken devolution as a chance to cut excessive Scottish spending in particular. However, it understood the political imperative of lubricating devolution, and the challenge was not made.

The Treasury's remit has never run as powerfully within Scotland, Wales and Northern Ireland as it has in the rest of the country. In dealing with (say) the English education department, it could make spending increases conditional, requiring, for example, the adoption of targets for what it achieved. Scotland got the increase automatically. That loss of Treasury power will be even stronger post-devolution, because the minister responsible in Scotland will not be a member of the government in England but of the Scottish government. Whatever its instincts, the Treasury has accepted that as a fact of life.

Some minor Treasury activities will disappear as a result of devolution. It will no longer have to deal with Scottish parliamentary estimates, for example (a chore unlikely to be much lamented). But much will continue in the traditional way. The Treasury is rightly determined to build informal relations with officials serving the devolved government in Scotland, rather than try to channel everything through the residual staff of the almost powerless secretary of state for Scotland (if indeed there is one).

Whether this will work is in the lap of the gods. One scenario has it breaking down swiftly. Scots politicians in particular, rather than running their own government, or putting up income tax in Scotland, might use their mandate as a platform from which to demand bigger and bigger subsidies from Whitehall. Naturally, officials look to ministers in general, and Treasury ministers in particular, to stand firm. Naturally, they are waiting to see if they will. For if they do not, devolution could yet prove a chink in the otherwise heavy armour of the Treasury against those who would spend more.

12 | Scandal Busting

The Treasury in the 1990s has taken on expanded responsibilities for financial regulation. This chapter discusses the prospects and pitfalls of the new regime.

Most of what the Treasury does it has always done – before Brown, before Burns, before quill pens gave way to typewriters and typewriters to e-mail. But there is one big exception: financial services. Only in 1993 did the Treasury take over responsibility for supervising the financial services industries from the Department of Trade and Industry. Only in 1998 did it complete its takeover, by taking over the regulation of general insurance from the DTI too. As it has turned out, this has been one of the most hectic bits of the Treasury ever since.

Quite why the transfer was made is not entirely clear. One argument had it that financial services regulation is shared between the government and the Bank of England, which has had prudential responsibility for supervising banks. The Bank of England and the Treasury already did a lot of work together on monetary policy. It was therefore sensible for them to work together on financial regulation too. A single meeting between the governor and the permanent secretary might then serve to deal with elements of both regulation and economic policy, where before the governor would have had to have a separate meeting with the permanent secretary of the industry department.

Another reason for the move is European practice. A lot of work in this area has been concerned with the negotiation and implementation of Brussels directives designed to bring about a single market in finance services. On the continent, such matters are mostly dealt with by financial ministers, who meet in the finance ministers' councils. It was awkward that in Britain the minister in charge was an industry minister, who might have to attend a meeting of finance ministers specially to discharge a little financial services business.

Not everyone involved believes that these were the key considerations. 'The Treasury just fancied getting their hands on it,' says one DTI official close to the takeover. 'People in the Treasury were pleased to get this work; it's a good piece of business which fits well with the other bits of business we do,' says one Treasury official.

The Treasury now has a quite large volume of work on financial services. For example, it was partly responsible for CREST, the accident-prone new system for settling Stock Exchange transactions, though the Bank of England took on the detailed work. Controlling derivatives falls to the Treasury. In 1994, it took over responsibility for detecting money-laundering – an unusual job for the Treasury in that it required hands-on work which it did itself, rather than the supervision and control of others. It vets the rule books of overseas stock exchanges which want to be recognized in the UK. Getting out to look at them is 'an amazing job for Treasury officials who are used to sitting in ivory towers', says one of those responsible.

Those who moved from the DTI to the Treasury with the change claim to have found it an unpleasant experience. 'The Treasury seemed a soulless place. They all sat at their desks behind the walls. Our staff were quite affected. They did not want to come,' says one of them.

Treasury condescension was at its worst. 'They regarded themselves as a big cut ahead of the rest of Whitehall. They tried to dismiss our people as ex-DTI. Someone said at top management board that they were "amazed by the quality of staff coming from DTI"', one official, who did not enjoy being patronized, says.

The Treasury's culture, then even more than now desk-bound,

fitted ill with the work. It simply is not possible to do the job of financial regulation properly from behind a desk. 'We need to get people out, to get them to see what the world is like from the point of view of people selling life insurance, dealing in the currency markets,' says one senior official. 'Most of what we do works by influencing the behaviour of economic agendas. If we don't understand what influences them it's a mug's game.'

Yet manning levels were soon cut to the Treasury norm. 'I just can't spend 40 per cent of my time seeing outsiders,' says a senior official. The official responsible for the European directives confessed, 'It would be nice to go to Brussels more often and nice to know what people really are doing to implement the directives. But I don't get there very much.' Many would say that it would be more than nice: that without going regularly to Brussels the job could not be done properly. A staffing regime like that is indefensible.

One official openly speculates as to what would happen if more than one crisis broke at once. 'What if we had a BCCI and a pensions scandal at the same time?' he asks. Certainly the work could not wait. 'If something goes wrong in this area, it is catastrophic,' another points out. It is surely an area where any sensible organization would build in spare capacity.

The Treasury has thought about the problem. If it happened, it says, it would formulate an ad hoc team to move in and help out. It is a solution that relies on the Treasury's legendary capacity to move fast in a crisis. However, the idea that the stability of the financial system should rest on a group which has had only hours to master it is not entirely reassuring.

Tough times

The Treasury takeover of responsibility for financial services took place at a tough time. Partly this was because of the legislative structure which the Treasury inherited. The massive Financial Services Act 1986 must rank as one of the most unsatisfactory ever passed by Parliament. Tory ministers had been torn: between a growing realization that more had to be done to regulate financial services to avoid financial scandals and rip-offs and strong pressure from the industry to be allowed to get on with the job. The result was a dog's breakfast.

For most financial services, government exercised only a general overview. One statutory body, the Securities and Investment Board, was charged with maintaining regulation below that, setting the general principles and so on. Below the SIB, however, were a cluster of so-called self-regulatory organizations (SROs) to do the day-to-day work of supervision and to punish firms who broke the rules.

'Self-regulatory' was a misnomer. One SRO, the Personal Investment Authority (PIA), for example, was governed by a board half of whose members were appointed to represent the public interest, not the industry. It had powers that far exceeded those that would be granted to most self-regulatory bodies. Its rules had the force of law, and those who broke them could be fined or expelled from the industry. It could even stop a firm from doing business instantly if it doubted its stability. Once it had issued a so-called intervention notice, it was illegal for the firm to conduct any business without the PIA's specific say-so. The financial services industry was given the illusion it was policing itself, but the reality was otherwise.

This three-tier system was unsatisfactory, since it was never clear who was accountable for what failings. Meanwhile large chunks of financial services were outside the system altogether: building societies were separately regulated; mortgage lending was in the hands of the Council of Mortgage Lenders, which had no disciplinary powers; separately regulated too were professionals such as solicitors who sold financial services on the side; general insurance such as motor and household insurance was dealt with entirely separately, though it was often sold by the same firms as sold investment products; the Bank of England regulated banks; and so on.

Moreover, the financial services industry is one that changes very rapidly. Modern financial products were often unheard of ten years ago. Who then talked derivatives? The boundaries between firms are changing all the time. It thus requires a nimble regulator. 'The financial services industries' rate of change has accelerated and accelerated. There is a real problem sometimes of a mismatch between its speed of change and that of the regulatory system,' says one official.

In the hands of clear-sighted Treasury officials, therefore, you might think that the case for radical reform was irresistible. But it was not so.

The birth of the new system under the 1986 Act had been traumatic. The politics were immensely complicated. The prospect of starting again was not enticing. The dangers of things going sour while you did it were real. 'The immense cost of change in this area outweighs the predictable gains over the long term on any discounted present-value analysis. The frictional costs are huge. People were badly scarred by the setting up of the SIB; there was chaos as they were designing the rule book. You have a long piece of legislation that may take years to get through.'

The Treasury also has a more subtle reason for treading cautiously in this field. It is simply this: if something goes wrong in financial regulation, and people lose money, it may end up paying the bill.

Barlow Clowes was an example. Lots of people lost money which they had deposited with Mr Clowes. They were middle-class people, many of them pillars of their local Conservative associations. And they moaned. The government resisted and eventually gave way, paying out £153 million in compensation. In the early 1990s, the Treasury still had twenty people mopping up in the aftermath of Barlow Clowes – chasing debts, answering letters from MPs and so on.

In that period, too, the Treasury had to worry that it would be presented with a very much bigger compensation bill. In the mid-1980s, the government had become enthusiastic for personal pensions, which people could take out and then transport around from job to job. So enthusiastic was it that it paid big bribes to people to contract out of the state's own pension scheme, the State Earnings-Related Pension Scheme (SERPS), to join private schemes.

The private schemes saw a great opportunity. Such products are very rewarding to sell. Typically a quarter of the value of the eventual pension goes not to the pensioner but to the provider, in charges. So they piled into the market. Many of those who bought were sold good pensions at fair prices. A large number, however, were sold pensions that were inappropriate for their circumstances. Many gave up good company schemes to do so.

The Treasury dilemma was this. Clearly, the scandal could not be allowed to rest where it lay. Clearly those who had been mis-sold had to be compensated. But the danger was that someone would point out that the whole blame did not lie with the companies involved. Much of it lay with the government, who had set the whole thing off.

If the government was to blame, might it not also be that the government should pay? This was no small matter. The latest estimate of the total compensation bill is £11 billion, equivalent to some £200 for every man, woman and child in the country.

The trick was to get the arm's-length bodies to do the work: the SIB and the PIA. The only people they could make pay were the firms. Ministers meanwhile spoke with forked tongues, deploring the scandal but getting involved as little as possible.

That changed with the change of government. New Labour did not feel responsible for a scandal that had been created under the Tories. So, as we have seen (in Chapter 2), Helen Liddell, the Treasury minister in charge, bludgeoned the big financial institutions into line.

The bigger result of the change of government, however, was that Treasury officials' reservations about a reform of financial regulation were swept aside. Treasury officials were presented with implementing in short order a large and controversial reform whose details were extremely complicated. Powerful financial institutions were expressing powerful views as to the form it should take. Moreover, there was bound to be a hiatus between the announcement of change and the passing of the necessary legislation.

An ingenious scheme was rigged up so that the new regulator, the Financial Services Authority, could start doing its job before legislation. Howard Davies, whose time as a Tory special adviser was forgiven by ministers, was put in charge. Mr Davies is a highly effective manager of change, but, even so, it was a formidable task – especially without legislative powers. When it looked as if the legislation to set the FSA up properly might be delayed, he personally went to see the prime minister to persuade him to give it priority.

The new legislation was to be subject to a new procedure. First, it was published in draft so that those with an interest could comment on it. Then it was announced that it would be examined in detail in Parliament by a new joint committee of the Commons and Lords. Finally, it was agreed that, if it could not be passed in full in the 1998–9 session of Parliament, it should be started on again in the 1999–2000 session where the previous session had left off. Until then, bills which failed to pass both houses inside one annual session simply fell.

In early 1999, the new FSA system seemed to be sailing along like a duck. Underneath, however, there was some frantic paddling going on. The Treasury, the FSA and the rump self-regulatory organizations were doing their best to make everything work. If all goes well, the Treasury's reservations about radical change may seem in retrospect fussy. If, heaven, forfend, it does not, old Treasury hands will be able to mutter: 'We told you so.'

Minding Eurobusiness | 13

Neither Eurofanatic nor Europhile, the Treasury is having to adapt radically
to meet the realities of life in the European Union.

A criticism often heard of the Treasury is that it has failed to adapt
to British membership of the European Union. Euro-enthusiasts, in
particular, tend to think of the Treasury as an essentially Eurosceptic
body which has underestimated the impact of Europe and failed to
promote its economic advantages in the corridors of power.

At the heart of this criticism lies a fundamental misunderstanding.
It is perfectly true that the Treasury is sceptical about Europe. This
attitude is a function of its general institutional attitudes: a suspicion
of grand schemes and visions, a congenital hostility towards state
spending, a concrete and material assessment of where Britain's
national interests lie, together with an understanding that they are
servants of their political masters and must pay court to their preoccu-
pations. Naturally, they resist the blandishments of enthusiastic Europeans, who seem to think that Britain will catch economic advantages
from being part of the European project rather as people in a crowded
room catch colds.

But this scepticism over the benefits of Europe does not mean
that the Treasury has been blind to the implications of Europe for
Britain, and to the way it works. Until 1997, it worked for a Eurosecept-
ical government. Under Kenneth Clarke it is true that the chancellor
did not share that Euroscepticism, though he was to some extent
fenced in by the policy of the government. But before that, it worked

under a true Eurosceptic in Norman Lamont, and more ambiguous ones in John Major and Nigel Lawson. There was no disguising the frustration of some officials with ministers during the Tory years. 'Most serious member-state delegations were paying attention to how things would work whereas the dominant feature in our approach was "How can we avoid any Brussels control of what we do?"' says one senior official.

In those circumstances it is perhaps remarkable that, wherever the politicians were, the administration was constantly adapting itself to the reality of European Union membership. Now, under Labour, 'the government is putting a great deal of effort into putting the relationship with Europe on a sounder footing', one senior official says.

Treasury views on Europe vary, but even the most sceptical official would not deny the growing importance of the European Union in the Treasury's work. The future of the Treasury is bound up with the future of Europe and Britain's policy towards it. It intrudes everywhere.

Britain and the euro

Probably the most important economic issue facing Tony Blair's government will remain the European single currency. Now it is going ahead, must Britain join?

The Treasury is not naturally either for or against European Monetary Union. It asks only, 'Will it work?' Before the general election, the senior officials responsible tended to the view that it was too risky to join at once, and therefore that they would advise a new government against immediate entry.

The exchange rate has always been an important factor in determining domestic monetary policy. Indeed, if ever Britain joined EMU, there would not be a separate domestic monetary policy any more. Interest rates would then be set by the European Central Bank, of which the governor of the Bank of England would be but one member. The Treasury's monetary directorate, under Gus O'Donnell, already produces a monthly *Eurozone Monitor*, discussing monetary conditions in Europe as a whole.

Indeed, the role of the Bank of England's Monetary Policy Committee would change dramatically if Britain joined the single currency. Quite what should happen to it is up for debate. The MPC could not after entry play a decisive role. The rules of the European Central Bank forbid any of the members of its governing council to be mandated about how they cast their vote. However, if the MPC was then working well, it might have some role to play. One possibility is that the MPC would become the governor's expert advisers. Another is that they would become somehow more representative of economic interests more generally, briefing him on Britain rather than advising him on Europe.

The government's policy on the single currency is 'prepare, then decide'. One kind of preparation – thinking about the implications of entry – is the job of Mr O'Donnell and his team.

On 27 October 1997, Gordon Brown appeared before MPs to set out the government's policy on entry, which – despite much yawing on the timing – has remained in place. He laid down five tests to be passed before Britain went in:

1. Whether there can be sustained convergence between Britain and the economics of a single currency.
2. Whether there is sufficient flexibility to cope with economic change.
3. The effect on investment.
4. The impact on our financial services industry.
5. Whether it is good for employment.

There is another team in the Treasury which is dealing with preparations for the euro of a very different kind. Britain joining the single currency requires more than intense cerebration; there are also practical things that have to be done on a big scale – for example, preparing company and government computers to deal in euros. 'It would be a fat lot of use if we ended up saying "The economics are wonderful, but sod it, we can't join anyway,"' says one official.

The team charged with this work is most unusual for the Treasury. It does a hands-on job of work. It has had to run the government's information campaign on the theme: 'The euro is here.' It managed to account for 12 per cent of the Treasury's total budget on a £7.5 million campaign of television and radio ads. Concentrating on small and medium-size enterprises, on the dubious premise that big business will do the job of its own accord, it has successfully adopted a high profile rare in Whitehall and without parallel in the Treasury. 'What it has achieved, it has achieved despite the Treasury, not because of it,' one jaundiced Whitehall observer says.

The team has had to prepare the public sector for change. For example, the Department of Social Security runs the most complicated computer systems in Britain; it will need major change before it can cope with payments in euros. The team is also charged with preparing a detailed changeover plan for use if and when Britain does actually join the single currency.

Officials recognize that Britain's influence long term will depend on whether it becomes a member. Naturally, if Britain stays out, it will have less influence than if it joins.

But, especially under the new government, Britain has not stayed aloof from the preparations the rest of Europe made for the introduction of the euro. It sought an equal voice over the workings of the new currency without actually being part of it, though it did not quite succeed. It even attempted to broker a compromise when the French and the Germans disagreed as to who should be the first-ever governor of the European Central Bank: Jean-Claude Trichet or Wim Duisenberg. 'Britain has made an enormous contribution to the euro, in particular to the stability pact. We have put time and effort into it, even though we haven't been members of it,' one official says.

Organizing for Europe

That is apparent when you talk to the Treasury about how it organizes its European dimension. The answer is long and untidy. But then it is bound to be. Since Europe affects nearly everything the Treasury does, it permeates all parts of the organization. 'How you deal with Europe is not a puzzle with a solution. It is a problem with no single answer,' says one senior official.

EMU entry is an example. It is not dealt with by that part of the Treasury which is in charge of its international affairs. Instead, advice on EMU entry comes from an entirely different team. It is based in the bit of the Treasury under Gus O'Donnell which deals with domestic monetary policy, on the grounds that, with entry, the distinction between domestic and European monetary policy would disappear.

Yet, despite this, it is Sir Nigel Wicks, head of the Treasury's international directorate, and not Mr O'Donnell, who until recently chaired the EU's monetary committee (though Sir Nigel's alternate is drawn from Mr O'Donnell's directorate). Whatever the logic says, Sir Nigel's unrivalled European contacts made this seem the most desirable division of labour.

Managing for the euro is very far from the only bit of the European Union which poses organizational problems for the Treasury. For example, what do you do about agricultural spending? On the one hand, it is largely determined by EU policy. On the other, agriculture is a UK spending department, with a programme of its own.

In fact, this side of European work has been removed from a specifically European team and given to the team charged with monitoring agricultural public expenditure. The actual negotiating in Brussels is largely done by the Ministry of Agriculture, MAFF. 'The sexiest Ministry of Agriculture work,' according to one worldly Treasury observer, 'is to indulge in and pursue UK interests in European market-rigging in favour of farmers.' The Treasury, which is opposed to market-rigging and to producer subsidies, can obtain leverage over such behaviour through a team that is responsible for approving MAFF spending.

Another organizational conundrum revolves round the division of work on Europe between the Treasury and UKREP, the British government's office in Brussels. UKREP is run by the Foreign Office, but the Treasury has a senior official on secondment there. UKREP plays an invaluable role as the Treasury's eyes and ears in Brussels and often sits for it on working groups. However, the real work on individual European issues facing the Treasury increasingly falls to the Treasury officials directly concerned with them.

For one thing, the detail involved on specific issues is likely to exceed the capacity of UKREP. For another, what is needed is a network of personal contacts, together with the feedback on European style and attitudes that that brings. For example, the British pragmatic tradition is to write down as little as possible. The European, particularly the German tradition, is to put everything into law. There is a culture clash here (though the Scandinavian countries have become Britain's allies on the matter); it is important that London understands it.

Europe's expanding frontiers

Europe's role is expanding in other areas of economic policy too, and this involves Britain in new debates. Ecofin, the monthly meeting of European finance ministers, discusses matters such as the Commission budget and enlargement, but it also debates wider economic issues. Preparations for Ecofin, and for briefing the chancellor for its meetings, are coordinated within the Treasury's international directorate, working through a variety of cross-cutting interdirectorate committees.

Economic policy beyond monetary policy is now becoming more European. The European Employment Action Plan has been produced, a new venture for Europe, designed to create jobs and thus to make the EU more popular.

Britain resists the idea of harmonizing taxes in general. However, it actively promotes harmonization when this would encourage trade. Dawn Primarolo, a Treasury minister, recently chaired the European committee which recommended a long list of detailed harmonization measures. Almost all European countries have been brought up in the Christian (and Social) Democratic tradition where labour is not just a factor of production, but a dignified state, deserving legal protections. Though Britain's culture has deposits of that thinking too, it also has elements of the different American tradition, whereby those who do not work shall not eat, and free contract between employer and employee is king. Britain therefore follows a middle road between the two. Under Tony Blair, that middle road has acquired its own distinctive carriageway, in the form of an emphasis on welfare-to-work and active labour market policies, together with aggressive support for free trade.

The Treasury's mission is to propagate that thinking in Europe. Often, they claim that they have won the argument. Certainly they are heavily engaged in it: Steve Robson's directorate, the one charged with promoting growth and competition, increasingly has a European dimension.

Europe intrudes on the Treasury in some of its most mundane operations. For example, for financial services supervision and regulation Europe's impact is often as great as domestic law. Brussels' financial services directives aim to set rules which allow financial institutions to compete for business right across Europe, and not just in any one nation state. This generates complex and demanding work, which requires the full-time services of a senior Treasury official.

On the whole the Treasury reckons harmonization to be good for Britain. As Britain is strong in, for example, life insurance, it may be expected to capture a good share of an expanding European market. At the same time, harmonization makes certain kinds of policy impossible. Following the debacle of the mis-selling of personal pensions, some have called for pensions products to be regulated, for example, to limit what people can be charged for them. But such a policy might well founder on European law.

Perhaps most of all the Treasury is professionally concerned about budgets. Brussels will always want to spend more. It gains the kudos for new projects, while the bills fall on the ministers of member states. It follows that member states who do not want to spend more will usually find themselves opposing the European Commission, which can create a false impression of fundamental hostility.

Treasury parsimony knows few limits. By tradition, when a country is enjoying its term in the presidency of the Community, it hosts a summit. Britain's was in Cardiff in June 1998. At these gatherings, similarly by tradition, journalists attending them are given a gift by the host nation; at Amsterdam, for example, in the autumn of 1997, the Dutch produced a suitcase on wheels, three pens and a small bottle of Dutch gin. Spendthrifts! When Sue Owen, the Treasury official responsible for coordinating EU matters, began planning Cardiff, the gifts were out straight away. Indeed, she was disgusted to be forced to agree to fund the journalists' centre at the conference. She did not see why the British taxpayer should subsidize rich news organizations – and it is hard to disagree.

Living in a Global World | 14

How the Treasury functions under globalization.

You utter a cliché within the portals of the Treasury at your peril.

These days we all speak of the global economy. We are educated to understand that nations count for nothing, being mere pawns on the great chessboard of international capitalism. Surely, never in economic history has the international side of policy making been more important. In the much-loved words of one IMF official, 'We live in a global world.'

The Treasury is less sure. If you say that international work is growing in importance, its instinct is to rehearse the reasons why it is not.

They cite, for example, the period after the Second World War. Britain had spent its stock of overseas assets fighting Hitler. The country was hideously short of dollars to pay for essential imports from America – the 'dollar gap'. The fixed exchange rate for the pound, then at the demanding $4.20, made matters worse. When Lord Keynes was in Washington negotiating for credits from the Americans, he was literally negotiating as to whether Britain's babes would have a crust that winter. Except when dealing with issues of aid and debt, the Treasury official today is rarely dealing in starvation.

Or think, they might go on, of the days before 1979 when exchange controls were in force, preventing people changing British money into foreign currency on any scale without prior permission. Running the controls was a job, giving power but posing teasing conundrums for the Treasury bureaucrats who devised the rules. You might not be deciding whether people starved or not but you were determining whether they could enjoy steak and *frites* in France.

Yet an excess of modesty would not be warranted. The international side of the Treasury has, after all, been heavily involved in arguably the three defining moments of British politics and economics of the past two decades.

The first was in 1976–7. The oil price crisis of 1972–3 had greatly weakened Britain's international position. What was left of it was further eroded by the Labour government's spending spree of 1974–5, when for once the Treasury entirely lost control over public spending. Never hubris without nemesis: Britain finally had to call in the International Monetary Fund, and accept successive waves of deflation as the price of its imprimatur on her policies. The Labour party has never fully recovered from the trauma; and the day the deal was signed has been dubbed 'the day that social democracy died'.

The role of the Treasury in the whole affair is still debated. Some Labour politicians reckon that they were ambushed by a Treasury ramp. Some allege that Sir Derek Mitchell, the senior Treasury man responsible for negotiations with the IMF, acted as a Trojan horse. Certainly, some officials enjoyed watching ministers struggling to cope with consequences of which they had been warned.

The second was 16 September 1992, 'Black Wednesday', when the government was forced to let sterling fall out of the Exchange Rate Mechanism (ERM) of the European Monetary System. The government had joined the ERM under (though despite the opposition of) Margaret Thatcher in 1990. However, under John Major, her successor, and Norman Lamont, his chancellor, membership of the ERM became ever more central to the government's economic strategy. Even as the British economy struggled with a strong currency, ministers made it clear that they thought ERM essential to keeping inflation down: ERM 'is not an optional add-on to be jettisoned at the first hint of trouble. It is and will remain at the very centre of our macroeconomic strategy,' Mr Lamont said.

The immediate cause of sterling's ejection from the ERM is clear enough. Tensions had already built up. In Germany interest rates were going up, to choke off the potential inflationary effects of reunification. That attracted money out of sterling into D-marks.

Because of Britain's inflationary record, much higher interest rates were required in Britain if investors were to be prepared to hold sterling rather than D-marks. On the day Britain left the ERM, interest rates started the day at 10 per cent. The British economy was, meanwhile, still in recession. Though in retrospect it had clearly begun to recover slowly in 1991, nearly a year before ERM exit, British politicians – particularly Eurosceptical Tories – blamed membership for unemployment and slow growth. So there was strong pressure on the government to withdraw. Since this in itself could lead to speculative pressure against sterling, the government had to insist that it would not consider such an option. Ministers declared their devotion to continued membership in ever more uncompromising terms.

Into this scenario was injected a looming and particular uncertainty. On 20 September, the French were to hold a referendum on the Maastricht Treaty on European integration. Whether they voted yes or no would have profound implications for the development of European monetary integration, and hence for the likely stability of European exchange rates. With the polls suggesting a close result – in the event a bare majority voted for the treaty – speculative pressures in the run-up to the referendum were inevitable.

Some observers are still inclined to blame Sir Nigel Wicks, the Treasury's senior international official, for what went wrong. The pressure could have been alleviated, so they argue, had Sir Nigel persuaded the Germans to allow a realignment in the ERM. The D-mark could have been revalued upwards, removing pressure on the pound and other weak currencies.

Sir Nigel chaired the European Union's official monetary committee for six years, winning the immense respect of his colleagues. If any official could have pulled off a realignment Sir Nigel could.

It is not clear that the Germans would ever have agreed to realign. So far as they were concerned, the mark was strong because of their success in keeping inflation down. They should not be forced to revalue it; rather, those whose currencies were weak should learn to match Germany's anti-inflationary virtue.

In any case, any chances of a solution of this character were blown not by Wicks, but by Norman Lamont, the chancellor. When European finance ministers met at Bath, on 4 September, Mr Lamont put up a blustering performance. Lacking humility, he berated his colleagues for their failure to do what he thought right – naturally reinforcing their determination not to do it. A more subtle diplomat might have done better.

Treasury officials blame ministers too for the mess that was made of the day of exit. With sterling under pressure, Black Wednesday was bound to be a tough day. However, the politicians took over to make it a tougher one.

The Treasury had a plan worked out, set out in its so-called 'war book', for what should happen if sterling's membership of the ERM became unsustainable. It involved a negotiated temporary withdrawal, followed by a forced realignment of European currencies the following weekend.

The politicians departed from this plan in two ways. First, Mr Major insisted on calling in Kenneth Clarke and Michael Heseltine, the two 'big beasts' of his Cabinet, to share decisions with Mr Lamont and himself. If they were to sink, he obviously calculated, they should sink together, so that no one could use the debacle to challenge him afterwards. But Mr Clarke and Mr Heseltine, perhaps caught off balance, were committed Europeans. They insisted that at any rate a token effort should be made to stay in the ERM. So instead of simply withdrawing, British interest rates were raised – first to 12 per cent and then, hours later, to 15 per cent. This had no impact on sterling, which was too far gone to respond to such medicine. It did make a tremendous impact on the public, who saw their mortgages going up and their homes going west with them for a few traumatic hours. Reducing interest rates back to 10 per cent after exit made no difference. The British public, having witnessed these shenanigans, were not disposed to trust the Tories with the economy again.

The second political judgement compounded this. The Treasury's plan was to rejoin the ERM at a new rate as soon as possible. This was vetoed by the prime minister himself. Once Britain was out, he insisted, it was out. His party never liked the ERM; he would not be able to persuade it to join again once out. When Normal Lamont claimed, some weeks later, that he was 'singing in the bath' as a result of ERM exit, he talked for many in his party. This, then, was a purely political judgement, for which officials cannot be blamed.

A core Treasury skill is to explain after an event why the way it turned out was in fact for the best in the best of all possible worlds. That is so of ERM exit. Membership, they say, was what first gave a strong monetary anchor to British economic policy and was responsible for permanently lowering British inflationary expectations.

The economic effects of leaving the ERM turned out to be less severe than anyone expected. The pound soon stabilized. There was no renewed burst of inflation. And economic recovery eventually gathered strength.

None of this excuses Treasury officials, however, as ministerial warnings of the effect of leaving the ERM had been based on Treasury warnings to them. The Treasury indeed thought that ERM exit would be a serious setback. The Treasury was wrong.

In any case, whatever the economic balance sheet, the political balance sheet was splashed with red ink. The impact of ERM exit on the Treasury was traumatic. As a direct result the chancellor was destroyed. Only a weak prime minister such as Mr Major would have refused his chancellor's resignation, so letting him struggle on for eight traumatic months. The end, though delayed, was inevitable. Mr Lamont, complaining bitterly, was sacked on 27 May 1993.

The wider effects on politics were dire for the government. The Tories had been re-elected in the April 1992 general election because people did not trust the competence (and the designs on their pockets) of a Labour government. Withdrawal from the ERM seemed to demonstrate an even greater Tory incompetence. The tax increases which necessarily followed it did nothing to restore their popularity. And, meanwhile, the issue highlighted Tory divisions over Europe, which meant that they fought the 1997 election as a disorganized rabble. If some future historian has to write the definitive account of the strange death of Tory Britain, ERM exit will play a large part.

The third great international event in which the Treasury was central in recent years is the financial crisis which began in the summer of 1998. Here we have to be much more tentative, as the story is not over and its denouement remains uncertain. What is clear is that developments during the summer exposed defects in the management of the international economic system – and that Gordon Brown and the Treasury decided to give a lead in putting them right.

The crisis started in Asia, as Asian financial institutions came to be seen to be increasingly unstable. There followed the Russian wave, culminating in the country's debt default. Though the Russian economy was not big enough to be significant in substance, that could have caused contagion, with a wave of defaults following it. In the short run it did cause a liquidity crisis in the US, which the Federal Reserve Bank moved swiftly and successfully to deal with. Then there was the third wave beginning with the collapse of LTCM, a hedge fund, and continuing through Brazil's long-resisted de facto devaluation in January 1999.

'There are periods,' says one senior official, 'in which the international system ticks over, punctuated by periods of crisis. Crises have to be very bad before anyone will do anything: the costs of making changes are incredibly high. But this crisis is the worst of the last fifty years, just below that before Bretton Woods. Like the plumbing in a house, you don't think about it until it goes wrong. Then you look at the design.'

It was initially seen as an Asian mismanagement problem, but now the faults of Western banks, lending without proper thought, are also seen. What was known as the 'Washington consensus' – free markets, unregulated exchange markets – has now passed its high point.

What made the crisis an interesting time for British officials was the particular stance of the chancellor. His approach to international economic matters had many parallels with his domestic agenda. He favoured transparency in policy, including monetary and exchange rate policy. He wanted codes of conduct, and guidelines to stop people trying to make policy on the hoof. He did not so much want new institutions as better coordination between institutions already in existence. In particular he favoured a much closer relationship between the International Monetary Fund and the Bank for International Settlements, which is responsible for such international regulation of private banking as exists. As president of the G7 industrial countries in 1998 he was instrumental in setting up a standing committee to coordinate all this.

Beyond that, a further set of issues came out of the crisis. In particular, is there a need for an international lender of last resort, bailing out those who lend to international banks with liquidity problems, just as domestic central banks bail out domestic banks? Mr Brown has pressed strongly for the private sector to take on more responsibility for the stability of the system.

Of course, Britain is only one of the G7 and by no means the most powerful. On transparency, the Americans are closer to Britain than are the Europeans. But on better regulation and supervision of private banks, the US and the UK have moved towards the more interventionist European position. Overall, there is still a gap between interventionist Europe and free-market America, with Britain brokering from a position in the middle.

Even now, the Treasury resists the cliché that international work is bound to grow in importance. Europe, they agree, is all going one way, towards ever-closer links, but internationally the Treasury is less sure. The upsurge as a result of the 1998–9 crisis may be merely cyclical.

But in one sense, internationalism is bound to grow. That is in the influence of one country's policies on those of others. As a result, the Treasury is a much less insular and self-satisfied place than it used to be. And improved communications help it to build knowledge. For example, time zones matter much less when you can take calls on mobile phones while travelling, or swap e-mails with no delays.

Privatization is an example of one area where Britain has strong claims to have led the world. Treasury officials, as we have seen, proselytize for it around the world (selling, so they claim, lots of business for British financial institutions off the back of it).

But sometimes the trade flows the other way. The Treasury did not know that Labour was going to win the 1997 general election. Still less did it know that it was going to give the Bank of England independence, a policy which the party had discreetly omitted from its manifesto. Yet the Treasury had sensed that, globally, the tide was running for independent central banking. It had invested in acquiring intellectual knowledge of those countries which had introduced it. New Zealand was one example. When, therefore, the policy had to be worked up in a single weekend after the election, it had that knowledge ready for use. The New Zealand model is quite close to the British model. And the Treasury is investing further in such knowledge: antipodean hawks have been brought over on secondment to the Treasury to teach it the lessons for Britain.

The Treasury and abroad

So international work at the Treasury remains important, and at times of paramount importance. How is it managed? Even as the top layers of management were being stripped away from Great George Street, the international sector still merited the leadership of a top official – in the familiar oldspeak, a second permanent secretary. This makes Sir Nigel Wicks, its holder in 1999, a member of the civil service's inner elite. While the Treasury still defends the cuts in staffing made as a result of the Fundamental Expenditure Review, it is inclined to think that the international side is one area where it is, if anything, understaffed.

Sir Nigel Wicks might at first meeting seem an unlikely candidate for such high authority. In his late fifties he still retained a boyish look: in moments of anxiety he was forever sweeping a long lock of hair off his forehead. He had been in the job for more than ten years, which made him one of the longest-established of his breed. This is typical of international finance, he says, where if anything other countries keep their officials in post for longer. Trust across frontiers is something which cannot be established in the twinkling of an eye.

Even before Sir Nigel took this post, he had been used to top jobs. He was economic private secretary to the Labour prime minister, James Callaghan; then, later, the chief private secretary to Margaret Thatcher, serving both with equal devotion. He has also been Britain's representative in Washington at the International Monetary Fund. Without side or pomp, he is famous for two things: his immense discretion and his contacts.

No journalist has ever claimed that they got a scoop from Sir Nigel, who trades in common-sense bromides. Unflashily, he works hard to maintain his international contacts. In the year ending December 1992, he had spent eighty nights abroad, undertaken fifteen day trips to Europe; and gone on 107 flights, spending a total of ten days and nineteen and a half hours in the air.

Sir Nigel's stock has ebbed and flowed in recent years. Unfairly, some ministers tended to blame him for the ERM debacle. (The alternative, after all, was to blame themselves.) But Sir Nigel is very much Gordon Brown's kind of official: genuinely expert, with the right contacts and a willingness to pursue the ministerial agenda loyally. Amongst other European nations, Sir Nigel's long chairmanship of the monetary committee has won him an extraordinary reputation. 'They think he is a demigod in Europe,' says one official observer.

Sir Nigel's empire is a huge one. It includes oversight of the man who currently does his old job of representing Britain at the International Monetary Fund (see below). One of his team supervises Britain's aid budget, unusually controlled from outside the spending divisions of the Treasury because of its international ramifications. That official is also in charge of monitoring public spending on the Commonwealth Development Corporation and on the British Council.

Sir Nigel supervises export credits (see below), and with that goes the job of negotiating for an international level playing field on such credits taking place under the auspices of the Organization for Economic Cooperation and Development (OECD). Aid to Eastern Europe, a particular interest of Mr Lamont's during his chancellorship, required the setting up of a special division under a middle-ranking official.

Trade policy is also his. Britain played a strong role in the negotiations on the General Agreement on Tariffs and Trade that was concluded successfully in 1994 and is involved in current (1999) negotiations designed to liberalize overseas investment. So he is in overall charge of British thinking on the future of international economic institutions and, as we have seen, of bits of its European policy. Whether international policy is or is not more important than it used to be, his remains one of the most important posts in British officialdom.

Our man in Washington

It is possible to spend a whole career at the Treasury without ever having a desk outside Whitehall. But if you do get out, there are few more exciting jobs to get out to than the Washington-based job at the IMF – or rather the three jobs which are brought together in one senior Treasury man there.

One of these is British executive director of the International Monetary Fund, the most powerful of the world's international economic organizations. Another is executive director at the World Bank, its sister organization for third-world development. But there is a third and quite separate function, as economic minister at the British Embassy. This involves reporting on America's economy and representing Britain in economic negotiations with the Americans.

The IMF board meets on Mondays, Wednesdays and Fridays, and the Bank's on Tuesdays and Thursdays, which does not leave much space. 'People ask me how I divided myself up. I say, "I spent 50 per cent of my time on each," ' says David Peretz, a former holder of the job.

In each job there is back-up. For the Bank and the Fund there is an alternate director. In the case of the Fund, by tradition, he or she comes from the Bank of England. In the case of the World Bank, he or she is recruited from Britain's aid ministry, the Overseas Trade Administration. There is a full-time economic and financial counsellor in the Embassy, a Treasury person temporarily assigned to diplomatic duties. They in turn have a team of two: a more junior Treasury official and, for reasons that are essentially historic, a specialist in labour.

All British representatives abroad tend to moan that their power is not what it was. Once upon a time, home was linked to abroad only by slow ships; an ambassador was necessarily left to his own initiative. Now instructions can be transmitted by phone or fax in the twinkling of an eye. If anything decent comes up, likely as not some minister will scent publicity and rush to take over.

But the IMF job is better than most. For one thing, its occupant is a director of the IMF. Britain is one of only five countries to appoint a director of its own. The director has duties, not only to his own country, but to the institution which he helps direct. 'The job is somewhere between being a representative of Britain and someone who has the fiduciary duties to the institution that a non-executive director has to his company,' says one recent incumbent. 'If ever there was a conflict between what was the good of the institution and what London wanted – and in practice there never has been a conflict – then I would have to make my own decision. But probably I'd have to look after the good of the institution first, because those are the terms of reference of the executive directors.'

For another, the job enjoys a degree of practical freedom. True, the chancellor of the exchequer is a governor of both the World Bank and the IMF, with the governor of the Bank of England his IMF alternate. Both will attend the September meetings of the Bank and the Fund. But the man on the spot knows more than the man in Whitehall. 'I do not on the whole get instructions from London,' says one director. 'I get guidance.' On a whole lot of issues concerning faraway countries of which Britain knows little, he may not even get that. That English is the working language can help. Japanese directors seem to spend much of their time translating things for Tokyo.

'I arrived in the US two days before Iraq invaded Kuwait,' Mr Peretz recalls. 'I spent a good deal of time dealing with the consequences of that. For example, there was World Bank lending to the countries adversely affected. The Gulf Crisis Coordination Committee was channelling money to Egypt. Egypt, Cyprus and Turkey had large tourist earnings that were affected, and there were large movements of people returning to Bangladesh and to Pakistan.'

Then there was the break-up of the Soviet Union, the subject of a four-institution study carried out jointly by the IMF, the Bank, the OECD and the European Bank for Reconstruction and Development. The Soviet Union wanted to join the IMF. They chose Britain to broker that, partly on account of its 'immensely effective foreign affairs machine, and the most effective diplomatic service in the world. We had a very effective director in the IMF, it goes without saying.' The work was 'quite controversial; quite difficult; quite fun'. The fund in turn provided the rules to try to make sure that the money which the West put into the Soviet Union was not going to waste, or into Swiss bank accounts for bureaucrats, but was leading to the kind of economic programme that could produce results.

The break-up of the ERM had its consequences for the IMF too. The fund had been caught by surprise by Black Wednesday, and its managing director, Michel Camadessus, knew it. In the aftermath, IMF monitoring was stepped up. It has been active too in the management of the 1998–9 crisis, trying to coordinate its activities with those of the World Bank and of the nearest thing the world has to an international banking regulator, the Bank for International Settlements in Basle.

The board holds regular discussions of the world economy and exercises surveillance over the major economies. In all this, the British director has an important contribution to make. 'We more than pull our weight in international discussions,' says one former director.

Meanwhile, the director is supposed to be overseeing reporting to the government on the American economy. Naturally, the Treasury claims to provide in-depth reporting beyond what is done by the newspapers: for example, the British embassy prepared a detailed assessment of the economic effects of President Clinton's health-care proposals. The director also has to deal with important one-off issues: for example, unitary taxation, the plan to tax all firms on the basis of their worldwide results, with disastrous effects on British companies. He was the one who had to ring round to find out what the vice-president, Al Gore, really meant when he said that Russia's economy needed 'more therapy and less shock', when, on the whole, Britain thought shocks were precisely what Russia needed.

Forecasting abroad

To prepare forecasts of Britain's economy, the Treasury also prepares forecasts of the world economy. These in turn rely on their forecasts of how individual countries abroad will perform. Economic counsellors in Britain's embassies do much of the reporting on which those forecasts are based, but the actual forecasting is not done in Sir Nigel's bit of the Treasury. This is primarily because the forecasts for Britain have to iterate with the world forecasts for a coherent picture to emerge. 'It's very important when you are forecasting to have responsibility for everything,' says one official. 'You can't have independent barons or you get a difference of approach.'

Economic counsellors in embassies lead a full life. They will of course read the domestic forecasts for each country, work their own official contacts and keep in touch with local opinion. At a time, however, when all Treasury jobs have come under minute scrutiny, it is perhaps surprising that these jobs have survived.

The era when governments had a monopoly of forecasting is long gone. Comprehensive forecasts for individual economies are now prepared at a higher level: the IMF's in particular. Meanwhile, private forecasting has proliferated with the expansion of financial markets. The regular circulars, for example, of city firms such as Goldman Sachs are as likely to contain in-depth coverage of Germany's economy, or Japan's, as they are of Britain's.

Anyway, as we have already seen, forecasting ain't what it used to be. As less and less importance attaches to forecasts, and as more and more decent forecasting is available from outside the Treasury, it is not easy to justify these economic counsellor positions. It remains to be seen whether they survive.

Export credits

Export credits is an area of Treasury business that deserves consideration, since they illustrate rather well the Treasury's beleaguered position. Export credits are guarantees given by government to companies that they will get paid for exports to other countries. The British government in the shape of the Export Credit Guarantee Department (ECGD) pays the companies and then gets the money back from the countries who had bought the goods.

Export credits have enthusiastic supporters. They are supported by firms who want to sell to unstable countries without worrying if they will get paid. They are supported by the Ministry of Defence, which chooses to act as spokesman in Whitehall for dealers in defence equipment. They are supported by the Department of Trade and Industry, which is similarly solicitous of the interests of industry. In behind them weighs the Foreign Office, which sees it as its job to sell things abroad. And they are supported by lots of politicians who think they sustain jobs in their constituencies. Besides, if Britain does not offer them, how will we compete with countries that do? So when the ECGD comes to the Treasury and asks, for example, for permission to extend credits to export to the Lebanon, the Treasury knows that it will have to fight if it is to resist.

So there have been lots of export credits granted. The record, according to the officials responsible, have not been good: ECGD in 1994 had provision for bad debts of around £7 billion on premium income.

For the Treasury as the taxpayer's representative, that constitutes a failure – and raises the fundamental question of whether we should have export credits at all. The result, around 1990, was a review of the subject, designed to see if export credits could be privatized. Short-term finance could be, the review concluded, and it was, to a Dutch company. But so far as medium-term policy goes, the scale of the risks are such that there is no private-sector company that is large enough to take it over. Even a commercial bank would be stretched and, given the underwriting record, they would not want it anyway.

The Treasury has made some headway in controlling export credits. For example, a new system was introduced whereby, before credit was granted, a proper assessment of the downside risk had to be made. The question that had to be answered was: is there a 2.5 per cent risk of us losing half the money we have put in?

For a while after the review, things went relatively well. Much of the backlog of debt was repaid. However, that was primarily because the world economy was going relatively well. And in 1998 that came to an end. Losses from the financial crisis of 1998–9 have yet to be assessed. But as one Treasury man says, 'The thing is inherently unstable. When things go wrong, you inevitably take a bath.'

This case perhaps illustrates the extent of and limits to Treasury power. Yes, the Treasury was powerful enough to get the subject looked at. Yes, it was strong enough to get rid of one part of the business. But it would be surprising if deep down the Treasury thought that underwriting private-sector debt was the business of government. It would be astonishing if it had not occurred to it to split the existing debt up and sell it off to a variety of private providers for what it would fetch. As for new debt, the Treasury might well think that if other countries wish to waste taxpayers' money subsidizing exporters, then that is for them. So far as Britain is concerned, if private bankers will not provide private capital, then capital is probably best not provided.

But that line has not prevailed. 'If a right-wing Conservative government was not prepared to get rid of export credits,' one official says, 'how likely is it that a government of the centre-left will do so?' 'Not very likely,' is the implied answer, which means that, though

Treasury officials would never say so, the review's findings were no more than the best available compromise.

'We will never get rid of it. We just need to try to keep the losses down,' one Treasury official sadly concludes.

15 | Parliament: Friend or Foe?

Relations between Parliament and the Treasury are complex. Both institutions, however, would benefit from more powerful parliamentary control.

Parliament's main job, under the British constitution, is to scrutinize the executive. The Treasury's main job is also to scrutinize the executive. The two should therefore be allies. Yet if you look at the record of recent years, this is not how things appear to have panned out.

On some grand set-piece occasions Parliament has simply refused to accept elements of the chancellor's budget (see below). These are occasions when the Commons has been playing its grand role in the cockpit of politics. Here, it is natural that from time to time conflict between Parliament and the chancellor should arise; that far from being his ally, the Commons becomes his enemy.

Yet it is not only over such matters that, in practice, Parliament and Treasury fail to work together. Smaller conflicts arise all the time. The Treasury often seems unwilling to give Parliament in general and its Treasury Select Committee in particular more information than it is forced to. The Treasury has never made common cause with Parliament's own spending watchdog, the Public Accounts Committee. For no very good reason, the government works off two sets of accounts: its own, and another artificial set, the estimates, which is what it gives to Parliament.

The reason for all this lies partly in history, and in Parliament's reluctance to modernize itself. It also lies in the traditional suspicion with which Whitehall views Westminster.

The relationship is far from simple. For a start, neither Parliament nor the Treasury is a single united entity with a single purpose.

The Treasury comprises both permanent officials and ministers. Often they work as one, but they also have subtly different interests. Officials are cautious, careful and necessarily bureaucratic; ministers are also cautious, but they are always tempted to make a splash and are usually impatient of bureaucratic restraint. Officials do not rely on Parliament for their reputations; even today, ministers do. Officials seek objective truth; ministers pursue political truth. And these differences colour the different attitudes of ministers and their officials towards Parliament.

Officials often welcome Parliament's assistance in scrutinizing other departments. They are often glad of the restraints of parliamentary procedures which, though often absurd, do put the brakes on ministerial impatience. However, officials tend to be angered by the special pleading of MPs for particular vested interests. Moreover, there is no hiding the fact that officials are on average cleverer than, and invariably better briefed than, MPs. Due official deference to MPs' democratic legitimacy is often tempered by understandable impatience with the quality of those whom the electorate has chosen.

Ministers welcome Parliament in so far as it provides a forum where they can show off their skills and advance their careers. They hate it, however, in so far as it is also the source of the banana skins that can trip them up. They are less interested in the quality of their fellow MPs than they are in their voices and votes, which help decide their standing in their party and even their standing in the outside world.

Parliament is not an institution with a single purpose either. To take one obvious difficulty, one set of its members supports the government; they do not usually want to embarrass ministers. Another set represents the opposition, and they want to use every opportunity to undermine ministers. So government MPs generally, rebels aside, will be in the business of constructive but not excessive scrutiny.

Opposition MPs generally are in the business of destructive forensic scrutiny.

Moreover, this complex drama is played on a complex mix of stages. There is what happens on the floor of the Commons, whose essence sadly remains that of confrontation and conflict. This essence, even more sadly, is carried over into the standing committees, the committees of MPs whose job it is to scrutinize legislation. Ministers want their bills and nothing but their bills.

There is now for the first time a sign of change here. More bills are being published in draft. As we have seen, the massive Financial Services and Markets Bill is one. Some, particularly the less controversial ones, are being scrutinized first, not by standing committees, which are confrontational, but by select committees, which are less so. In any case, much of the most important work is not done on the floor of the chamber or in the standing committees but in the more constructive select committees. We turn now to the work of two of those committees: the Treasury Select Committee and the Public Accounts Committee.

The Treasury Select Committee

Of all the select committees of the Commons, the Treasury Select Committee is the one ambitious MPs want to be on. Its subject matter is that at the heart of government, covering everything that falls within the Treasury remit and the work of the Bank of England besides.

For most of the past twenty years it has been chaired by distinguished parliamentarians: Edward du Cann, Terence Higgins and now Giles Radice. The three less distinguished parliamentarians, John Watts, Tom Arnold and Matthew Carrington, who chaired it between Mr (now Lord) Higgins's departure in 1992 and before Mr Radice's election in 1997, did not last long enough to weaken its reputation.

Its membership has also been well above the Commons median

in quality. Though for some reason a favoured home for fanatical anti-Europeans (Austin Mitchell, Labour, then the late Nicholas Budgen and now Teddy Taylor, Conservative), it is also a training ground for younger members set for the economic heart of government. Charles Clarke, Labour, who joined the committee in May 1997, was one of the first of the new intake to become a minister. Many expect Ruth Kelly, another of that intake, to join him soon. 'Its quality depends on the chairman's taking it seriously and on not having too many eccentrics,' says the current chairman, Giles Radice.

Sometimes, partisanship is displayed in the workings of the committee. In 1998, the committee, at Mr Clarke's behest, agreed certain remarks on the length of time it would take before European Monetary Union either proved itself or failed. The opposition slyly latched on to these and interpreted them as supporting the Tory policy of staying out of EMU for two parliaments. They did this by leaking them, out of context. Gordon Brown was very cross, and not just with the Tories.

But there are more occasions when the spirit of the committee is essentially bipartisan. Then it is at its best, because it asks questions in public which no one else is able to ask in the same way.

The press watches its proceedings, with leading economic journalists as well as the press gallery reporters often attending important sessions. And because it is reported, its reports are also well read.

A number of distinguished economists have served as its advisers. Before preparing a recent report on the Bank of England, the committee held a private seminar with outside experts, including a former governor of the Bank of England, Robin Leigh-Pemberton, now Lord Kingsdown, and a former chancellor, Nigel (now Lord) Lawson. It has even had that Commons rarity, a colourful committee clerk. Philip Hensher is now a writer of critically acclaimed novels, including *Kitchen Venom*, which is set in the House of Commons.

Until the election it also had an important subcommittee scrutinizing the civil and public services, though public services now have their own select committee. A subcommittee of the Treasury Committee does, however, scrutinize the Treasury's six Next Steps agencies, which include the Registry of Friendly Societies and the Royal Mint.

In the early 1980s, it served as something of a focal point for critics of the government's new monetarism. Though it never attacked it head on, what could be read between the lines was quite enough to vex the whips. The tradition continues, with its remarks on the euro only the latest of the many times when the chancellor has been angered by its findings. 'If you are a control freak like Gordon Brown you are bound to have an uncomfortable relationship with the committee,' says one MP.

It can even claim to have been in the forefront of some important changes of policy. The committee became a champion of greater independence for the Bank of England even when the last Tory government was dithering about it. It articulated the targets that the bank should be set and the way in which it should interrelate with Parliament.

The committee recently sought to extend its power in one major way, by arguing that the governor of the newly independent bank should be subject to confirmation by the Treasury Committee itself. There were strong arguments for this. It seems reasonable that the people's representatives should have a chance to quiz the nominee who might otherwise emerge from an old boys' network. There was also a counter-argument. The whole point of the reform was to put the bank 'above politics'. But if the governor was subject to confirmation, that would undermine his independence. Moreover, mid-term, a governor might seek to adjust his behaviour to that most likely to gain parliamentary approval.

Despite the strength of the counter-argument, some Treasury officials would apparently not have minded if confirmation hearings had been agreed, though ministers were unenthusiastic. But elsewhere in Whitehall the feeling was different. No power is as precious to the

British executive as the exclusive power of appointment, and this toe in the water of parliamentary involvement in such matters sent waves round Whitehall. It was vetoed.

The committee did hold hearings to interview members of the Monetary Policy Committee, however. Beforehand, the Treasury was ambiguous about this idea. Gus O'Donnell, the senior official responsible for monetary policy, had previously served in Washington. Watching senate confirmatory committees crawling over the details of people's private lives had left him with a jaundiced view.

In the event, he was pleasantly surprised. The hearings were well handled. They focused on the professional capacity of MPC members to do the job. For the future, therefore, the Treasury Committee represents another disincentive to ministers to try to put their poodles on the committee, since they would be publicly exposed. Here is another example of the Treasury and Parliament as allies.

Its influence in helping to bring about independence for the Bank of England is not the committee's only recent success. It also had some influence over the creation of the new Financial Services Authority. The committee, in successive reports, was critical of pension mis-selling by the insurance industry, which had ripped off consumers. It did not think much of the speed with which the existing regulator, the Personal Investment Authority, got to grips with it. It even, most unfairly, criticized the PIA's saintly chairman, Joe Palmer, because he had once been group chief executive of one of the companies, Legal and General, which had mis-sold.

The committee also took the Bank of England to task for its handling of the BCCI scandal. Partly in consequence of these inquiries the reputation of the British system of financial regulation sank. Labour in opposition decided on the dramatic reforms which it pushed through in government.

The committee treads on politically sensitive territory. Since the 1970s, Scotland's share of public spending has been set according to the Barnett Formula, named after a former chief secretary to the

Treasury. This ensured that the Scots enjoyed more than their due share of the taxpayer's money. If inflation had gone on as it was when the formula was negotiated, Scotland's bonus would gradually have been reduced. It didn't, and the Scots continued to roll in clover.

With the coming of the Scottish Parliament, and the challenge to Labour there from the Scottish National Party, resources for Scotland was a highly sensitive issue with government. The least said, the general Cabinet view was, the better.

The Treasury Committee demurred. Its report, though factual rather than prescriptive, demonstrated the illogicality of the formula. Gordon Brown, a Scottish MP, was not best pleased. But some Treasury officials, who had been pointing out the absurdity of Scotland's favourable treatment for years, were less unhappy.

There could be no better example of the communality of interest between the select committee on the one hand and the official Treasury on the other. Why then is the Treasury not more forthcoming with the committee? Why so often when Treasury officials appear before it do they appear to be saying as little as possible, playing for time?

Partly this reflects the general Whitehall view of select committees. There is no tradition of openness and a long tradition of caution. But this is slowly diminishing. The modern official is less instinctively cagey than his predecessors. More and more officials are being actively trained to appear before select committees. More and more have had experience of the ordeal of doing so. The system is learning by doing.

But this greater openness will continue to be limited so long as the constitutional doctrine of ministerial accountability to Parliament holds sway. Doctrine states that officials appear before committees only as the instruments of their ministers. They should of course be as helpful as possible, and provide the committee with factual information, but the views they defend are those of their ministers.

This is a product of Whitehall's Faustian pact between officials and ministers. It is a power-sharing agreement. Ministers will retain a monopoly over the right to decide; officials will retain a monopoly over the right to advise. Ministers will get all the public glory when things go right in return for taking all the public odium when things go wrong. Officials will not claim credit but neither will they take blame; their power will remain subterranean.

It follows that the job of officials, when they appear before select committees, is principally to avoid embarrassment for their ministers. They must not be caught saying anything that appears to shed doubt on the policies of their ministers; or which exposes contradictions; or which uncovers the deals struck by their political masters. Blandness is all.

In practice, this doctrine is not entirely adhered to. Different officials strike different balances between their duty to their ministers of being discreet and their duty to be honest and open with Parliament. Sir Alan Budd, for example, a loyal ministerial adviser, nevertheless leaned over backwards to give the committee as much information as he could.

'Some Treasury officials treat it as a potential ally. Officials are there to defend their masters but they need not put up a total wall,' says Mr Radice. You have to learn to read between the lines. An official who says, 'I am confident that the public-spending targets will be hit,' is saying something stronger than an official who says, 'Ministers are confident that the public-spending targets will be hit.' Hints can be given that not every belief a minister holds is shared by his officials. Attention can be drawn to one bit of a minister's statement or one paragraph of an official report while another less palatable bit is ignored. A more or less vehement answer may indicate more or less commitment to its contents. It is hard to recall a recent incident of an official saying something which could be quoted against his minister. But you can sometimes tell where the official Treasury opinion really stands.

For the chancellor, as for his officials, an appearance before the select committee is not without its difficulties. It is, even for someone of chancellorial self-confidence, a testing business. The chancellor's life in general comprises set speeches before chosen audiences. Such audiences are often deferential, and sometimes admiring. Even in the House of Commons, replies to questions are carefully scripted; it is very rare nowadays for a minister to say something at question time that gets him into hot water. Out of it, media soundbites can be polished and rehearsed, with the aid of professional spin doctors. Even press conferences are under the chancellor's control. He calls them; he decides which questioners to invite; and he can generally limit them to half an hour.

An appearance before the Treasury Committee is very different. The chancellor is summoned. Questions will last up to two hours. The answers are recorded verbatim. The cameras record all. A slip or a hesitation will be noted, seized on, punished. 'They don't want to say anything that could be used against them,' says Mr Radice.

At the same time, an appearance is an opportunity. As an event, it can attract public attention.

A sensible chancellor is aware that the committee can be on his side. Chancellors for example are under constant pressure to spend, spend, spend. The Treasury Committee appreciates the need for the sums to add up. It has constantly supported a tough fiscal stance. When, as too often happens, the chancellor has been forced by colleagues to allow too much spending, the Treasury Committee notices. Its possible censure can be used as a weapon against the spenders. 'If the chancellor is relaxed about criticism, the committee can be an ally,' Mr Radice says.

The chancellor needs to take the committee seriously, but not to get into a stew about it. There are limits to how hostile it is likely to be. A majority of its members will generally be members of his own party. Although party discipline is not as strictly enforced in select committees as it is on the floor of the House, this is a relative matter. A select committee member who asks hostile questions of his own minister will be in deep water with the whips. Probing questioning need not be a barrier to career advancement for a government MP on the committee, but there are limits. Ms Diane Abbott, a Labour left-winger, was removed from the committee after the 1997 general election, though she was given the consolation prize of a place on the Foreign Affairs Select Committee. Though clever, and black, Ms Abbott is not likely to become a minister.

As for opposition MPs, they can ask what they like. But a minister in trouble with them can use the normal weapon of his trade in the British system: abuse. At the end of the day, the governing party has the majority to vote the opposition down.

These factors help to delineate the limits to the committee's role. It cannot go too far. If it gets above its station, it will eventually be put down. *In extremis*, the whips could always stuff it with placemen.

It therefore has to use discretion as well as valour. It has never sought to criticize the government head on. Its differences are conveyed subtly, in nuances.

In the summer of 1998, the chancellor announced his three-year spending plans. The Treasury press release referred to 'a £19 billion investment in education', as if this was a single year's increase. The headlines next day took the bait. The Treasury Committee did not. 'There is thus no cash bonanza of the type which newspaper headlines might suggest,' it said in its report ('The New Fiscal Framework and the Comprehensive Spending Review', Proceedings of the Committee, Vol. 1, 27 July 1998, 960–61), 'but a steady increase in real resource. We recommend that, for the sake of transparency, in future the government should refer to annual increases over the previous year rather than a cumulative total.'

It could have put this somewhat differently. For example, 'Brown published phoney figures designed to fool the public. Be warned, Gordon. You've been rumbled.' As it was, the muted version was enough to displease the chancellor once more.

The Public Accounts Committee

On the green benches outside a Commons committee room, a gaggle of grey-suited men cluster, clutching gargantuan briefing folders. One amongst them, apparently their boss, is as grey as his suit, eyes black-rimmed from too little sleep, hands refusing to stay still. Even the most august permanent secretary, used to the effortless power of the mandarin, is apt to quail at the thought of an appearance before the Public Accounts Committee (PAC), Parliament's most venerable scrutinizer of public expenditure. One permanent secretary due to appear blocked out his diary for five days for preparation.

Occasionally, the work of the PAC springs into public prominence. In 1993, the committee published an investigation into the government's £234 million support for the government of Malaysia to pay for a dam in Pergau. The money had been made available following a deal between Margaret Thatcher, then prime minister, and the Malaysian prime minister, Mahathir Mohamad. The problem was that the money had been made as part of Britain's aid programme. Yet it appeared to be linked to agreements on trade. The government was thus using money voted by Parliament for one purpose for something different.

Sir Tim Lankester was then the permanent secretary of the Overseas Aid Department. In that capacity, Sir Tim was accounting officer for the department; it was his job to certify that all the money it had spent had been spent legally and economically. Sir Tim, a man of compelling integrity, refused to sign for the Pergau money. It could not be justified, he believed, to the PAC. He kept his job, but many believe that revenge was taken later. He was subsequently a frontrunner for another permanent secretaryship, but failed to get the job. He retired.

The government did its level and disgraceful best to keep Pergau quiet. Without Sir Tim, it might have succeeded. But behind Sir Tim stood the PAC, as implacable a guardian of righteousness as he was himself. There could be no better example of the enduring value of detailed parliamentary scrutiny.

The Public Accounts Committee is unlike any other select committee. It is by convention chaired by a member of the opposition. Until 1997, it was headed by Bob Sheldon, a respected Labour former Treasury minister. In 1997, he was succeeded by David Davies, a former Tory minister who, at the age of only forty-eight, had a career ahead of him if the Tories ever won again.

Unlike every other committee, it has a big staff: some 780 in 1998. By comparison, most select committees have two or three clerks. This staff is headed up by the comptroller and auditor general. This august official is appointed not by the government but by Parliament. He is accountable to it alone.

Most select committees are bipartisan up to a point. The PAC, however, is pretty well wholly bipartisan. It has not divided on party political lines in recent years. Well-chaired, as it has been, it is usually hard to tell from which party a member asking questions comes.

Its range is enormous. Between January 1998 and the summer recess that year, it had published sixty-one reports. The Ministry of Agriculture was examined on tackling Common Agricultural Policy irregularities. Highlands and Islands Enterprise was studied for its value-for-money performance measurement. The Private Finance Initiative contracts for Bridgend and Fazakerley Prisons were crawled over. Even the Queen did not escape scrutiny in the investigation into 'Property Services in the English Occupied Royal Palaces: Responsibilities for Royal Household Remuneration and the Provision of Accommodation'. It is a formidable output.

However, despite this, the PAC has critics. Some indeed believe that it is not the power in the land it used to be.

This is unfair. There has been a general passing of power from Parliament to the media outside. Parliamentary rebuke, though painful to ministers and civil servants alike, no longer represents the mark of shame which it used to. And so the PAC, like every instrument of Parliament, is bound to appear weaker than it was.

However, it cannot escape all blame. The committee has failed to adapt to this shift from inside Westminster to the media outside. Though its reports are published, and duly distributed to the press, no serious attempt is made to interest the press in them. As they are usually, in their detail, what most journalists regard as boring, they are widely ignored. One good press officer would do more for the PAC than a score more investigating officers.

Secondly, reading its reports, it is hard to escape a feeling that the PAC has failed to modernize its techniques. The frontier of controlling public spending is full of innovation. There are new values and techniques: targeting, incentivization, the encouragement of new public management, of individual enterprise, even of risk. In the PAC's bit of the game, however, old values and techniques seem to dominate: it follows paper trails; it counts candle ends; it rebukes administrative error. The contrast with the Audit Commission, which performs similar functions to the PAC with regard to local authorities and health trusts, is striking.

No doubt, the PAC could point to many examples where it has behaved as if it was a modern institution. But then, to take another ancient institution at random, so could the Jockey Club. It does not prevent the overall impression being that it is reactive, fuddy-duddy and insufficiently bold.

Thirdly, the PAC is always *post facto*. It scrutinizes the government's accounts, not its plans. It makes no attempt to look at how the money is going to be spent before it has been spent. The horse has to have bolted before the committee checks the stable door.

Post facto scrutiny is not a function to be pooh-poohed. Obviously it picks up things that have gone wrong. It does hold those who have erred to account. You would not decry a company's auditors because its directors had made wrong decisions.

The fact that expenditure may be scrutinized in future by the

PAC is an incentive to its controllers to scrutinize it now. British government by consent remains remarkably uncorrupt. The PAC can claim a modest share of the credit for that.

The PAC therefore has an important function. Its standing may not be unchallenged, but it is a far from negligible standing. However, its limits mean that it is quite clearly not sufficient to constitute in itself adequate parliamentary control. For that, other mechanisms are required.

The cockpit of the nation

Control, real control, requires something more than the PAC and the Treasury Committee. It requires a stronger will from the House of Commons to control the executive.

And yet, on the big things, it rarely does. Very occasionally, it is true, the chancellor will lose a measure from his budget: Kenneth Clarke was forced to raise other taxes to restore revenue lost when the House turned down his increase in domestic fuel duty in 1994. These are rarities. Far more often the budget goes through unchanged.

Merit does not come into it. In Britain's confrontational party system, an opposition party spots an opportunity. Whether it can bring it off or not does not depend on opposition MPs. They can be relied upon to troop through the anti-government lobby at the whips' behest. Indeed, save for the great debates on Europe from the 1970s to the 1990s, it is hard to recall an occasion when individual opposition MPs have chosen to vote against their whips and with the government.

Whether the government is defeated or not does not depend on merit. It depends on the government's majority, and whether it is sufficiently large to be rebellion-proof. And then it depends on whether there are sufficient of its supporters sufficiently disenchanted to make common cause against it with the parliamentary enemy. This system can on occasion produce good theatre. But it has little to do with good government. Indeed it impedes it even more than the formal record of defeats suggests. For every actual defeat, there have to be reckoned the things the government ought to have done, but hasn't, for fear of defeat.

Every serious look at housing for thirty years has concluded that mortgage interest relief is wholly without justification. Even the Duke of Edinburgh, by proxy a substantial homeowner, signed a report to that effect in 1985. But successive chancellors have been wary of getting rid of it. Partly, it is true, this is because they feared the homeowner vote in the country, but equally they hesitated for fear of parliamentary rejection. Even today, MIRAS (mortgage interest relief at source) survives, albeit at a reduced 10 per cent rate.

Some may see this as an example of the power of Parliament to represent the people. Others would prefer a more logical approach to policy making.

Parliament devotes quite a lot of time to debating economic issues. There is the lengthy set-piece debate on the budget. There used to be a long debate on the public-spending white paper and there was a one-day debate on the 1998 Comprehensive Spending Review. A day in the debate on the Queen's Speech setting out the legislative programme is devoted to Treasury matters. When the economy is going awry, the opposition is likely to choose economic policy for one or more of their 'supply days', when they choose the subject.

If the chancellor is really on the rocks, these can be parliamentary occasions. More usually, the debates are ill attended. The speeches are predictable, partisan and ill informed. Parliament, meanwhile, rarely gets round to debating on the floor of the House the reports of its own select committees, including those of the Treasury Committee.

The Commons does not help itself by its failure to review its ancient ways of controlling public spending. The inadequacies of its budget arrangements are laughable. It still passes 'estimates' and 'supplementary estimates' for government spending, based on numbers entirely different from those in its real spending plans. Only technical experts can reconcile the two. Important items may get only one line in the estimates, no more than is devoted to trivia. Though the House of Commons has, on occasion, as we have seen, changed the chancellor's taxing plans, it has never changed his spending plans.

This accounting may improve in future: for example, it is intended that estimates are folded into resource accounting in a single system of reporting to Parliament. But MPs all too often hang on to the illusion of power in preference to its substance. There is no tradition of the House of Commons that is so outmoded as to be easily disposed of in the face of the conservatism of some of its older members. This reform may yet fail at their hands, though all who want good government will wish otherwise.

In any case, it would be a missed opportunity to reform the accounts without also reforming the way Parliament deals with them. What is needed, not just for Parliament's sake but for the nation's, is genuine involvement by the people's representatives in public-spending decisions.

Chancellors can treat Parliament largely with contempt. They may not even bother to be much around the Commons. Kenneth Clarke prided himself on being a 'House of Commons' man, in touch with all shades of opinion, though, as it turned out, he was not much good at adjusting to opinion in his own party. Norman Lamont, too, was a natural Commons man, though less affable when weighed down by the office of chancellor than before or after.

On the other hand, Nigel Lawson was not keen on the Commons. Gordon Brown would rather MPs came to Number 11 than he go across the road to them. It would be hard, studying recent chancellors, to conclude that the Commons men amongst them were more successful. Indeed those chancellors who despised the House of Commons and its denizens as a necessary evil have on balance the better record.

This cannot be right. Of course, Parliament will never recover the position as cockpit of the nation which it held in Victorian times. But it is not a cockpit the nation needs. It looks to Parliament to check that its money is spent wisely and well; that the right taxes are raised with efficiency and justice; and that economic policy is properly scrutinized and assessed. Parliament, the efforts of the Treasury Committee and the PAC not withstanding, is failing in its job. It needs to change.

Better scrutiny

'Don't muck around with the Treasury . . . Do muck around with Parliament.' That was the conclusion of Heclo and Wildavsky's classic study of public-expenditure control, already cited. 'The analytic staff capabilities of Parliament cry out for improvement . . . cosy clientelism can develop between . . . legislative committees, executive bureaux and outside interests . . . Parliament needs a budget committee cutting *across* departmental lines . . . the staff available to MPs should be increased . . . as should institutional staff serving Parliament and its committees as a whole.'

The second edition of Heclo and Wildavsky dates from 1981. Seventeen years later, Parliament's analytic staff remains exiguous. Select committees, the Treasury Committee apart, continue to be too much influenced by lobby groups and their calls for more resources for their causes. And Parliament still does not have a committee specifically charged with looking at public spending across the water-front. The choice of priorities made by the Treasury and the Cabinet goes unconsidered by Parliament.

Sadly, therefore, it is necessary to repeat Heclo and Wildavsky's 1981 prescription. Yes, Parliament should set up a select committee specifically charged with examining the government's expenditure plans and priorities. It should not be its principal task to look at the overall level of spending: that should remain the remit of the Treasury Committee. But it should crawl over the budgets of each individual department. Even more important, it should look at the relative rates of growth in those budgets and ask: do the government's spending priorities match its strategy?

If such a new committee is to work, the following are required. Firstly a leading parliamentarian, preferably one with Treasury ministerial experience, should be appointed its chairman. Secondly, he must do everything in his power, with the House's support, to stop its being stuffed with whips' trusties. Thirdly, it must be properly staffed: not as heavily, perhaps, as the PAC, but with a core permanent team of fifty to a hundred, who might be a mixture of government officials, academic experts and those with knowledge of audit. Fourthly, though it must look at budgets department by department, it ought also to look at the 'wicked issues', issues that are the province of more than one department, such as social exclusion, to see how taxpayers' money is being used in them. Fifthly, it should produce an annual report on government spending as a whole, drawing on individual reports during the year. That report should be the subject of a debate, preferably a debate of at least two days, on the floor of the House of Commons.

As we have seen above, Parliament is potentially an ally of the Treasury, and particularly an ally of Treasury officials. Of course, responding to such a committee would inevitably mean more work on top of a workload which is already excessive. But wise officials would welcome such scrutiny. It would strengthen the Treasury's hand against spendthrift departments. It would provide a forum for a sensible (though inevitably politically charged) debate on priorities. It would be another weapon in the Treasury's war against waste.

The Treasury, as we have seen, is an institution that understands power. So far, that has disposed it towards hoarding power, and keeping other powerful institutions under its thumb. But its own interests would be served by sharing more power with Parliament. A more open and accountable Treasury would also be the more effective Treasury that Britain needs as it moves into the third millennium.

16 | The Way Ahead

This chapter reviews briefly the themes of this account of the Treasury; suggests some of the ways in which it might evolve from here on; and gives a positive verdict on its record.

As we have seen, the thousand-year history of the Treasury has been punctuated by periods of rapid change, and periods of fierce controversy. Few, however, match the turbulence of the 1990s, where the Treasury was at the centre of the downfall of one government, and at the helm of the strategy of its successor.

That change should be particularly rapid in the 1990s is no surprise. The accelerating speed of change, with all its exhilarations and terrors, is the cliché of our age.

The turbulence in the Treasury is surprising, however, in one regard: it comes in a period of relative stability in our nation's economic affairs. The ERM crisis, it is true, was by any standards a big one; and the difficulties of the world economy in 1998 could easily have become one. But if you were a Martian, studying the economic data for Britain in the 1990s but ignorant of the accompanying history, you would see an unusual steadiness. Economic growth has been continuous, except for a hiccup in 1998–9. Inflation has been kept down. Unemployment has come down. The fashionable Jeremiahs, predicting disaster and peddling alternative nostrums, have proved wholly wrong.

In the past, the great changes in the Treasury have followed events causing economic turmoil. These have sometimes been political. For example, parliamentary control over spending evolved from the shift of power to Parliament, away from the monarchy, and then later from the growth of democracy. The increasing sophistication of public-expenditure control has its roots in a large increase in public expenditure's share of the national wealth, and this in turn reflected the rise of the industrial working class and its demands.

Changes have sometimes been geopolitical. Wars have nearly always led to greatly increased powers for the Treasury. More recently, globalization has transformed the Treasury's attitude to free markets in capital and currencies, changing its role and reducing its control.

Changes have also sometimes been economic. For example, Treasury guilt at its role in the Great Depression caused it to accede too readily to the unrealistic expectations heaped upon it for the thirty years or so following the Second World War.

In general, a stable economy leads to a stable Treasury, but that has not been the case over the past decade.

The revolutionary decade

Revolutions, or at any rate peaceful revolutions, are not always seen as such in their time. Each element in them may seem minor; and the smallness of the parts distracts attention from the bulk of the whole.

Yet, by any account, the Treasury is a very different place with a very different role at the end of the 1990s from what it was in the beginning. To summarize:

1. Having effectively given up on an activist fiscal policy in the 1970s and 1980s, it has now shed responsibility over monetary policy to an independent Bank of England.

2. It has moved from public-expenditure control exercised through detailed use of its veto power to a more general (though tough) control of public-expenditure totals, devolving the detail to departments while monitoring their performance with unprecedented thoroughness.

3. It has become much more flexible about the boundaries between public and private provision, both in terms of the use of private money for public purpose and in terms of the adoption of private-sector accounting methods and appraisal techniques for public expenditures.

4. It has undergone a profound internal organizational revolution, and this has stripped out management layers, increased economic professionalism and redirected itself towards a more task-oriented rather than a role-oriented model.

5. It has become much more global in outlook, appreciating the limits on the freedom of action of a single nation state; it has also become much more European in outlook.

These changes are starkly stated. As the Treasury is packed with sceptics, you would find people there to scoff at each of these points, and to suggest that, beneath the surface, nothing has really changed. To such sceptics, one can only say: stand back, you are seeing the trees but not the wood.

The future

It cannot simply be assumed that the trends in evidence in 1999 will be sustained. For each, it is possible to imagine a reversal.

1. Devolution of power over monetary policy to the Bank of England may seem irreversible. But what if, with an election impending, unemployment rose sharply? What if, despite that, the Bank's monetary policy committee insisted on high interest rates to fight inflation? What if there were riots on the streets?

2. Devolution of power over public-expenditure control may seem irreversible. But what if departments abuse their new freedoms? What if they do not perform well? What if the chancellor's political

position within government becomes less dominant and party pressures for a loosening of controls mount?

3. The introduction of private-sector values and private-sector cash into the public sector may seem irreversible. But what if there is a series of scandals: of private-sector rip-offs of taxpayers? What if public-sector employees start feathering their own nests as their private-sector counterparts do? What if an awareness of the sheer cost of financing from taxes the return to private shareholders and debt holders spreads – as it has recently in Scotland over the use of private money to build public hospitals?

4. The internal revolution at the Treasury may seem irreversible. But what if more than one economic crisis occurs simultaneously, so stretching its capacity to manage crisis? What if it turns out that greater flexibility means that the basic jobs are not being done properly and administrative scandals result? And what if it fails to maintain quality? To an outside observer, its staffing now seems frighteningly slim for the tasks it undertakes, and the present quality of its Treasury upper echelons disguises a lack of strength in depth.

5. Globalization in particular may seem irreversible. Yet it has already been accompanied by a rise in the spirit of nationalism not only in Scotland and Wales but in England too. Though globalism is a fact of life, it is also a peculiarly threatening fact of life; and it is still possible to imagine a political reaction against it. Would the Treasury's attitudes to Europe easily survive the election of a truly Eurosceptical Tory government?

The future of the Treasury

None of these scenarios represents the most likely outcome. Amongst weather forecasters, it has long been recognized that it is not easy to outperform a forecast which says simply: 'Tomorrow will be the same as today.' Similarly with the Treasury, it is most likely that tomorrow will be the same as today. The same as today in terms of the underlying institutional values of probity, austerity, caution and reason; the same in terms of current economic philosophy, the same in terms of carrying through and further the changes which have already been made to fit the Treasury for its functions in a modern economy.

The Treasury of the future is likely to be even more strategic, more performance-oriented, leaner and fitter, more European, more global. The Treasury of the future is likely to be less inclined to macro-interventionism, less veto-happy, less rigid, less bureaucratic and less insular.

That said, one should avoid political, economic or institutional determinism. None of these developments simply happen by themselves. All of them require human beings to do things, to change things. For all the weight of the Treasury's great history, its character at any particular time reflects the nature of the people who work there and the decisions they take.

Its history has been made by individuals as well as by external forces. The Treasury today, for example, would be a different place were it not for its mid-nineteenth-century flourishing under William Gladstone as chancellor and Lord Trevelyan as permanent secretary.

Similarly, the 1990s have been marked by the dominance of one very good chancellor, Kenneth Clarke, and one potentially great one, Gordon Brown. Lords Burns, permanent secretary for most of this period, is a more controversial figure; but history will rank the Fundamental Expenditure Review as one of the greatest reforms that the Treasury has ever seen. Since it was an unforced change, driven through in the face of much sceptical opposition, Lord Burns too has exercised an influence for good that will long survive his departure.

To end where we started, the Treasury has few friends. Nor should it have. No one has said that better than King James I, quoted earlier: 'All Treasurers, if they do good service to their masters, must be generally hated.' And certainly even the modern Treasury does plenty to ensure that the supply of its enemies is kept up, sometimes beyond the level necessary for the effective discharge of its duties.

However, our verdict on the Treasury should not depend on whether it, as an institution, is loved or hated, or on whether we find its denizens congenial or not. Just as it seeks performance from those it controls, so performance is the only measure by which it can itself be judged.

Put simply, is Britain a richer country as a result of the Treasury's work? Is it a more stable country? Is it a more equitable country? Is it governed in a way that mitigates against corruption?

To all these questions the answer is 'yes'. For all its manifest failings, its infuriating bad habits, its misjudgements and mistakes, the Treasury does a difficult job well. For low salaries, for little thanks, at the cost of grinding labour punctuated by periods of acute stress, generally favouring the public interest over personal interests, and providing a serious, considered and now even a successful core to the country's governance, the Treasury deserves, though it would never expect, quiet praise.

Index